# Politics as Religion

# Politics as Religion

*Emilio Gentile*

Translated by George Staunton

PRINCETON UNIVERSITY PRESS

PRINCETON AND OXFORD

First published in Italian under the title *Le religioni della politica:*
*Fra democrazie e totalitarismi*
© 2001, Gius. Laterza & Figli. This translation of
*Le religioni della politica* is published by arrangement
with Gius. Laterza & Figli S.P.A., Roma-Bari.

English translation Copyright ©2006 by Princeton University Press
Published by Princeton University Press, 41 William Street,
Princeton, NJ 08540
In the United Kingdom: Princeton University Press,
3 Market Place, Woodstock, Oxfordshire 0X20 1SY

Library of Congress Cataloging-in-Publication Data
Gentile, Emilio, 1946–
[Religioni della politica. English]
Politics as religion / Emilio Gentile; translated
by George Staunton.
p. cm.
Includes bibliographical references.
ISBN-13: 978-0-691-11393-7 (cloth : alk. paper)
ISBN-10: 0-691-11393-9 (cloth : alk. paper)
1. Ideology—Political aspects. 2. Religion and politics.
3. Political psychology. I. Title.
HM641.G4613 2006
306.2–dc22        2005044498

British Library Cataloging-in-Publication Data is available

This book has been composed in Sabon

Printed on acid-free paper. ∞

pup.princeton.edu

Printed in the United States of America

1  3  5  7  9  10  8  6  4  2

At different periods dogmatic belief is more or less common. It arises in different ways, and it may change its object and its form; but under no circumstances will dogmatic belief cease to exist, or, in other words, men will never cease to entertain some opinions on trust and without discussion. If everyone undertook to form all his own opinions and to seek for truth by isolated paths struck out by himself alone, it would follow that no considerable number of men would ever unite in any common belief.

But obviously without such common belief no society can prosper; say, rather, no society can exist; for without ideas held in common there is no common action, and without common action there may still be men, but no social body. In order that society should exist and, *a fortiori*, that a society should prosper, it is necessary that the minds of all the citizens should be rallied and held together by certain predominant ideas; and this cannot be the case unless each of them sometimes draws his opinions from the common source and consents to accept certain matters of belief already formed.

—Alexis de Tocqueville, *Democracy in America*, vol. 2, chapter 2

It makes you wonder whether the modern world, which studies and reads, and therefore should be emancipated from myth and many natural terrors, really is, when taken as a whole, freer from prejudices, and does not give into much more dangerous prejudices.

—Jacob Burckhardt, *Griechische Kulturgeschichte*

But there is no need of gods nor secret conspiracies to drive men towards the most absurd catastrophes. Human nature alone is quite sufficient.

—Simone Weil, *Let's Not Fight the Trojan War Again*

# CONTENTS

# ACKNOWLEDGMENTS

I wish to thank my friends Stefano Falco, Maria Fraddosio, and Roberta Suzzi Valli for their assistance while I was writing this work. Without their help, it would be a different but not a better book.

More than a quarter century has passed since I first met Vito Laterza. He was in his office and I was there to hand over the manuscript of my first book published by his company. A few years ago, I suggested the idea for *Politics as Religion* in that same office. He was very keen on the project and encouraged me to write it. I am very thankful to him for that and much more besides. My only regret is that the delay in its completion has robbed the book of his critical eye, just as his death means that I was unable to ask his permission to dedicate the work to him, as I had fully intended.

*Introduction*

# THE SACRALIZATION OF POLITICS

THE DOLLAR AS A RELIGIOUS SYMBOL

An American dollar bill, with its portrait of George Washington, is a religious symbol. This assertion may surprise readers. Some might find it extravagant, paradoxical, or just plain blasphemous, because it mixes religion, the maximum expression of all that is sacred, with money, the utterly commonplace object representing all that is profane. Others might think that I am using the dollar as a metaphor for the way in which we have come to treat money as a god. In reality, however, the religious symbolism of a dollar bill has to be seen as something literal.

This can be demonstrated by observing the back of the banknote. In the center, there is the inscription, "In God We Trust." This is the national motto of the United States, which was officially adopted on 30 July 1956 under the presidency of Dwight D. Eisenhower, but it had already appeared in 1862 on a two-cent piece. A slightly different version, "In God Is Our Trust," is to be found in the patriotic song "The Star-Spangled Banner," popular since 1814 and adopted as the national anthem by Congress in 1931. The two faces of the Great Seal of the United States appear on either side of the motto. The seal was chosen in 1776 by Benjamin Franklin, Thomas Jefferson, and John Adams and approved by Congress on 20 June 1782 after exhaustive scrutiny. On one side, we find the American eagle with spread wings, with the arrows of war grasped in one claw and an olive branch in the other, while its beak holds a ribbon with the wording of another national motto: "E Pluribus Unum" ("one made up of many"). The sentence consists of thirteen letters, one for each colony that gave birth to the new republic. Above the eagle, there is a constellation of thirteen stars, set out so as to create a figure surrounded by a glittering halo. On the other side of the religious motto is the image of an incomplete pyramid, made up of thirteen layers of squared-off blocks of stone. These blocks represent self-government, and the unfinished state of the edifice signifies that new states can be added to the American republic. The date of the Declaration of Independence is inscribed on the lowest layer of stone blocks in Roman numerals, MDCCLXXVI. The base of the pyramid is surrounded by a ribbon that bears the inscription taken from Virgil's poetry, "Novus Ordo Seclorum" ("a new order of ages"). The eye of God looks down from above the sacred triangle, and above that there appears another thirteen-letter sentence from Virgil in pride of place within the heavens, as though the words were uttered by some voice from above: "Annuit Coeptis" ("He has approved our undertaking").

To all intents and purposes, the dollar bill is therefore a religious symbol because it expresses a profession of faith and confers an aura of holiness on the people of the star-spangled republic, its origin, its history, its institutions, and its destiny in the world. Although the words and images on the banknote have an incontrovertible religious meaning, it is not clear what religion they are supposed to express. The United States is a country with many religious confessions, and it is perhaps still the most religious of the modern industrialized nations. However, the American republic is not a confessional state, and it does not attribute a privileged status within its institutions to any one religion or church. There is not a single reference to God or divine providence in the Constitution of the United States, which was adopted in 1787. In 1791, the First Amendment to the Constitution guaranteed the freedom of all religious confessions, and explicitly refused to assign the role of Established Church to one particular religion.

In spite of this, the United States officially professes its faith in God, and since the time of the Revolution, the American nation has believed that it has a special mystical relationship with God, one that has been sealed by a sacred covenant. The American people consider themselves to have been chosen by God to fulfill a historical mission for the benefit of all mankind. The Declaration of Independence, which was approved by Congress on 4 July 1776, starts by asserting that the American people wish "to assume among the powers of the earth, the separate and equal station to which the Laws of Nature and of Nature's God entitle them," and concludes with an appeal "to the Supreme Judge of the world for the rectitude of our intentions," while claiming "a firm reliance on the protection of divine Providence."

The reference to the American nation's election by God also appears in the Pledge of Allegiance to the Stars and Stripes, an obligatory pledge that was introduced into the school system at the end of the nineteenth century and is recited before lessons can start. On 14 June 1954, Congress decided to add the assertion that the United States is "one nation under God" to this declaration. The appeal to God is also to be found in the most solemn declarations by presidents of the United States. From the beginning, all heads of state have sworn allegiance to the Constitution at their investiture using the formula "So help me, God," and in their inaugural speeches they have invoked God or the Almighty to guard over their country. The first Catholic president, John Fitzgerald Kennedy, started his inaugural speech by declaring that he has sworn before the American people and Almighty God, and he ended by calling for God's blessing on the American nation, "knowing that here on earth God's work must truly be our own."

There is not, however, a contradiction between the principle of the separation of church and state asserted by the Constitution, and the profession of religious faith expressed by the mottos, symbols, and political rituals of the United States. The reason is that faith in God or the Almighty as expressed in symbols and political rituals of the American nation is the manifestation of a particular form of religion, one that does not correspond to any particular religion professed by the citizens of the United States. It is a *civil religion*, by which we mean a system of beliefs, values, myths, rituals, and symbols that confer an aura of sanctity on the United States as a political entity, and on the country's institutions, history, and destiny in the world.

The American civil religion has its own "holy scriptures," the Declaration of Independence and the Constitution, which are treasured and venerated like the Tables of the Law. It has its own prophets, such as the Pilgrim Fathers. It celebrates its own sacred heroes such as George Washington, the "American Moses" who freed the "new people of Israel" from slavery under the English and led them to the Promised Land of freedom, independence, and democracy. It venerates its martyrs, such as Abraham Lincoln, the sacrificial victim assassinated on Good Friday of 1865, after the American nation had been subjected to the purifying fires of a cruel civil war to expiate its guilt and reestablish the hallowed nature of its unity and mission. John Kennedy and Martin Luther King Jr. then became further examples of martyrdom for this civil religion, alongside the figure of Lincoln. Like all religions, this civil religion has its own temples for the veneration of its leading figures, such as the monument to Washington, the Lincoln Memorial, and Arlington Cemetery, where the tomb of the Unknown Soldier is revered as a symbol for the citizens who fell to save their nation. Finally, the civil religion has its sermons and liturgy: the presidential inaugural speeches, Independence Day on 4 July, Thanksgiving Day, Memorial Day when the war dead are commemorated, and other collective ceremonies that celebrate personalities and events in American history turned by myth into a "sacred history" of a nation elected by God to fulfill its particular mission in the world.

The civil religion of the United States derived from Protestantism, and for more than a century it displayed the unmistakable imprint of Puritanism and the biblical tradition. As time went on, however, it began to differentiate itself and became an explicit and direct reference point and a purely civic credo that coexisted with both Christian and non-Christian confessions. Given the freedom that the state accords all religions, the American civil religion respects all traditional religions, whether or not they are Christian; and for their part, the religions pay homage to the sacred nature of the nation, its institutions, and its symbols. The flag of the United States is displayed in many churches above the altar or pulpit.

## The Sacralization of Politics

Thus we come to this book's central argument. The American civil religion is the first historical example of a *religion of politics* in the modern era. By a religion of politics I mean a particular form of *sacralization of politics* that has occurred in the modern era after the political realm had gained its independence from traditional religion. By taking over the religious dimension and acquiring a sacred nature, politics went so far as to claim for itself the prerogative to determine the meaning and fundamental aim of human existence for individuals and the collectivity, at least on this earth. A religion of politics is created every time a political entity such as a nation, state, race, class, party, or movement is transformed into a sacred entity, which means it becomes transcendent, unchallengeable, and intangible. As such, it becomes the core of an elaborate system of beliefs, myths, values, commandments, rituals, and symbols, and consequently an object of faith, reverence, veneration, loyalty, and devotion, for which, if necessary, people are willing to sacrifice their lives. The resulting religion of politics is a religion in the sense that it is *a system of beliefs, myths, rituals, and symbols that interpret and define the meaning and end of human existence by subordinating the destiny of individuals and the collectivity to a supreme entity.*

The sacralization of politics as a modern phenomenon differs from other historical forms of sacralization of political power. Throughout history and since the most ancient times, political power has been shrouded in holiness. It was either identified with the divine or considered its direct emanation, as in the case of the pharaohs of Ancient Egypt. In Greek city-states and republican Rome, the religious dimension was indistinguishable from the city religion: the sacred nature of political power was incorporated into the civic institutions. In imperial Rome, the deification of the emperor personalized the hallowedness of power and was superimposed on the city religion. With the advent of Christianity, the fusion between religion and politics was shattered, giving rise to a new sacralization of power in which the church obtained a spiritual primacy over the state. In Christian monarchies from the Middle Ages until the sovereignty of the people appeared on the scene, the sacralization of power corresponded to the sacred nature of the divine right of kings, which was acknowledged and legitimized by the church, unless of course the monarch was also the head of the church, as in the case of Anglican England. For centuries until the Modern Era, this led to tensions, rivalries, and conflicts between the spiritual power of the church and the temporal power of the monarch, each claiming the primacy of its sovereignty made sacred by divine investiture.

During the Modern Era, the relationship between the religious and political dimensions and between power and sacredness entered a new phase that gave rise to the sacralization of politics, which reflected the affirmation of the primacy of the sovereignty of the state, secularization of culture, the loss of the church's spiritual hegemony in relation to the state and society, the subsequent separation of the church and state, the triumph of the principle of the people's sovereignty and the creation of mass politics. *Civil religions* and *political religions* represent the two main phenomena of sacralization of politics produced by modern society, and these are the categories that we will be using throughout this book. The difference between the two reflects the different attitudes and behaviors adopted in relation to traditional religions and the different solutions they find for the relationship between authority and freedom, and between the individual and the state.

*Civil religion* is the conceptual category that contains the forms of sacralization of a political system that guarantee a plurality of ideas, free competition in the exercise of power, and the ability of the governed to dismiss their governments through peaceful and constitutional methods. Civil religion therefore respects individual freedom, coexists with other ideologies, and does not impose obligatory and unconditional support for its commandments. *Political religion* is the sacralization of a political system founded on an unchallengeable monopoly of power, ideological monism, and the obligatory and unconditional subordination of the individual and the collectivity to its code of commandments. Consequently, a political religion is intolerant, invasive, and fundamentalist, and it wishes to permeate every aspect of an individual's life and of a society's collective life.

This conceptual distinction, which is so clear-cut in its theoretical formulation, must, however, take into account the existence of the wider variety of sacralization of politics in historical reality. These find themselves in intermediate positions between the two main categories, according to their different political, cultural and religious situations. For example, a civil religion may take on invasive, intolerant, and exclusive attitudes and forms of behavior in particular circumstances, in spite of existing within a democratic system. This differentiation needs to be remembered when examining the attitude adopted by a religion of politics in relation to traditional religion and the ecclesiastical institutions that represent it. A civil or political religion may derive from a traditional religion and may make use of the latter either directly or indirectly in order to develop a system of beliefs, myths, values, symbols, and rituals that confer a sacred aura on political institutions without subordinating the state to the church, as occurred in the United States, and without establishing a polemical or antagonistic relationship with churches and traditional religions. In totalitarian regimes, a religion of politics may enter into conflict with traditional religions, because it claims the primary role in defining the meaning and purpose of the existence of a certain collectivity and aims to subordinate the traditional religion to its own aspirations—when, that is, it does not want to destroy it altogether.

Sacralization of politics differs from various traditional and contemporary forms of politicization of religion, as in the case of Caesaropapism, whereby political power appropriates and exercises spiritual power through a traditional religion, or of other mergers between politics and religion that, this time, involve the traditional religion absorbing the political dimension or imposing direct political control. Hence, in both analytical and historical terms, sacralization of politics does not include theocracy, which is the historical form whereby politics is subordinated to a traditional religion through the exercise of direct political power; Shintoism, which is the national religion of imperial Japan; the Catholic Church's various political activities such as those in Poland under the communist regime; or even the fundamentalist religious movements that have taken power and apply their own religious principles to society and the state, as occurred in Iran following Khomeini's revolution.

Historically, the sacralization of politics, in the sense I have just explained, commenced with the birth of modern democracy and mass politics. Its origins are democratic, republican, and patriotic. The first real religions of politics appeared during the American and French revolutions as a set of beliefs, values, myths, symbols, and rituals that conferred a sacred quality and meaning on the new political institution of popular sovereignty. Subsequently, the sacralization of politics was given a further impetus during the nineteenth century by various cultural and political movements, such as romanticism, idealism, positivism, nationalism, socialism, communism, and racism, which all put forward global concepts of human existence by adopting various aspects of secular religions intent upon replacing traditional religions. These secular religions could be defined as religions of humanity. The affirmation of national states during the second half of the nineteenth century and during the twentieth century contributed more decisively and directly to the sacralization of politics. Everywhere, these states adopted myths, rituals, and symbols of varying degrees of complexity in order to confer a sacred aura on their political institutions, to exalt the fundamental principles and values of the national community, and to cultivate a collective identity among their citizens, which required them to feel a sense of duty, loyalty, and devotion toward both state and nation. As the principle of national sovereignty spread to the entire planet during the twentieth century, nationalism became the most universal manifestation of sacralization of politics in the contemporary world and merged with a wide variety of ideologies and cultural and religious traditions. In some cases it acted as a revolutionary force and in others as a conservative one, and it either challenged traditional religions or attempted to integrate them into its own system of beliefs, values, and aims.

The twentieth century has been the most fertile period for the sacralization of politics. The wars and political revolutions that forged the world we live in through the creation of new nations and states, and the liberation and emancipation of populations everywhere, were all carried out in the name of collective beliefs and myths that made politics something sacred and excited faith, enthusiasm, and devotion among their followers to the point that they were willing to lay down their lives. The greatest and most inhuman massacres, which involved the mass slaughter of millions of victims at the altar of deified political entities, were inflicted during the century by political movements that operated very much as fundamentalist and intolerant religious movements. Such movements claimed to determine the meaning and ultimate purpose of existence by distinguishing between humans who were the followers of Good and those who were the followers of Evil. The latter were ruthlessly and ferociously persecuted by every means at the disposal of these movements to the point of their annihilation.

The First World War, which was fought as an apocalyptic struggle between Good and Evil, exalted the nation and intensified the sacralization of politics in its nationalist manifestation. This then favored the creation of the new political religions of fascism and Nazism, while the Bolshevik Revolution, which was another child of the war, engendered an internationalist version of the sacralization of politics, and indeed it attracted an enthusiastic response and proselytized in every corner of the globe. Between the wars, Europe experienced the bewildering spectacles of great seas of people acclaiming the dictators of new totalitarian states as terrestrial demigods. These regimes were the churches of the new intolerant religion of politics that claimed to determine the meaning and ultimate end of individual and collective existence through an obligatory system of beliefs, myths, rituals, and symbols. The perception of fascism and bolshevism as political religions goes back to the 1920s. The concepts of "secular religion" and "political religion" were coined precisely in order to describe the novelty and originality of the totalitarian regimes that sprung up between the two world wars.

Fascism was the first nationalist totalitarian movement that fully displayed the characteristics of a political religion, as it indeed proclaimed itself to be. This was consistent with the irrationalist and mythical premises of its culture, which were used to establish a system of beliefs, myths, rituals, and symbols that deified the nation and state and celebrated the personality cult of "Il Duce" as a living myth. National-socialism, another political religion, did the same. On its altar it placed the Aryan race, the veneration of blood ties, and the Führer, Germany's savior and the messiah of the millennial Third Reich. It encompassed all public life in a complex tangle of rituals and symbols that evoked the ancient myths of the Germanic religion and blended them with the myths of modern racist paganism, which challenged the Christian churches.

However, something similar occurred in Soviet Russia during the same period. There, the totalitarian party professed an atheist and materialist ideology and came into conflict with all religions, which were considered an "opiate of the people." Bolshevism in power transformed its ideology into a dogmatic doctrine, the party into a church, and its leader into an earthly god. Lenin, who resisted the glorification of his person while he was alive, was immediately deified after his death in 1924 by the establishment of a cult around his embalmed body. His corpse was preserved and venerated in a mausoleum built in Red Square in front of the Kremlin Wall, very much in the manner of the ancient saints of the Orthodox Church. The sacralization of his thought, which became Leninism in its dogmatized form, opened the way to the sacralization of the Communist Party and the deification of Stalin, who was the brightest star in the universal communist firmament from the end of the 1920s until his death in 1953. After the October Revolution, Soviet communism recruited adherents in every part of the world without distinction of nation, race, ethnicity, or religion. It fused with a very wide range of traditions and cultures while conserving its original universalism. Its organization, the Third International, was simply the universal church of a political religion, and it continued to exist until the Second World War and had activists in every country and of every race. With this universality of principles and activism, the communist religion was clearly distinguishable from the fascist and national-socialist religions, in spite of the fact that it took on some strongly nationalistic connotations within the different movements and regimes it inspired. Indeed, fascism and Nazism were unshakable in their hostility to any form of universalism or egalitarian humanism, even though they, in turn, had ambitions to transcend the national state and enter an institutional and ideological dimension founded on new imperial communities. Ultimately they remained tied to nationalistic and racist concepts based on the principle of inequality between men, nations, and races.

Though the Second World War led to the definitive destruction of the fascist and national-socialist religions and condemned them to eternal damnation in the collective memory, it did not mean the end of the sacralization of politics. In the second half of the twentieth century, its intensity and durability varied and manifested itself in some of the old Western democratic states in a more or less explicit and institutional manner as a civil religion that coexisted peacefully with traditional religions. In other parts of the world during the same period, new or revitalized political religions appeared: new leaders were transfigured into living myths and venerated by the masses. Many lives were sacrificed on the altars of deified secular entities so that those entities could triumph. In Africa and Asia, the sacralization of politics was on the whole typical of the new states that emerged from the demise of colonialism. In these countries, the establishment of a system of beliefs, myths, and rituals that sacralized the independence struggle, the founding fathers of liberation, and the dominant party were an integral part of the plan to create unity and a collective identity. That same postwar period saw another phase in the expansion of the communist political religion, which was reinvigorated by pride in a great and powerful empire and the birth of more communist regimes in Europe, Asia, Africa, and Latin America. As in the Soviet Union, the new communist regimes that were created in the second half of the twentieth century took on the typical features of a religious institution as they imposed Marxist ideology as an indisputable truth, consecrated the party as the only depositary and interpreter of doctrine, celebrated rituals relating to revolutionary events and heroes, and worshipped the supreme and enlightened leader.

From the end of the Second World War until the end of the twentieth century, communism was, together with nationalism, the most universal manifestation of the sacralization of politics in the contemporary world, although its characteristics changed from one communist regime to another and from one period in their history to another. Following the collapse of the communist regimes, communism as a political religion has either disappeared or is in decline almost everywhere. In those countries where it is still in power, its sacralization has been considerably reduced in relation to the past, whereas various forms of nationalism continue to be the most universal manifestations of the sacralization of politics in the contemporary world, although the intensity varies. Everywhere in the world, buildings, monuments, and statues are used for the symbolic representation of the nation, its history, its institutions, and its heroes. Everywhere in the world, the national flag is considered a sacred symbol, and every state has an anthem that exalts the nation's virtues, glories, and immortality in a tone that can only be described as religious. Everywhere in the world, public holidays and majestic ceremonies are on the state's liturgical calendar, renewing and perpetuating the unity and identity of the nation through a ritual commemoration of historical events and personalities.

## The Purpose of This Book

I believe that the examples I have just given are sufficient to demonstrate the importance of the sacralization of politics in contemporary history. In recent years, studies of civil and political religions have become increasingly common among historians, of politics and of religions, not to mention sociologists, anthropologists, political scientists, theologians, art historians, and historians of social behavior. The interpretation of totalitarian movements and political phenomena as political or civil religions is still a matter of debate and controversy. Some scholars even dispute the very existence of such things; they consider the political phenomena that express secular religiosity through myths, rituals, and symbols to be nothing more than propaganda devices to seduce the masses. According to this point of view, anyone who studies a political phenomenon as a religion either does not know what a religion is or is the victim of an illusion, because he or she believes in the existence of a "never-never-religion," a conceptual equivalent of Peter Pan's island. Even if this were the case, the historian would still not be able to elude the problem of why the victims of a "never-never-religion" (i.e., those who believed in the existence of political religions) have become increasingly numerous, particularly during the period of totalitarian states and movements. When I speak of victims, I am not referring to believers in totalitarian religions but to their adversaries who considered them to be a real and deadly threat to human civilization. As we shall see, these victims included academics with wholly secular mentalities who were disinclined to let themselves be deceived by the illusion of nonexistent realities, such as Bertrand Russell and Raymond Aron. They also included Catholic believers, intellectuals, and militants such as Luigi Sturzo and Jacques Maritain, and Protestant theologians such as Paul Tillich and Reinhold Niebuhr. Given the competence of these thinkers on religious matters and the reliability of their observations on totalitarian religions, it is extremely difficult to understand how their perception of totalitarianism as a political religion could be the product of an illusion or attributable to their ignorance of what a religion is.

As someone who has been studying political beliefs and myths for more than thirty years, I have dealt with the sacralization of politics in contemporary history and have come across striking examples in the nineteenth-century struggle for Italian unification, in the modernist vanguard during the early decades of the twentieth century, and more particularly in fascism. I wrote an in-depth study of fascist political religion, *The Sacralization of Politics in Fascist Italy*, the original Italian edition of which went through several editions and has been translated into English and now French. It provoked a great deal of comment, most of it approving, and became the model or at least the inspiration for further research into the same field and on the question of civil and political religions. I mention the success of this previous work solely in order to demonstrate the current high level of interest in the sacralization of politics and more particularly the question of totalitarian religions among many academics in various disciplines. Further confirmation of this comes from the creation in 2000 of *Totalitarian Movements and Political Religions*, a journal entirely devoted to the study of these phenomena.

This work is a critical introduction to the study of the sacralization of politics through a combination of historical and theoretical analyses. It is supposed to provide the reader with the essential tools for identifying the general characteristics of the phenomenon by referring to significant historical examples and applying some preliminary definitions. It also aims to specify and distinguish civil and political religions according to differing historical circumstances and various ideological mixtures while identifying similarities, affinities, differences, and special features. The historical examples have been chosen with particular attention to the more exuberant and intense periods of the sacralization of politics, namely the era of the democratic revolutions in America and France, the First World War, and the era of totalitarian states. The preliminary definitions suggest an interpretative framework that could aid the conceptual clarification of a subject that continues to be highly confused. The review of the principle interpretations of the sacralization of politics, with the related bibliographical references, makes no claim to be exhaustive, but the intention is to provide the reader with the essential information for further examination of the questions and problems raised in each chapter, which I will briefly summarize here.

The first chapter deals with the general problem of a secular religion, of which civil and political religions are a particular manifestation, and looks at this in the light of the principal interpretations of religious phenomena in order to verify whether there is a religious dimension to politics *qua* politics and whether it is legitimate to study some political phenomena as civil and political religions. The next chapter outlines the historical background to the more important manifestations of the sacralization of politics in the eighteenth, nineteenth, and twentieth centuries. The third and fourth chapters are devoted to examining the relationship between the sacralization of politics and totalitarian states between the world wars; they combine theoretical analyses and historical accounts using the reports and interpretations of contemporary observers, philosophers, historians, sociologists, political scientists, and theologians. The fifth chapter takes up the historical profile again and deals with the principal manifestations of the sacralization of politics during the second half of the twentieth century. In the final chapter, I attempt to identify the theoretical nature of civil or political religion in relation to other ways in which the religious and political dimensions come together. To achieve this goal, I formulate definitions, distinctions, and explanations within the different contexts in which a religion of politics can manifest itself, in accordance with the conceptual differentiation between a civil religion, which involves forms of sacralization of politics in conjunction with democratic ideologies and regimes, and a political religion, which involves the sacralization of politics by antidemocratic ideologies and regimes.

The greater attention devoted in this book to totalitarian religions and especially to communist political religions is due to their greater importance in contemporary history. The sacralization of politics achieved its greatest presence and intensity in the modern world through totalitarian regimes. However, it must be pointed out that totalitarianism was not the inevitable result of the sacralization of politics, although the presence of the phenomenon was certainly one of the conditions that made totalitarianism possible. However obvious it might appear, it is also worth clarifying that the study of totalitarianism as a political religion does not imply that this aspect provides the only explanation of its nature and historical significance. The study of both democratic civil religions and totalitarian political ones draws the historian's attention to the political dimension, which is the predominant one in historical reality.

Whereas totalitarian regimes, by their very nature, lead inevitably to the establishment of a political religion (by turning their concept of life into a dogma, deifying the single party and its leaders, and imposing a cult and code of commandments to be obeyed), a civil religion is not always to be found in a democratic regime. Quite possibly, this civil religion will not operate through coercion and an institutionalized system of beliefs, myths, rituals, and symbols. Some people believe that no political collectivity could possibly maintain its unity and identity over time without creating some form of lay religion founded on a code of shared beliefs and civic values, which are needed to integrate the individual into society and to avoid disintegration and increasing internal fragmentation from conflicts of values and interests. This is meant to be particularly true of a collectivity organized on a democratic basis: according to this argument, no democracy can exist without a civil religion that educates its citizens in loyalty to its institutions and devotion to the common good. On the other hand, others believe that the creation of any type of civil religion, however noble its aims and ideals, could constitute a danger to democracy, because it would contain the inherent risk of tempting conformism, intolerance, and discrimination precisely because it is a form of sacralization of politics through a system of beliefs, myths, rituals, and symbols.

This latter problem is briefly referred to at the end of this work, which deals with the religions of politics as they have been experienced in the past and not as a problem for the present or the future. If by reading this book someone is inspired to dream up a religion of politics or to deplore its absence, this person would be acting contrary to the spirit in which it was written. However, the reader will be entering into the spirit of the work if he or she is encouraged to take seriously all the manifestations of the sacralization of politics, which have for so long been ignored or treated with scathing contempt out of a misplaced desire to demystify. All too often they have been seen as mere propaganda expedients or remnants of past superstitions revamped as political devices.

From a historical and theoretical point of view, the controversies over the existence and nature of civil and political religions, and over the categories used to interpret them, are very probably destined to continue for some time, as always happens with historical problems that concern the meaning of human existence and our judgment of it. A debate about the existence of the religions of politics has nothing in common with a debate about the existence of life on Venus. This is particularly true of the historical experience of totalitarian political religions, which took up so great a part of the history of the twentieth century with consequences that profoundly marked human destiny and our consciousness of who we are. The experiments in totalitarianism were a reality: at the time of their triumph, totalitarian regimes exercised a fascination that equaled the power of a religious movement, and like religions they inspired fanatical enthusiasm, implacable hatred, generous sacrifice, ferocious brutality, hope of redemption, and campaigns of annihilation.

# Politics as Religion

# *Chapter* 1

# A NEVER-NEVER RELIGION, A SUBSTITUTE FOR RELIGION, OR A NEW RELIGION?

> Our logical apparatus is an imperfect instrument. The
> word, that indispensable aid, always has the tendency to
> deceive us with its splendid appearance of immediate
> truth, and the more the balance of time is shaken, the
> greater the danger of words that pretend to pass for wis
> dom. On the other hand, our debate should be as simple
> as possible. We will leave profound lucubration to others.
> —Johan Huizinga

## SECULAR RELIGION

Civil and political religions belong to a more general phenomenon, *secular religion*. This term is used to describe a more or less developed system of beliefs, myths, rituals, and symbols that create an aura of sacredness around an entity belonging to this world and turn it into a cult and an object of worship and devotion. Politics is not alone in this: any human activity from science to history or from entertainment to sport can be invested with "secular sacredness" and become the object of a secular cult, thus constituting a secular religion. In politics, however, the term "secular religion"[1] is often adopted as a synonym for civil religion or political religion.

There does not appear to be any doubt about the attribution of the concept of "civil religion" to Jean-Jacques Rousseau, who introduced it to define a new citizen's religion that he considered essential for democracy. This civil religion was to be distinct and different from Christianity, and in some ways antagonistic to it. During the nineteenth and twentieth centuries, the term "secular religion" was explicitly adopted to define ideologies and ideals that intended to replace traditional metaphysical religion with new humanist concepts that created a cult of humanity, history, nation, and society. On the other hand, the concept of "secular religion" is commonly attributed to the French sociologist Raymond Aron, who used it in an article written in 1944 to define doctrines that promise the salvation of mankind in this world.[2] In truth, the expression had been in use since the early thirties. The editor of a collection of essays on dictatorship, which was published in 1935, observed that the novelty of contemporary dictatorship in relation to dictatorships of the ancient world was to be found in the "powerful technique of controlling the masses by means of propaganda through radio, cinema, the press, education and a secular religion of their own creation."[3] In 1936, the Protestant theologian Adolf Keller wrote that bolshevism had transformed the scientific philosophical system of Marxism into a secular religion.[4] Two years later, the English journalist Frederik A. Voigt conducted a comparative analysis of Marxism and national-socialism, treating them as secular religions.[5]

The concept of a secular religion was therefore already in use in the thirties as a definition for the forms in which totalitarian regimes created political cults. As for the term "political religion," it is generally attributed to the Austrian philosopher Eric Voegelin, who published *The Political Religions* in 1938.[6] Here again, the term had been used before the publication of Voegelin's book; Condorcet had used it at the time of the French Revolution.[7] Abraham Lincoln defined reverence for the laws handed down by the Constitution and the Declaration of Independence as the "political religion of the nation."[8] Luigi Settembrini called the Giovine Italia (Young Italy), a nationalist movement of *Risorgimento*, a "new political religion."[9] Fascism explicitly used the term since the twenties to define its own fideistic and totalitarian view of politics. In 1935, the Austrian historian Karl Polanyi studied the "tendency for National-Socialism to produce a political religion,"[10] while the American theologian Reinhold Niebuhr applied this term to Marxism and communism.[11]

Even though these terms have been in use for some time, it was only in the mid-sixties that civil and political religions became the subject of systematic research and debates, which at times could be extremely impassioned. You only have to recall the long debate provoked by the article on American civil religion that the sociologist Robert Bellah published in 1967.[12] After defining religion as "a collection of beliefs, symbols, and rituals with respect to sacred things and institutionalized in a collectivity," Bellah asserted that there was a religious dimension to politics alongside the traditional religions but distinct from them. Borrowing the term from Rousseau, he defined it as a civil religion, one that had been developed and institutionalized through a system of beliefs, symbols, and rituals that conferred a religious significance on the American national experience.[13]

In more recent times, secular religion has increasingly become the object of new studies as a phenomenon in the political world. These studies have mainly concentrated its ritualistic and symbolic features, often dissociating them from the beliefs, myths, and dogmas of which they were an expression, in order to treat them solely or principally as useful political instruments in the conquest and maintenance of power.[14] Today we can turn to numerous studies that contain detailed descriptions and comparative analyses of the principal manifestations of the sacralization of politics in both democratic and totalitarian states, although the definition of secular religion is still the subject of fierce debate. The controversy inevitably also involves civil and political religions and their specific characteristics.[15]

Doubts have been expressed about the actual existence of an American civil religion.[16] Objections have also been raised to the concept of secular religion, and there are those who firmly reject the idea that any political phenomenon could be defined as a religion. For example, those who argue that only belief systems that refer to a supernatural being can be considered *true* religions argue that there can be no such thing as a secular religion. For them the term "secular religion" is a kind of conceptual oxymoron on a par with "square circle." Others argue that we should avoid using the term "religion" to describe political movements that adopt forms of words, rituals, and symbols of a religious kind, and at the very most are willing to concede that such movements could be defined as "pseudo-religions" because they are simply political phenomena that dress themselves up in religious garments in order to beguile the masses. Yet others claim that calling a political movement a religion is nothing more than making use of a metaphor. This means that the political movement cannot be considered a real religion and studied as such. In conclusion, these viewpoints suggest that secular religion and therefore civil or political religion simply does not exist. Anyone who says anything else has mistaken a metaphor for reality and does not know what a religion is. Alternatively, they are victims of an illusion that led them to believe in a "never-never religion."

Clearly, the definition of a religious phenomenon plays a decisive role in this controversy over whether there is a secular religion in the modern world. If, for example, your definition of a religion is premised on the existence of a supernatural divinity, then you would be justified in denying that a belief system that considers a secular entity to be sacred could be a religious phenomenon. However, if we accept this definition, we would be obliged to deny that Buddhism is a religious phenomenon, because it does not allow for the existence of God, whereas the Nazi political religion could be considered a religious phenomenon, because it did not deny the existence of a god, even though it dressed that god up in its own ideology. However, not all scholars link religious phenomena to the presence of a supernatural divinity.[17] This presence is not considered indispensable by sociologists and anthropologists, who interpret religion as a social and cultural phenomenon, namely a system of beliefs, myths, rituals, and symbols that express the common principles and values of a collectivity. Fundamentally, there are various interpretations of religious phenomena, and some of these make it possible to include some political phenomena within the wider context of religious phenomena.

## Beguiling the Masses

At the end of the nineteenth century, Gaetano Mosca, one of the founders of political science, provided us with a classic formulation of what we could call the *crowd manipulation* interpretation of religion and the sacralization of politics perceived as a mere expedient and artifice made up of seemingly religious myths, symbols, and rituals that are consciously adopted for propagandistic and demagogic reasons. In *The Ruling Class* (original title: *Elementi di scienza politica*, 1895), Mosca discussed churches, religious sects, and political parties in the same chapter, and put founders of religions and founders of sociopolitical schools within the same category. He observed that the latter "ultimately are quasi-religions stripped of the divine element." According to him, religious sects and political parties operate in the same way, and "as long as their followers are loyal to the flag, they cover for and excuse their worst villainies." As far as they are concerned, *whoever wears the habit* immediately becomes someone quite different. Mosca believed that the ritualistic, symbolic, and fideistic aspects of political movements were a secular form of Jesuitism used to dupe and beguile the masses:

> One notes, on close inspection, that the artifices that are used to wheedle crowds are more or less alike at all times and in all places, since the problem is always to take advantage of the same human weaknesses. All religions, even those that deny the supernatural, have their special declamatory style, and their sermons, lectures, and speeches are delivered in it. All of them have their rituals and their displays of pomp to strike the fancy. Some parade with lighted candles and chant litanies. Others march behind red banners to the tune of the "Marseillaise" or the "International". . . . All religions and all parties which have set out with more or less sincere enthusiasms to lead men toward specified goals have, to varying degrees, used methods similar to the methods of the Jesuits, and sometimes worse ones. . . . In our day sects and political parties are highly skilled at creating the superman, the legendary hero, the "man of unquestioned honesty," who serves, in his turn, to maintain the luster of the gang and brings in wealth and power for the sly ones to use.[18]

No further studies or consideration into the nature of a civil or political religion are required for those who share this interpretation: it is simply a demagogic expedient to gain the support of the masses. The historian Alphonse Aulard applied this interpretation to the religious manifestations of the French Revolution, such as the cult of the Goddess Reason and the Supreme Being. He argued that the revolutionary cults were only stop-gap solutions that were imposed by the war and dreamed up to promote patriotism among the masses and to incite them to fight against the Revolution's enemies at home and abroad.[19] Similarly, Guglielmo Ferrero in 1942 interpreted the sacralization of politics as the legitimization of power by surrounding it with "an almost religious fervor that exalts it and confers a transcendent virtue upon it":

> This exaltation can only be perceived through an emotional crystallization of admiration, gratitude, enthusiasm, and love around the principle of legitimacy that transforms its imperfections, limits and lack of common principles into something that is absolute and inspires devotion. This fervor and this total, sincere, joyful but partly illusory acknowledgment of the superiority of power causes legitimacy to achieve its complete maturity and highest degree of effectiveness, which then transform that legitimacy into a kind of paternalistic authority.
>
> What are the means for achieving this fullness of legitimacy? There are many devices that can be used, but art has always been one of the most powerful. Painting, sculpture, and architecture did not just cooperate with monarchies and aristocracies of the *Ancien Regime*, but with governments of all times and all places, by presenting the masses with magnificent works that demonstrate the greatness and excellence of power in relation to the mediocrity of the world and people's mundane lives. . . . We should add to these the parades, processions, military reviews, triumphal displays, warrior assemblies, great public festivals, the pomp of great religious, and civil celebrations and other such ceremonies.[20]

According to this interpretation, the representation of politics through myths, rituals, and symbols can never be considered a religious phenomenon, but has to be explained exclusively in terms of a conscious *invention* of myths and ritual practices of an essentially utilitarian and instrumental nature. They are demagogic expedients needed for finding new ways to establish, preserve, and reaffirm the legitimacy of power in a mass society.[21]

Many historical examples can confirm that this has indeed been the origin and nature of some manifestations of the sacralization of politics. On the other hand, the theory that all the manifestations of the sacralization of politics can be explained by the *crowd manipulation* interpretation is not very convincing, particularly if it is applied to the religious aspects of mass movements, which do not always prove to be simply a means to an end. By restricting itself to utilitarian explanations of the sacralization of politics, the *crowd manipulation* interpretation effectively attempts to resolve in an oversimplified way the weighty and complex question of the

irrational dimension of *faith* and *belief* in mass politics and more generally
in human experience as a whole.


## THE NEED FOR FAITH


The *fideistic* interpretation of religion, as argued by Gustave Le Bon at
the end of the nineteenth century, makes the existence of civil and political
religions appear plausible. According to Le Bon, the concept of religion
does not necessarily presuppose the existence of a transcendent divinity.
The gods are figments of our imaginations: "It was undoubtedly man who
created the gods, but he then became subjugated to them immediately
after their creation. They are not the products of fear, as Lucretius claims,
but of hope, and therefore their influence springs eternal. . . . Of course,
the gods are not immortal, but the spirit of religion is eternal. This spirit
becomes torpid for a period, and then reawakens as soon as a new divinity
is created."

Le Bon, who studied the psychology of the crowd, considered religion
in whatever form it manifested itself to be the expression of an irrepressible human sentiment. Religion originates in the most peremptory of
human instincts, namely "the need to submit oneself to a divine, political,
or social faith, whatever the circumstances."[22]

> This sentiment has very simple characteristics, such as worship of a being
> supposed superior, fear of the power with which the being is credited, blind
> submission to its commandments, inability to discuss its dogmas, the desire
> to spread them, and a tendency to consider as enemies all by whom they are
> not accepted. Whether such a sentiment apply to an invisible God, to a
> wooden or stone idol, to a hero or to a political conception, its essence al-
> ways remains religious. . . . A person is not religious solely when he worships
> a divinity, but when he puts all the resources of his mind, the complete sub-
> mission of his will, and the whole-souled ardour of fanaticism at the service
> of a cause or an individual who becomes the goal and guide of his thoughts
> and actions.[23]

The religious beliefs produced by this sentiment are the primordial
force that created and established empires and civilizations.[24] Religion's
strength is to be found in its power to mold and transform the character
of a human mass by inculcating shared feelings, interests, and ideas in the
individuals that make it up. It thus produces a formidable power to generate enthusiasm and action and to channel individual and collective energies toward a single purpose, the triumph of their beliefs: "The majority
of historical events were created indirectly by the variation of religious

ideas. The history of humanity is parallel to that of the gods. The birth of new gods has marked the dawn of a new civilization."[25]

Le Bon used the example of the French Revolution to back up his interpretation of the sacralization of politics, as the world then saw "what the religious spirit is capable of, given that it really was a new religion that was being established, and its inspiration was motivating an entire people. The divinities that were then flowering were undoubtedly too fragile to last, but while they lasted, they exercised an absolute dominion."[26] He believed that modern society, in which there was a clash between declining traditional religions and mass aspirations to find new divinities and new credos, would be fertile ground for the creation and affirmation of new and powerful secular religions. Le Bon believed socialism to be an example.

Other thinkers who studied socialism during the first few decades of the twentieth century also adopted this kind of approach. When he was studying the sociology of political parties, Robert Michels observed that the masses "experience a profound need to prostrate themselves, not simply before great ideals, but also before the individuals who in their eyes incorporate such ideals. Their adoration of these temporal divinities is the more blind in proportion as their lives are rude."[27] Henri De Man, a scholar and socialist activist, considered the affirmation of socialism as a new collective religion to be based on faith, which was a "psychological need" of the masses. It originated and continually drew sustenance and vigor from an "eschatological instinct" that transformed class solidarity from a purely economic motivation into a "cause for ardor." De Man added that as soon as this transformation occurs, it is followed by "phenomena of mass psychology that are so little the emanation of a rational awareness of one's interests" that they can only be described "using the vocabulary of the history of religions and the psychology of beliefs." The most important of these phenomena is the eschatological instinct, the "nostalgia for better conditions in the future," which appears as an "absolute good," and it was this "trend towards the absolute that infused the socialist workers' movement with its eschatological and religious nature." According to De Man, this eschatological yearning was "the common and almost Christian basis to all the systems of myths and symbols that express the emotional life of the socialist movement," commencing with the fundamental myth of the Revolution, which "so powerfully evokes emotions that recall the eschatological visions of the Apocalypse, the end of the world, the Last Judgment, the Kingdom of God, etc."[28]

The fideistic interpretation approaches the study of the religious aspects of political movements from the opposite end, because it does not claim that leaders are always alone in the artificial production of political myths and rituals to deceive and control the masses. On the contrary, it accepts that myths and rituals can also be the spontaneous expression of the masses, produced by their need for faith and beliefs, which they then satisfy by their devotion to a leader or an ideology that promises them well-being and salvation. A civil or political religion, perceived in this manner, is not just an artifice and can actually constitute a new religion that responds to the mass's need for faith and fresh beliefs to direct their lives, as particularly occurs during periods of profound upheaval when long-established faiths are in decline and the hope of a better world becomes more compelling.

## SOCIETY'S GODS

The *functionalist* theory of religion developed by Emile Durkheim in 1912 is in part related to the fideistic theory of religious phenomena. He believed that religion "is a unified system of beliefs and practices relative to sacred things, that is to say, things set apart and surrounded by prohibitions—beliefs and practices that unite its adherents in a single moral community called a church."[29] Its function is to elevate people beyond themselves and have them live a superior life in the collectivity to which they belong. Religion is the condition in which the individual, in a psychological state of "effervescence," that is of elation and enthusiasm, transcends himself or herself through deep involvement in the collectivity to which he or she belongs as a result of shared beliefs. In this sense, religious experience "is above all warmth, life, enthusiasm, the exaltation of all mental activities, the transport of the individual beyond himself."[30]

For Durkheim, religion does not require the presence of a supernatural being, because it is nothing more than the expression of the totality of collective life. The divine is the society itself, and society venerates itself. "Religious representations are collective representations that express collective realities; rituals are ways of acting that are generated only within assembled groups and are meant to stimulate and sustain or recreate certain mental states in these groups."[31] The individuals who constitute a community feel unified and maintain that unity for as long as they share a set of beliefs and practice the rituals required by those beliefs. "Religious force is the feeling the collectivity inspires in its members, but projected outside and objectified by the minds that feel it. It becomes objectified by being anchored in an object which then becomes sacred, but any object can play this role."[32] Religious beliefs express the unity and identity of a collectivity, while rituals are forms of actions that serve to evoke, maintain, and renew the unity and identity of a social group through their reference to sacred entities, which can be objects, animals, persons, or ideas. Shared beliefs relating to sacred objects, such as the flag, the motherland, a form of political organization, a hero, or a historical event are mandatory beliefs in that the community will not tolerate their rejection or desecration. "For us the fatherland, the French Revolution and Joan of Arc are *sacred entities* and will not allow anyone to offend them."[33] According to Durkheim, therefore, even systems of collective beliefs, myths, and rituals that are institutionalized so as to reaffirm regularly the identity and unity of a political collectivity are religious manifestations or, more specifically, a secular religion that is not necessarily connected to faith in the existence of a supernatural being. He uses the experience of the French Revolution to show the propensity of a social group, particularly during periods of "collective effervescence," to create new divinities through the deification of its beliefs. During the early years of the Revolution, under the influence of widespread enthusiasm, there was public support for a new religion with its own dogmas, symbols, altars, and festivities, which spontaneously made sacred such entities as the Motherland, Freedom, and Reason, which originally had been purely secular. The Revolution attempted to gratify officially these "spontaneous aspirations" by establishing the cult of Reason and the Supreme Being.[34]

Durkheim claimed that the studies into revolutionary cults by the historian Albert Mathiez confirmed his own considerations on the French Revolution, and these studies had in turn used Durkheim's concept of religion.[35] In opposition to Aulard, Mathiez considered revolutionary cults to be spontaneous manifestations of a new religion that originated from the political experience of Revolution. He defined it as a "true religion," albeit an ephemeral one, because it contained all the fundamental elements common to all religions: *faith*, i.e., a set of obligatory beliefs that are asserted as indisputable dogmas, and *worship*, i.e., a set of symbols and rituals through which the beliefs are manifested. The political essence of this religion was *patriotism* and the messianic expectation of *regeneration*; its dogmas were the Law, the Constitution, Equality, Liberty, and the Sovereignty of the People.[36]

The functionalist interpretation considers the origin of any religious phenomenon to be a fundamentally spontaneous product of a united collectivity, and therefore it does not exclude the possibility that the birth of new religions that deify society and politics is in fact a religious phenomenon. Indeed, the majority of scholars studying civil religions, perceived as systems of beliefs, myths, principles, and symbolic behavior that express the fundamental values of a society, subscribe to the functionalist theory.

## MANIFESTATIONS OF THE SACRED IN MODERNITY

Finally, the existence of a civil or political religion appears plausible, if we refer to the concept of the sacred developed by the German theologian

Rudolf Otto in 1917.[37] According to his theory, the sacred, which he considers to be "a category of interpretation and valuation peculiar to the sphere of religion,"[38] is an inexpressible spiritual experience that cannot be understood rationally and occurs in the presence of the *numinous*. This term, which was coined by Otto, refers to the manifestation of an immense, mysterious, and majestic power that, through its enthralling and awe-inspiring nature, invokes a feeling of absolute dependency in whoever experiences it, but at the same time it produces an irrational energy that "engages man's sentiments, drives him to 'industrious fervor' and fills him with a boundless dynamic tension both in terms of asceticism and zealousness against the world and the flesh, and in terms of heroic behavior by which the inner excitement erupts into the external world."[39] Religions originate from the numinous experience of the sacred.

A theoretical presupposition is required in order to claim that the political dimension could never be the stage of numinous experiences and manifestations of the sacred. Throughout history, political power has always been invested with a sacred nature, even when not directly identified with a divinity. According to religious anthropology, absolute power is an essential attribute of the sacred, while political anthropology explains that an aura of sacredness always emanates from those who hold power. In the modern age, the state, having freed itself from the sanctification conferred on it by traditional religion, can appear as a numinous reality and an enthralling and awe-inspiring power that invokes a feeling of absolute dependency. Even modern warfare can be perceived as a violent experience of the sacred and therefore facilitate the formation of new religious beliefs directed toward secular entities, such as the nation, the people, or the race. Perhaps it is no coincidence that Otto's book on the sacred was published during the First World War and was an immediate success. The Italian philosopher Adriano Tilgher explicitly turned to the theory of the numinous in order to interpret the proliferation of the new secular religions that after the First World War took the place of the religions of Humanity, Progress, and Science, "through which Western civilization attempted to fill the vacuum left in the spirit by the decline of Christianity."[40] At the beginning of the Great War, following the decline of nineteenth-century secular religions, the "numinous sentiment," wrote Tilgher in 1938, "wandered in a state of freedom and purity in search of new objects and terms on which to discharge itself, just as a lightning charge wanders in search of a place in which to discharge itself. Just after the war, it discharged itself on *new* objects: the State, the Fatherland, the Nation, the Race, the Class, which were entities which had to be defended against mortal dangers or one of which everything was expected."

> The period after the [First World] War witnessed one of the most startling outbreaks of pure numinousness ever recalled in the history of the world.

We witnessed the birth of new deities [*numines*] with our own eyes. You would need to be blind and deaf to all current realities if you were unable to realize that for very many of our contemporaries State, Fatherland, Nation, Race, and Class are objects not just of enthusiastic veneration but also of mystical adoration. They are terms belonging to a numinous sentiment because they are perceived as presences that boundlessly transcend daily life and as such they evoke all the contradictory and ambivalent feelings that are to be found within the numinous: love and terror, and enthrallment and fear. They generate impulses of mystical adoration and devotion. . . . The twentieth century promises to add a few interesting chapters to the history of religious wars (which the nineteenth century believed were over): that is my prophecy which in all probability is about to be proven correct.[41]

Numinous situations in the world of modern politics occur during revolutions, when politics becomes a place of violent "collective effervescence" and can indeed be a numinous experience. The forces that produce it and manage to successfully dominate it can assume a sacred aura, because they appear as manifestations of a majestic and terrible power. In the modern era, the revolution in itself has become a sacred secular entity in the manner in which it is imagined, desired, pursued, and experienced.

Finally, modernity could be a favorable situation for the birth of new religions, to the extent that it is a period of violent upheavals that destroy millennial certainties and drag humanity into a vortex of continuous change. "The entire contemporary world is again in search of a religion," Benedetto Croce wrote at the beginning of the twentieth century. He argued that the problem of modern civilization was above all a religious problem:

Religion derives from the need for a concept of reality and life, and for direction in relation to them. Without religion and without this direction, you cannot live or you live unhappily with a divided and confused spirit. Of course, it is better to have a religion that conforms to philosophical truth than a religion based on myth, but it is better to have any religion based on myth than no religion at all. Given that no one wishes to live unhappily, everyone in their own way endeavors consciously or unconsciously to create a religion for themselves.[42]

During the same period, Durkheim foresaw that modernity would favor the creation of new religions even outside the traditional field of the historical religions, as had occurred in the French Revolution, because modernity produces situations of disintegration, uncertainty, anomie, and continuous agitation. Every society feels the need to reaffirm and renew "the collective sentiments and ideas that form its unity and its personality."

Now, this moral remaking can be achieved only by means of meetings, assemblies, or congregations in which individuals, brought into close contact, reaffirm in common their common feelings: hence those ceremonies whose goals, results, and methods do not differ in kind from properly religious ceremonies. What essential difference is there between an assembly of Christians commemorating the principal moments in the life of Christ, or Jews celebrating either the exodus from Egypt or the giving of the ten commandments, and a meeting of citizens commemorating the institution of a new moral charter or some great event in national life?[43]

Modern man had lost his faith in the traditional religions, but his need for religion remained very much alive. However, attempts to satisfy that need, such as the revolutionary cults or the project to establish a secular religion of humanity organized by the positivist philosopher Auguste Comte, who had taught Durkheim, all proved to be short-lived. Because of its irrepressible need, the French sociologist concluded, humankind would never cease to invent new gods and new religions.

In short, the ancient gods grow old or die, and others are not yet born. . . . But this state of uncertainty and confused agitation cannot go on forever. A day will come when our societies will once again experience times of creative effervescence and new ideas will surge up, new formulas will arise that will serve to guide humanity for a time. And having lived during these times, men will spontaneously experience the need to revive them through thought now and then, that is, to sustain the memory of them by means of festivals that regularly recreate their fruits. We have already seen how the French Revolution instituted a whole cycle of festivals to preserve the principles that inspired it in a state of perpetual youth. If the institution quickly perished, that is because revolutionary faith lasted only for a little while; disappointments and discouragement rapidly followed after the first moment of enthusiasm. But although the work was aborted, it allows us to imagine what it might have been under other conditions; and everything leads us to think that sooner or later it will be taken up again. There are no immortal gospels, and there is no reason to believe that humanity is henceforth incapable of conceiving new ones. As for knowing in advance the symbols in which the new faith will be expressed, if they will or will not resemble those of the past, if they will be more adequate to the reality they are meant to translate, this is a matter that surpasses human faculties of prediction and is, moreover, beside the point.[44]

Today many of those studying religious phenomena believe that the modern age is not undergoing an irreversible process of secularization involving the gradual disappearance of the sacred from an increasingly cynical world, but is rather a situation in which there is a continuous *metamorphosis of the sacred* in politics and in other dimensions to human activity. The historian of religion Mircea Eliade has observed that the experience of the sacred is not at all foreign to the conscience of modern man who claims that he has now been liberated from ancient religious beliefs and has become "nonreligious man." This liberation is entirely an illusion for many people, because this "nonreligious man descends from *homo religiosus* and, whether he likes it or not, he is also the work of religious man; his formation begins with the situations assumed by his ancestors." Modern man rebels against his past and attempts to free himself from it, but "do what he will, he is an inheritor. He cannot utterly abolish his past, since he is himself the product of his past."

> For . . . nonreligious man *in the pure state* is a comparatively rare phenomenon, even in the most desacralized of modern societies. The majority of the "irreligious" still behave religiously, even though they are unaware of the fact. . . . But the modern man who feels and claims that he is nonreligious still retains a large stock of camouflaged myths and degenerated rituals. . . . Strictly speaking, the great majority of the irreligious are not liberated from religious behavior, from theologies and mythologies. . . . In short, the majority of men "without religion" still hold to pseudoreligious and degenerated mythologies.[45]

In the contemporary age, the sacred has displayed tenacious resistance and an extraordinary vitality.[46] Secularization disengaged the sacred from institutional religions that had tempered it in their dogmas and rituals, and let it go "wild," to use the sociologist Roger Bastide's expression, by which he meant free to find new ways of manifesting itself in every human activity until it is eventually brought under control by other dogmas and rituals. The "death of the established gods" does not at all mean "the disappearance of the establishing experience of the sacred in search of new forms in which to embody itself,"[47] and the death of God, proclaimed by Nietzsche, "is not necessarily the death of the sacred, since the experience of the sacred constitutes an essential dimension for mankind."[48]

From this point of view, then, the experience of the sacred does not exhaust itself with the advance of secularization. "What is generally called the 'process of secularization' often obscures the savage proliferation of religiosity," writes the anthropologist Claude Rivire, for whom it is undeniable that "the sacred (*fascinans* and *tremendum*) is a fundamental anthropological dimension, whose domain cannot be limited to that of the established religions, nor even to its manifestations to a sociography of religious practices."[49] As has been observed by religious historian Giovanni Filoramo, while it is true "that secularization has deprived traditional religions of a whole series of domains by rendering them profane and autonomous, it is equally true that these domains are once again

creators of the sacred, independent of the traditional religions."[50] In a
modern society, sacredness therefore constitutes "one of the possible ways
of putting socially shared meanings in order and creating some coherence
around them. To be more precise, the process of sacralization is triggered
when individuals and groups of people confer an absolute value on objects and symbols in order to make sense of their individual or collective
existence (they consecrate them and therefore isolate them)."[51] The modern thus becomes in part a "place for the creation of the religious," in
that "while modernity has undoubtedly secularized traditional religions,
it is not however irreversibly antagonistic to religion and the sacred in
general." On the contrary, "modernity's restructuring favors in turn the
emergence of rationales and dynamics based on sacredness and religiosity
that never disappeared."[52] During the period of modernity, other faiths
have appeared alongside faith in the supernatural, and these have sacralized different aspects of human activity. The sociologist Salvador
Giner has observed that modern times, although apparently in many ways
insensitive to the supernatural, have very often replaced it with "social
transcendence," such as

> the myths of revolution, nation, new eras, scientism, new man, complete
> liberation, communion with nature and the universe, eternal health, hedo-
> nism as the only way to live, and many others are now forms of transcen-
> dence, whether they are separate or joined in various combinations and
> whether or not they are linked to supernatural religions. Thanks to them,
> we have encountered a barrier to the process of desecration of the world that
> started with the Renaissance. These myths are the material on which the
> secular metamorphosis of the ancients who have returned to life consolidated
> its position.[53]

In the modern era, expressions of the sacralization of different aspects
of human life have multiplied using history, philosophy, art, and, last but
not least, politics. The political philosopher Manuel García Pelayo has
written that there are eras or social groups within a particular era that do
not perceive politics solely as "an order in which human life has to develop and an essential field like any other, but as the ontological foundation and root of human existence." Consequently, they expect politics
not just to resolve particular problems, but rather "the entire problem of
existence":

> In short, by introducing religious practices into politics, they experience poli-
> tics as a life and means of salvation, either because they believe, as the ancient
> world did, that salvation, although the work of the divine, is revealed
> through a political system established by a charismatic figure with a sacred
> nature or because man, in spite of having lost his belief in God, has not lost

his sense of being an unfortunate soul and he still places all his hopes of salvation in a political doctrine or system. This phenomenon has given rise to what some people call "political religions." We will not dwell upon the rights and wrongs of this term, but it is at least clear that certain ideologies and certain political movements cannot be fully understood without the assistance of definitions that were originally religious although now translated into non-religious categories.

Modern politics has thus become, according to the religious sociologist Jean-Pierre Sironneau, "the preferred terrain for the creation and expansion of the sacred in secular societies."

It is a fact that our contemporaries have tended to direct part of their religious aspirations and passions toward politics, transform political ideologies into myths, and look on many political leaders or dictators as divine and heroic figures. Modern politics is full of "sacred" persons. These figures are both terrifying (*tremendum*) because they possess all the (technical, military and psychological) power of the modern state and have enormous capacity to impose their will and reek destruction, and reassuring (*fascinans*) because they represent a providential force capable of providing protection and safety to modern man who has been uprooted and ground down by the great industrial and urban complexes. Politics has produced the idols of our time. . . . Politics reveals more easily the traditional expressions of religions, namely myth, ritual, communion and faith. Politics have taken on the role of legitimizing the social order that in the past was carried out by religion.[54]

In conclusion, it appears entirely legitimate to consider the sacralization of politics a *modern ieropahany,* that is, a manifestation of the sacred in modernity and to study civil and political religions as new forms of religiosity that originated during the modern era and belong to it. Max Weber, who was very much the theoretician of disillusionment with the modern world, wrote in 1890 that the ancients had not been definitively banished but were to return in another form: "The ancient gods, disenchanted and therefore transformed into impersonal powers, rise from their graves and reassume the eternal struggle between them in the hope of conquering the supremacy of life."[55] The experience of totalitarian religions authorizes us to argue that politics was the battlefield where the new gods fought for supremacy over men during the twentieth century. Those who witness the advent of totalitarian religions were certainly convinced of this, and they considered such religions to be a deadly danger to humanity.

## Chapter 2

# CIVIL RELIGIONS AND POLITICAL RELIGIONS

*From Democratic Revolutions to Totalitarian States*

> Once religious faith (in the traditional sense of the word)
> had gone, people desperately searched for a new system
> of beliefs and general principles around which to re-
> group themselves and in which to find the reason within
> their innermost selves for living in a worthwhile fashion.
> They thus created an endless number of new "churches,"
> according to their social class: some found followings
> in the salons, others amongst intellectuals and still others
> amidst the working people.
> —Antonio Gramsci

## A Citizen's Religion

The sacralization of politics in the modern era commenced with the democratic revolutions of the eighteenth century, but its roots went back to the
humanistic idealization of the Greek and Roman civic religion; the new
secular concepts of life, society, and the state; the Masonic tradition of
rituals and symbols; and ultimately the Enlightenment culture itself.[1] The
specifically political conditions that made its birth possible were affirmation of the principal of a state's sovereignty in relation to the church and
the glorification of the nation as the supreme ideal entity to which the
citizen owes loyalty, devotion, and commitment.

The concept of sovereignty developed by modern theoreticians of the
absolute state laid the foundations for the sacralization of politics because
it was created out of secularized theological concepts that transferred the
attributes of divinity to the state and thus conferred upon it a sacredness
no longer dependent on consecration by the church. Almighty God had
now become the omnipotent legislator.[2] Subsequently, the Enlightenment
took its polemic against ecclesiastical religion and the hegemony of the
church to the point of proclaiming the primacy of the state over religious
matters too. In 1770 Abbot Guillaume Raynal argued:

> It is not the state that is made for religion, but religion that is made for
> the state. First principle. The general interest is the rule that must govern
> everything that exists within the state. Second principle. Only the people, or

the sovereign authority that is its custodian, has the right to judge whether any institution conforms to the general interest. Third principle. . . . The examination of a religion's dogmas and discipline are the sole concern of this authority. . . . Only this authority can proscribe an existing cult, adopt a new one or do without one altogether, if this is in its interests. . . . There is no other council outside the sovereign's assembly of ministers. When the administrators of the state are gathered in assembly, the church is in assembly. When the state has pronounced its view, the church has nothing to say.[3]

The Enlightenment made an important contribution to the sacralization of civil society and the nation by elevating them to the status of supreme bodies and values for the modern citizen. An essay on the new freedom of thought that was published in Amsterdam in 1743, asserted "civil society is, as it were, the only divinity that [the philosopher] can acknowledge on the earth; he venerates and honors it with probity, constant attention to his duties and a sincere desire not to be a useless and troublesome member of it."[4] In 1755, Abbot Coyer argued that the nation is "a power as ancient as society itself and founded on nature and order; it is a power superior to all the powers that it establishes within itself, and it subjugates to its laws all those who command in its name as well as those who obey. It is a divinity that accepts gifts only to lavish them, that demands love rather than respect, that smiles when providing assistance and sighs when casting down its thunderbolts."[5] Love for one's country, wrote Diderot in his article on the nation in the *Enciclopedie*, "leads a high standard of morals, and this leads to love for the land of one's fathers": "Love for the fatherland is love for the laws and the prosperity of the state, and is particularly strong in democracies. It is a political virtue by which an individual surrenders his own interests and gives preference to the public interest over his own. It is a sentiment, and not based on any knowledge; it can be shared by the lowliest person and by the head of state."

The Enlightenment was convinced that a well-ordered society could not do without some form of collective religion that educated the individual to place the public good above personal interest. In 1749 Benjamin Franklin, when concerning himself with the education of the youth of Philadelphia, argued "the Necessity of a *Publick Religion*, from its Usefulness to the Publick," which had to be inculcated in young people through the teaching of history.[6] It was precisely in relation to the cult of the nation and the duties of the citizenry that the ideal of a new civil religion based on the principles of deism, natural rights, and civic virtue came to be formed in the second half of the eighteenth century. It drew on the ancient model of republican religion and was perceived as the ideal foundation for ensuring the moral unity of the body politic and for instructing citizens in awareness of the common good, a sense of civic duty, loyalty to institutions, and devotion to the nation. Jean-Jacques Rousseau claimed in 1756 that people cannot do without a religion when they form a society:

> As soon as men live in society, they need a religion that holds them together. There has never been and never will be a people without a religion. If no one provided a people with a religion, then they would provide themselves with one or very soon be annihilated. Anyone who does not believe in a future life is necessarily a coward or a madman in any state that can demand its members to sacrifice their lives, but we know only too well the degree to which hope of a future life can drive a fanatic to despise his earthly existence. Free the fanatic from his visions and give him the same hope as the prize for virtue and you will have made a true citizen of him.[7]

Rousseau developed these premises in *The Social Contract* (1762) to produce the concept of a new civil religion as the indispensable spiritual bond maintaining political unity in a new national state founded on popular sovereignty. Underlying this concept, there was the need to overcome the division created by Christianity, which had separated the "theological from the political system" by establishing its church on earth. This had shattered the unity of the body politic, bringing about "the internal divisions which have never ceased to trouble Christian peoples." He argued that the only solution to this evil was to follow Thomas Hobbes's proposal for "a reunion of the two heads of the eagle, and the restoration throughout of political unity, without which no State or government will ever be rightly constituted."[8] This solution led to the rejection of Christianity, because this religion "so far from binding the hearts of the citizens to the State, . . . has the effect of taking them away from all earthly things. I know of nothing more contrary to the social spirit."[9] Democracy therefore needed "a purely civil profession of faith of which the Sovereign should fix the articles, not exactly as religious dogmas, but as social sentiments without which a man cannot be a good citizen or a faithful subject." The dogma of the civil religion had to be "few, simple, and exactly worded, without explanation or commentary." Rousseau himself suggested what they should be: "The existence of a mighty, intelligent and beneficent Divinity, possessed of foresight and providence, the life to come, the happiness of the just, the punishment of the wicked, the sanctity of the social contract and the laws." These were the "positive dogmas" of the civil religion, whereas the only "negative dogma" was intolerance. Rousseau condemned intolerance and the religions that practiced it, such as the "exclusive national religion," while he demanded the acceptance of all those religions that tolerated others, but only "so long as their dogmas contain nothing contrary to the duties of citizenship." The principle of tolerance did not extend to those citizens who failed in their duty of loyalty to the precepts of the civil religion after having accepted them:

While [the sovereign] can compel no one to believe them, it can banish from the State whoever does not believe them—it can banish him, not for impiety, but as an anti-social being, incapable of truly loving the laws and justice, and of sacrificing, at need, his life to his duty. If any one, after publicly recognizing these dogmas, behaves as if he does not believe them, let him be punished by death: he has committed the worst of all crimes, that of lying before the law.[10]

In this manner, civil religion conferred sacredness on democracy. Rousseau attributed an equally sacred role to the governors of his republic who were responsible for renewing and teaching the citizenry in particular to love their country. Democracy had the supreme purpose of moral education that molded the citizens' consciences so that they were wholly devoted to the good of the fatherland and to worshipping as a divinity held up before them.

When first he opens his eyes, an infant ought to see the fatherland, and up to the day of his death he ought never to see anything else. Every true republican has drunk in love of country, that is to say love of law and liberty, along with his mother's milk. This love is his whole existence; he sees nothing but the fatherland, he lives for it alone; when he is solitary, he is nothing; when he has ceased to have a fatherland, he no longer exists; and if he is not dead, he is worse than dead.[11]

Rousseau wrote in the *Considerations on the Government of Poland* (1771) that education "must give souls a national formation, and direct their opinions and tastes in such a way that they will be patriotic by inclination, by passion, by necessity."[12] The establishment of a civil religion necessarily presupposed the existence of a didactic state, which had to take responsibility for the moral renewal of each individual who then is integrated through education into the moral community of the body politic:

He who dares to undertake the making of a people's institutions ought to feel himself capable, so to speak, of changing human nature, of transforming each individual, who is by himself a complete and solitary whole, into part of a greater whole from which he in a manner receives his life and being; of altering man's constitution for the purpose of strengthening it; and of substituting a partial and moral existence for the physical and independent existence nature has conferred on us all.[13]

American and French revolutionaries, as disciples of the Enlightenment, were the first politicians of our modern age who took up the task of providing the people with new institutions. They were convinced that no democracy would be able to survive without a common faith inspired by civic virtues and by loyalty and devotion to the state and fatherland, because it would be continuously threatened by the selfishness of individuals. The first civil religions were born therefore to consecrate the legitimacy of democracy and subordinate particular interests to the common good.

## THE NEW PEOPLE OF GOD

The American civil religion started to form during the War of Independence, and developed during the nineteenth century, particularly after the Civil War. It coexisted with numerous traditional religious confessions in a general climate of mutual tolerance, in spite of the prevailing puritan roots of the American civil religion and the close association of its principles and values to the Christian tradition.[14] The formation of the American civil religion was actually facilitated by the existence of religious pluralism, which prevented a single religious confession from assuming the role of Established Church, even though Protestantism maintained its decisive hegemony over the shaping of the republic's civil religion until the middle of the twentieth century, and this actively sustained patriotism and the spirit of liberalism. The American civil religion was the result of religious, ideological, and political syncretism, to which Protestantism, the Enlightenment, and republicanism all contributed. In this sense, the American civil religion constitutes a unique phenomenon in the history of sacralization of politics because of its particular historical characteristics and its continuing presence over the last two centuries of American history, although it has gone through different stages. It could be argued that it is the only example of fully developed civil religion that provided a religious dimension to politics independent from traditional religions, while still appealing to a transcendent God. It achieves this without entering into conflict with traditional religions; indeed, it has their support and cooperation in building a system of beliefs, myths, values, and symbols relating to the American nation, the majority of which derive from the Old and New Testaments as far as their essential structure is concerned.

Alexis de Tocqueville was the first to realize the fundamental role of religion in American democracy. After his visit to the United States, he wrote in 1835: "In France I had almost always seen the spirit of religion and the spirit of freedom marching in opposite directions. But in America I found they were intimately united and that they reigned in common over the same country."[15] This was the reason for the fundamental importance Americans attributed to religious faith as the basis of the republican democracy, without however giving a privileged status to any confession or church. "Religion in America takes no direct part in the government of society, but it must be considered the first of their political institutions;

for if it does not impart a taste for freedom, it facilitates the use of it."[16] According to Tocqueville, the religious dimension of American democracy did not only involve political institutions and their functions, but affected the entire interpretation of the meaning of American history, the Revolution, and the new era heralded by the creation of the United States. Thus the foundations of the American civil religion were laid, and by civil religion we mean the expression of a religious dimension that sacralizes the institutions of the republic by providing categories, myths, principles, and values through which the newly founded nation interpreted its origin, role, and mission in the history of mankind. Sacredness was bestowed upon American democracy with the mediation and cooperation of the traditional religious confessions but with a tendency for the civil religion to take on an independent existence while producing a system of beliefs, myths, rituals, and symbols that actually made a cult of the American nation, its institution, its history, and its heroes, albeit a system that constantly referred to the supreme spiritual sovereignty of an impersonal God and Omnipotent Being. Francis Grund, an Austrian diplomat who emigrated to the United States, observed in 1837 that religion had been the foundation of the more important American colonies, had held together their small communities, had assisted Americans in their war of independence, and had incited them to defend their rights. But that was not all; it had also taught the citizens of the republic the value of liberty and had suffused their civic awareness and patriotism with a religious spirit.

> It is with the solemnities of religion that the declaration of independence is yet annually read to the people from the pulpit, or that Americans celebrate the anniversaries of the most important events of their history. It is to religion that they have recourse whenever they wish to impress the popular feeling with anything relative to their country; and it is religion which assists them in all their national undertakings. The Americans look upon religion as a promoter of civil and political liberty; and have, therefore, transferred to it a large portion of the affection which they cherish for the institutions of their country.[17]

From the very early years of its existence, the United States had been involved in a *transfer of sacredness* from traditional religious confessions to the political dimension of the new republic, which continued uninterrupted although with varying degrees of intensity over the following two centuries of American history, contributing to the formation of that "public religion" for which Franklin had so wished. It was a public religion that mixed together the biblical theology of Puritanism, the rationalist deism of the Enlightenment, and the beliefs, myths, and symbols emerging from the growing patriotism of the new republic. From the very beginning it reworked the events of its own origins as a heroic epic and a "sacred history" whose further developments unfolded under the benevolent eye of the Almighty.[18]

The American revolutionaries, who had been educated in the religious and civic traditions of Puritanism as well as Enlightenment philosophy, lived through the War of Independence as though it were a religious experience and interpreted it in terms of the eschatological myths of Protestant millenarianism.[19] They were convinced that they were a new people chosen by God and a new Israel that was about to implement the divine will and contribute to the rebirth and salvation of humanity.[20] The War of Independence and the foundation of the United States were compared with the Exodus, the arrival in the Promised Land, and the establishment of a new Jerusalem, the "city upon a hill" destined to become a beacon to all humanity. The founding father were glorified after their death as earthly gods and placed in the nation's Pantheon. Monuments and temples were dedicated to their memory.[21] Washington was sanctified as a new Moses who liberated the new Israel from slavery by taking it to the promised land of liberty and independence. The date of his birth (19 February) became a federal holiday.[22]

An American writer considered the birth of the United States to be the "event next in importance to the birth of Christ,"[23] and the beginning of a new era in which the American people had the task of restoring humanity to the rightful path. The myth of rebirth, which was to have a pivotal role in all civil and political religions, was to be found in American culture from the very beginning of the republic, not only as an ideal projected toward implementation in the future, but also as an actual reality existing the conscience, values, and principles of the new American society: immigrants from Europe acquired a new dignity as citizens along with liberty and equality. The regenerative myth of "new man," which was to become the fundamental aspiration of all civil and political religions, was American man himself as far as American patriots were concerned. American man was supposed to have freed himself from the evils of the Old European World through his moral revival in the New World. Liberty and the boundless spaces transformed immigrants into a new people, wrote Hector St. John Crèvecoeur, whose famous account of his experiences as an American colonial farmer was published in 1782: "Every thing has tended to regenerate them. New laws, a new mode of living, a new social system. Here they are become men. . . . Here individuals of all nations are melted into a new race of men, whose labors and posterity will one day cause great changes in the world." The American, he concluded, "is a new man, who acts upon new principles."[24] The United States was the promised land for all peoples of the earth who sought liberty, dignity, and happiness.

During the nineteenth century, the civil religion developed through the exaltation of the American people who had been elected by God and the mission he gave them to seek the welfare of all of humankind. The belief that the United States' mission came from God was consolidated and popularized through presidential speeches, sermons, historical accounts, literature, and school education. It became the last and fundamental myth of the American civil religion.[25] The messianic essence of the American nation, according to the writer Herman Melville, was in the divine nature of its democracy, which conferred "august dignity" on every human being, "that democratic dignity which, on all hands, radiates without end from God; Himself! The great God absolute! The center and circumference of all democracy! His omnipresence, our divine equality!"[26] Democracy in the United States was confirmation that the American people had been called by God to carry out great deeds for the good of all humanity:

> We Americans are the peculiar, chosen people—the Israel of our time: we bear the ark of the liberties of the world. . . . God has predestined, mankind expects, great things from our race; and great things we feel in our souls. The rest of the nations must soon be in our rear. We are the pioneers of the world; the advance guard, sent through the wilderness of untried things, to break a path in the New World that is ours. In our youth is our strength; in our inexperience, our wisdom. At a period when other nations have but lisped, our deep voice is heard afar. Long enough we have been skeptics with regard to ourselves, and doubted whether, indeed, the political Messiah had come. But he has come in *us*, if we would give utterance to his promptings.[27]

The American Civil War gave added impetus to the American civil religion in the second half of the nineteenth century. It was fought by both sides in the conviction that each was defending the fundamental values of the American nation in order to remain loyal to the mission God had bestowed upon them. The experience of the Civil War provided a tragic and prophetic dimension to the republican religion, which up until then had been marked by optimistic pride. This was enhanced by Abraham Lincoln's religious interpretation of the war and its meaning. Lincoln was a man of deep religious consciousness, although not a member of any church. He perceived history as the implementation of God's will, and firmly believed that God had chosen the American people to carry out his work in history. He considered the nation's mission to be the defense of the "government of the people by the people for the people."[28] He had a mystical concept of the Union, which he identified with liberty and democracy, and he interpreted the Civil War as a punishment for the disunity of the American people, who had broken their sacred pact with the Omnipotent. It was therefore a martyrdom required in order to regenerate the American nation and make it again worthy of God's mission. The

United States had to regain humility in relation to its responsibilities to the Omnipotent through suffering: Lincoln told Congress at the end of 1862, "We shall nobly save, or meanly lose, the last, best hope of earth."[29]

The experience of the Civil War provided the American religion with new myths, symbols, and rituals, which also derived from the transposition of sacred Christian models onto the civil and political spheres. The celebration of Thanksgiving Day was established during Lincoln's presidency in 1863 as a family ceremony of national devotion to God. The consecration of war graves and the cult of fallen soldiers then became the new rituals, of the republican religion, which were celebrated on Memorial Day since 1868. The myth of regeneration was renewed through the experience of the Civil War with the concept of sacrifice and death as a form of expiation in order for the nation to be reborn and unity safeguarded, a concept that came to be represented symbolically by the assassination of Lincoln, the victim sacrificed for the salvation of the Union and therefore the whole of humanity.[30] Lincoln immediately entered the pantheon of the American civil religion and took pride of place alongside Washington. Now the son who had sacrificed himself for the Union and for democracy sat beside the nation's founding father. Since 1866, Lincoln's date of birth (12 February) has been celebrated in many northern states in memory of their president.[31]

Following the Civil War and particularly in the final decades of the nineteenth century, faith in democracy stayed at the very center of the civil religion, but its values, myths, rituals, and symbols did not extend to those who were not Anglo-Saxons and were excluded from society and its institutions, such as Native Americans, blacks, immigrants of non–Anglo-Saxon races, and those who were not of the Protestant religion. Racism in various forms was a component that underlay the civil religion since the birth of the United States, and it was not eliminated by the victory of the Union over the rebel states of the South. Indeed, hostility toward minorities of outcasts and marginalized persons thought to belong to races of inferior civilizations and to believe in false faiths found its moral justification in the civil religion of Anglo-Saxon whites. This hostility was supposed to be a sacrosanct aversion to those who for various reasons could be considered the incarnation or agents of Evil, or in any case enemies of the American religion. The United States was glorified not so much as the promised land and refuge for the forsaken and persecuted of the world than as a great imperial power that had to spread the superior civilization of the Anglo-Saxon race around the world. The myth of a people chosen by God to carry out a mission of salvation for all mankind became extraordinarily popular in the second half of the nineteenth century and was used to justify wars of conquest and expansion by the republic of the star-spangled banner. The impact of industrialization and global competition caused faith in democracy to be increasingly identified with faith in the "manifest destiny"[32] of the American nation, now conceived as the onus on the Anglo-Saxon race to expand. Seen in this light, the civil religion's accentuation of its nationalistic, racist, and imperialist tones tended to take on the characteristics of an intolerant and fundamentalist political religion that reserved full membership of the national community blessed by God to Americans of Anglo-Saxon stock. Shortly after the end of the Spanish-American War, Albert J. Beveridge, a popular Republican senator, produced an explicit and conceited expression of the new imperial version of the American mission required and watched over by Divine Providence:

> It is a glorious history our God has bestowed upon His chosen people; a history whose keynote was struck by Liberty Bell; a history heroic with faith in our mission and our future; a history of statesmen who flung the boundaries of the republic out into unexplored lands and savage wildernesses; a history of soldiers who carried the flag across the blazing deserts and through the ranks of hostile mountains, even to the gates of sunset; a history of a multiplying people who overran a continent in half a century; a history of prophets who saw the consequences of evils inherited from the past and of martyrs who died to save us from them; a history divinely logical, in the process of whose tremendous reasoning we find ourselves today.[33]

Thus, the civil religion assumed an openly nationalistic and racist nature that prevailed until the First World War, when the American nation's fundamental principles and values of liberty and democracy once again began to prevail. President Woodrow Wilson, a religious man who believed in the religious role of politics and in the American people's divine mission, justified the United States' participation in the First World War as a duty to God and to humanity in order to defend, save, and spread liberty and democracy in the world.[34] The Americans went to war as a crusade to save civilization from the modern Huns and were exhorted to fight from the pulpit of nearly all the churches, which united under the symbols of patriotic religion to exalt the American nation's mission and reassure their congregations that God was on their side in the holy war against the Antichrist now incarnated by imperial Germany.[35] The war was perceived as an apocalyptic battle of Armageddon and the final struggle between the forces of Good and Evil. The war dead were beatified as martyrs sacrificed in order to achieve the destiny of the American nation under God's will, and the struggle was to lead to the regeneration of mankind and a world safe for democracy.

## FRENCH DEMOCRACY IN SEARCH OF A CIVIL RELIGION

The events surrounding the sacralization of politics in France differed very considerably from the American experience, but in modern Europe, a religion of politics first made its appearance following the Revolution of 1789. Like the American Revolution, the French Revolution was caught up in an atmosphere of messianic and eschatological religious enthusiasm.[36] The political and religious immediately became entangled with each other, and this was reflected in the way supporters and enemies of the Revolution experienced and interpreted revolutionary events. Catholic reactionaries saw the Revolution as the act of the devil, especially when it took an anti-Christian direction.

New symbols, such as the Altar of the Fatherland, the Tree of Liberty, and the tricolor cockade, were spontaneously produced by the revolutionary exuberance, and they represented the new beliefs evoked by the fall the Ancien Régime and the messianic expectancy of a new era. Along with the establishment of new rituals relating to the nation and the celebration of fundamental revolutionary events such as the taking of the Bastille and the abolition of the feudal system, they made a decisive contribution to the sacralization of revolutionary ideals and events.[37] The Declaration of Rights and the Constitution were made sacred by the civic oath of the citizenry, and became the Ten Commandments of the new revolutionary faith. They were engraved on metal and stone for display above the altars of the fatherland as objects of veneration and worship. In a largely spontaneous manner, they thus combined to create the constituent parts of a civil religion in the sense that Rousseau had hoped for: a system of beliefs, myths, rituals, and symbols that conferred a religious meaning on the Revolution itself as a great messianic event marking a period of renewal.[38] After having regenerated France through the Revolution, the French people were to re-create the ideas of Liberty, Fraternity, and Equality for humanity as a whole.

The myth of regeneration projected onto the "new man" was the original core around which the revolutionary religion arose and developed.[39] French revolutionaries believed in the regenerative powers of politics through the educative role of the new democratic institutions which had to be saturated with religiosity, because they felt certain that a state could not exist without a religion.

At the beginning, revolutionaries were not at all hostile to Catholicism as the dominant faith, nor did they wish to replace it with a new religion. The first public ceremonies of revolutionary France sacralized the nation reborn and its revolutionary ideals but also attempted to reconcile the Revolution with Catholicism. The Festival of the Federation, the first great collective celebration of revolutionary France, took place in Paris on 14 July 1790 and was a syncretic ritual combining Catholicism and the newly created revolutionary religiosity. An altar was placed at the center of a great amphitheater built in the Champs-de-Mars, where Bishop Talleyrand, a deputy for the clergy in the States General, celebrated mass while surrounded by two hundred priests, in the presence of the king and representatives of the National Assembly and before 300,000 spectators from all over France. Then everyone swore allegiance to the Constitution in accordance with the formula pronounced by Marquis La Fayette. After the Civil Constitution of the Clergy (12 July 1790), however, revolutionaries entered a war with Catholicism and undertook to create a new citizens' religion founded on the dogmas of Fatherland, Law, Constitution, and the new secular Trinity of "Liberty, Fraternity, and Equality." This involved transferring the sacred from the monarchy by divine right to the sovereign nation and the republic through the introduction of new festivals, rituals, and symbols.[40]

Once the fracture between the Revolution and the Catholic Church had occurred, revolutionaries took their inspiration directly from Rousseau and conceived a revolutionary religious program. They felt that their mission to renew their world could not be restricted to political and social reform. Religious reform was also needed if they were to carry it through to completion: "We certainly have the power to change religion," said a deputy to the Legislative Assembly on 1 July 1790.[41] The new state had to have a religious essence and role; as Rousseau had hoped, it had to unite "the two heads of the eagle" and fulfill the essential task of the new citizens' moral education.[42] The revolutionaries wanted to put the ideal of a civil religion and a didactic state in practice in order to raise future generations in the cult of the nation and its democratic ideals. They had a mystical faith in the regenerative powers of laws and institutions, but they also believed in the didactic role of festivals, rituals, and symbols as the instruments for inculcating the civil religion and revolutionary faith. Jacobins established new cults, such as the cult of the Goddess Reason or of the Supreme Being, and yet revolutionary politics itself became a new religion. Even though the attempts made by French revolutionaries to establish a new civil religion were short-lived, the legacy of their revolutionary faith proved to be lasting, if understood as the myth that the Revolution has a sacred regenerative power that creates a better world through the purification of violence.

Even those who did not hold this faith could see its importance in the revolutionary experience. Tocqueville wrote that the French Revolution had been "a political revolution which acted like and began to look like a religious revolution":

Observe the characteristic traits which make it resemble one: not only is it widespread, but, like a religious revolution, it is spread by preaching and propaganda. It is a political revolution which inspires conversions, and which preaches as ardently to foreigners as it acts passionately at home: think what a new sight this is! Among all the unheard-of things that the French Revolution presented to the world, this was certainly the newest. . . . The French Revolution operated, with respect to this world, in precisely the same manner that religious revolutions have acted with respect to the other world. It considered the citizen in an abstract manner, outside of any particular society, the same way that religion considers man in general, independently of time and place. The Revolution did not only ask what the particular rights of French citizens were, but what were the general political rights and duties of men. . . . Because the Revolution seemed to be striving for the regeneration of the human race even more than for the reform of France, it lit a passion which the most violent political revolutions had never before been able to produce. It inspired conversions and generated propaganda. Thus, in the end, it took on that appearance of a religious revolution which so astonished its contemporaries. Or rather, it itself became a new kind of religion, it is true without God, without ritual, and without life after death, but one which nevertheless, like Islam, flooded the earth with its soldiers, apostles and martyrs.[43]

Following the Revolution, the sacralization of politics followed a very different path in France than in the United States, one that was much more uncertain, troubled, and provisional in its outcomes, given its antagonism to traditional religion. It was the start of a long and bitter conflict between Catholicism and various civil religions that appeared in France in the wake of its revolutionary tradition during the nineteenth and early twentieth centuries.

The ideal of a new civil religion continued to be cultivated in France by cultural, social, and political movements that evoked the French Revolution and kept alive the sacralization of politics through the myths, rituals, and symbols of their republican and socialist faiths, or of the secular religion of freethinkers.[44] However, these movements encountered obstacles that prevented the new republic that arose after 1870 from following the example of the United States in the establishment of a civil religion: on the one hand, there was the predominance of Catholicism, and on the other, the profound diffidence of rationalist, positivist, and individualist secularism toward any form of civic education that played on the emotions and beliefs of a faith rather than through reflections and convictions based on reason.[45]

However, the Third Republic was strongly motivated to create a secular civic consciousness with recourse not only to rational education but also to emotional strategies based on symbols and rituals celebrating republican ideals and the cult of the nation. In 1880, the republic adopted the 14th of July as a national holiday to be celebrated every year and to renew ideological ties with the Revolution and keep the cult of the nation and belief in the common good alive among the citizenry.[46] With the outbreak of the First World War, patriotism became the principal factor in the rapid and intense sacralization of politics, which brought together traditional religions in the worship of the nation and sanctification of the citizen's civic duty to devote his life to the safety of his nation and ultimately to lay down his life for it. France after the war, like the other countries that took part in the conflict, witnessed a rapid growth in the cult of the war dead, a genuine expression of a civil religion and secular piety that renewed the sacred nature of republican ideals.[47]

## HUMAN, REVOLUTIONARY, AND NATIONALIST RELIGIONS

The two democratic revolutions of the eighteenth century produced some fundamental elements of the essentially mythical structure of a civil or political religion, and these elements appear to remain constant throughout the widely varying ideological adaptations and permutations of the various historical expressions of the sacralization of politics: the myth of regeneration through politics, the myth of the "new man," and the myth of the people chosen to create new institutions that will save the world.

The following century was populated by founders, prophets, apostles, and martyrs of new secular religions who believed that Christianity was defunct and who made a cult of humanity, history, revolution, society, art, or sex, thus multiplying the number of secular divinities in the world, as the historian Friedrich Heer has argued: "Certainly in the nineteenth century there were endless attempts by artists, philosophers, scientists, sociologists, to frame new religious concepts. The scope was infinite. The revivalist movements of theism, pantheism, and Christianity paraded as new religions, and with them the developing atheistic creeds."[48]

The ranks of founders and would-be founders of new religions included such figures as Saint-Simon, Comte, Mazzini, and Mickiewicz. They were prophets and theologians of new religions of society, humanity, and nation. "Humanity has a religious future—the religion of the future will be greater and more powerful than any religion of the past. Its dogma will be the synthesis of all creations and all the types of human nature: the social and political institution taken as a whole shall be a religious institution." This passage appeared in Saint-Simon's *New Christianity*, which was published in 1825 shortly before his death. He uttered the following words to his disciples from his deathbed: "Religion could never disappear from the world; it can only transform itself."[49]

During the nineteenth century, the sacralization of politics made considerable advances through revolutionary faith, political messianism, secularized eschatological visions based on new concepts of history such as Hegelianism and Marxism, and new philosophies that turned humanity into something sacred. Ludwig Feuerbach proclaimed that Man had to become God for Man, and in 1842 he added: "We must start to be religious once again; politics must become our religion, but it can only do so if we, in our perceptions, have a supreme value that makes our religion of politics."[50]

Nationalism was the new secular religion that became most widespread in the second half of the nineteenth century and in the century that followed, because of its ability to merge into different ideologies, institutions, and regimes by subjecting them to the primacy of the nation as a sacred supreme being.[51] New ways of mobilizing the masses developed from nationalism, using the "new politics" that sought to turn the abstract myth of nationhood into reality by involving the citizens in the secular religion of the fatherland with the assistance of symbols, rituals, and collective festivals.[52] Under the impetus of the cult of the nation, traditional monarchies also contributed to the sacralization of politics as they sought to renew the sacred nature of power by adapting it to the democratization of politics through the establishment of ceremonies and rituals that often claimed a false antiquity.[53] In reality, the contribution made by this form of sacralization of politics was somewhat limited, and it was in any case almost always indirect, as it remained substantially wedded to the traditional ecclesiastical consecration of the monarchy as an institution. Moreover, the use of traditional religion, even if modernized, as a means to legitimize power restricted the extent to which the sacralization of power could be transformed into the modern sacralization of politics. The latter was essentially a revolutionary or democratic phenomenon, and therefore more congenial to movements that challenged the sacred nature of monarchical power and asserted the sacred nature of the nation and the sovereign people.

The symbolic and ceremonial devices of new democratic states were more influential in the sacralization of politics, and these included the establishment of civic holidays and the spread of national symbols through architecture, town planning, and state monuments. Even in these cases, however, it was not always possible to establish an effective religion of politics. As we have seen in the case of France of the Third Republic, the prevalence of a secularist, rationalist, and individualist political culture among the ruling classes could constitute an obstacle to this development, as it resisted any idea of typically religious forms to celebrate the cult of the nation. They feared that this would have perpetuated irrational superstition and prevented the emancipation of the individual, as it used instruments that savored of demagogy or imitated those traditional religions against which secular and liberal culture had been fighting in the name of reason and liberty. The rulers of liberal states believed it necessary to educate citizens in the cult of the "religion of the fatherland," but they mainly attributed this task to schools and the armed forces. This explains why the contribution of nineteenth-century national states to the sacralization of politics was limited in spite of the considerable increase in their rituals, symbols, and myths, which were, however, to be used by totalitarian regimes as the groundwork for the foundations of their political religions.[54]

The sacralization of politics was further assisted by the creation of mass movements. These made ample use of the formulas and formats that derived from the religious tradition, as well as new rituals and symbols, giving rise to new fideistic relations between the masses and their leaders. The mass movements gave considerable impetus to the crystallization of secular entities into myths that were the core of their ideologies, and to political practices such as the all-absorbing dedication of the activist, which became a reason for and way of living. It is significant in itself that by the end of the nineteenth century sociologists had started to define mass movements, particularly socialism, as new religions. Even more significant was the fact that the very protagonists of these movements perceived them as manifestations of a new secular religiosity, and even wanted their activists to take on the spirit and mentality of religious movements. The contribution of George Sorel and his theory of myth to the sacralization of revolutionary politics was particularly fruitful from this point of view. Activists in revolutionary movements, which even proclaimed their atheism, were very happy to compare themselves with religious movements in order to define their concept of politics as a total experience and as a force for complete renewal that was supposed to lead to the creation of a new civilization and a new humanity. Mussolini, an atheistic socialist, argued for "a *religious* concept of socialism" in 1912. Antonio Gramsci proclaimed even more categorically in 1916 that socialism "is precisely the religion that has to kill off Christianity. It is a religion in the sense that it is also a faith with its own mysteries and practices, and because in our consciences it has replaced the transcendental God of Catholicism with faith in Man and his best energies as the only spiritual reality."[55] Equally, we should not underestimate the contribution of avant-garde modernism to the sacralization of politics, even if it was indirect. Its features included the search for a new religion perceived as the reconstruction of the totality of life, as a spiritual revolution, as an apocalyptic expectation of the great regenerative catastrophe, and as the invocation of new man and the messiah. Like the revolutionary movements, they contributed to the sanctification of violence as a holy instrument for the regeneration of humanity.

At the beginning of the twentieth century, the most decisive and productive stimulus to the sacralization of politics came from the First World War, which intensified the cult of the nation and produced new material for the creation of political religions and for their exploitation by totalitarian movements. Above all, the Great War contributed to both the sanctification of the fatherland and the politicization of historical religions, which in almost all countries took the side of the nation in its holy war against the Antichrist. Each belligerent state proclaimed that God was at the side of its soldiers and leading them to victory for the salvation of civilization and humanity. The war in itself was interpreted as a great apocalyptic and regenerative event desired by God, and this increased the legitimization of violence for the triumph of Good. For the first time, war propaganda fully developed the *image of the enemy* as the incarnation of Evil, and this was not unconnected to the appearance of the *enemy within* who lurks within the very body of the nation but does not belong to it, because he does not acknowledge its sacred nature and does not worship it with loyal and absolute devotion. Lastly, mass deaths affecting for the first time millions of men favored the reawakening of religious sentiment and generated new forms of secular religiosity linked to the experience of war. The symbolism of death and resurrection, devotion to the nation, the mystique of blood and sacrifice, the cult of heroes and martyrs, and the "communion" of the comradeship all contributed to the spread among combatants of the idea that politics was a total and therefore religious experience that was going to regenerate all forms of existence.

The cult of the war dead is probably the most universal manifestation of the sacralization of politics in the twentieth century. The sacralization of the nation in all the countries party to the conflict, with the exception of Russia, reached its peak during the First World War. Many modern states established the cult of the Unknown Soldier as a symbol for those who fell for the salvation of their fatherland. Symbolic representations of heroism and piety carved in marble or set in bronze perpetuate the memory of the war dead in the towns and villages of the countries that took part in the war, following the model used by churches for millennia to celebrate the lives of saints and martyrs. It was through the experience of the Great War that new states such as Canada, Australia, and New Zealand developed the original elements of a civil religion founded on the myth of the nation, and they gained their complete and definitive autonomy as states through their participation in the conflict. They used the myth of the Great War and the cult of the war dead as the nucleus around which to form an embryonic configuration of myths, rituals, and symbols, in which they expressed or attempted to condense and consolidate the new nation's sense of identity.[56]

Fascism and Nazism, both products of the war, derived the religious dimension of their politics mainly from the experience of the conflict, but in the formation of their totalitarian religions they also made conspicuous use of experiences and the considerable material accumulated by ancient traditions.

## THE FASCIST RELIGION

The perception of fascism by nonfascists as a new political religion goes back to the very moment it took power. Examples included several democratic antifascists from both secular and Catholic backgrounds who very quickly sensed that there was an inherent and necessary link in fascism between the totalitarian will to conquer the monopoly of political power and the way in which it conceived its own ideology as a fundamentalist and dogmatic religion that could not tolerate the coexistence of other political convictions and demanded that all Italians believe in its myths and celebrate its rituals.

In 1923 Giovanni Amendola, a liberal antifascist and victim of political thuggery, was probably the first to understand the intrinsic connection between totalitarianism and political religions:

> A party may seek to dominate public life, but it must not go beyond the confines of the private conscience in which everyone is free to seek refuge. But fascism did not so much aim to govern Italy as to monopolize the control of Italian consciences. The possession of power is not enough for fascism: it needs to possess the private conscience of all its citizens, it demands the "conversion" of Italians. . . . Fascism makes the same claims as a religion. . . . Fascism has the supreme ambitions and inhuman intolerance of a religious crusade. It does not promise happiness to those who do not convert, and it does not leave any room for hope to those who do not let themselves be baptized.

Amendola adopted the term "totalitarian" to describe the essence of fascism—and he may have been its inventor: "Truly, the fascist rising's most striking feature for those who will study it in the future will always be its "totalitarian" spirit, which does not accept that there will be tomorrows with dawns that will not be greeted with the Roman salute, just as it does not accept that today could give succor to souls who have not succumbed to its 'credo.' "[57]

During the same period, Novello Papafava, a liberal Catholic, observed that the Fascist Party was building a despotic state, while Mussolini had proclaimed himself "the sole interpreter and depositary of the new religion of the Fatherland":

> Thus we find ourselves before a new dogmatic religion with its own sacraments and its own infallible leader. Anyone who does not love his fatherland in accordance with Benito Mussolini's dogmas and the rituals he has decreed, is a heretic who shall be consigned to the purifying fire of the National Militia's rifles. Leaving aside the question of the value and significance of religions, it is well known that dogmatically organized religions derive their legitimacy from the fact that they consider themselves to be the depositaries of the revelation of absolute and transcendent divine truths. Now what was the revelation on which the honorable Benito Mussolini founded his dogma of the fatherland? Which particular divinity anointed his head?[58]

These observations appear all the more important and significant when you consider that they were expressed immediately after the advent of fascist power, when the majority of antifascists paid no attention to the manifestations of fascism's political religion and its own claims to be one. Indeed, they laughed at this aspect of fascism and saw it as proof of its ideological inconsistency and its precariousness as a political movement they believed was destined shortly to run out of steam.

The features of fascism that showed it to be a political religion, particularly its symbols and rituals, soon drew the attention of foreign observers in Italy after Mussolini took power. Immediately after the "March on Rome," the *chargé d'affaires* at the French Embassy in Rome informed his government that the lever fascism used for its insurrection was a fanatical "religious sentiment relating to the fatherland."[59] In 1924, a French journalist likened fascism's mysticism and revolutionary spirit to Jacobinism and compared the symbols and rituals of the two revolutions, which produced the common elements of a new "civic religion":

> The [French] Revolution had the altar of the fatherland, the tricolor cockade, the Tenets of the Constitution, the Column of the Rights of Man, the trees of liberty, the Fasces of Unity, funeral rites, and commemorative festivals in the form of processions, ceremonies, symbolic games, and educational amusements. Fascism has the altar of the fatherland, Lictorian Fasces, the Tablets of the Law (the decisions of the Great Council of Fascism), the trees of remembrance, the fascist school battalions, women's groups, brutal and threatening ways of expression, civil processions, absurd uniforms, a skull and cross bones sewn on black shirts, and the "Holy Militia" in place of the "Holy Mountain."[60]

Herbert W. Schneider, an American academic who lived in Italy from 1926 to 1927, spoke of a "fascist religion."[61] Schneider perceived in fascism "the rudiments of a new religion. Whether or not these will grow remains to be seen, but certainly there can be no doubt that already this new cult has taken some hold of the Italian heart and imagination." He considered the constituent elements of this new religion to be the cult of martyrs, the "deification of Il Duce," and the proliferation of rituals, symbols, and catechisms. While agreeing that the propaganda in the fascist liturgy had much that was artificial, this academic noted a "considerable and undeniable element of religious conviction and devotion in most Fascists, which transcends the limits of political strife and party tactics."[62] Fascism, he concluded, was "a genuine religion and has all the techniques of a religious cult."[63] Consequently, Schneider predicted that there would be friction and conflict between the fascist religion and the Catholic Church in spite of the apparent convergence of interests between the Vatican and the fascist regime.

The German jurist Hermann Heller was of the same opinion. He believed fascism to be part of the current based on the sacralization of politics, which started with Hegel and came down through nationalism to the new cult of violence and power fueled by activistic concepts of life and the experiences of the Great War. Heller wrote in 1931 that fascism worshipped the nation and in reality practiced a "polytheistic paganism," which was the inevitable result of fascist nationalism or any other fascism, and which, because of its totalitarian ambition, was forced to adopt an anti-Christian stance: "The state can only be totalitarian if it wants to reunite the church and state; this return to the past will only be possible through a radical rejection of Christianity."[64] According to the French jurist Marcel Prélot writing in 1936, the nature of the fascist state, which increasingly took on the features and functions of a church, demonstrated that this was the effective essence of fascism and the logic behind its policies:

> The totalitarian state extends its field of action far beyond the acknowledged dominion of the traditional state, and claims to constitute not only a political unit, but also an ethical and spiritual community to which citizens wholly and necessarily belong, given that the state itself is a church. . . .
>
> The fascist state has the mystical and genuinely religious bonds of a church. It exalts the principles of sacrifice and self-denial. It professes a heroic philosophy of life, an anti-hedonistic ethic, an anti-intellectual and anti-materialist concept of the world. It works for the advent of a new order that is essentially defined as spiritual.
>
> Like a church, the fascist state believes itself to have an edifying, educative, apostolic, and charitable mission. It devotes itself to the constant evangelization of the unenthusiastic and the nonbelievers. Like Catholicism, with its orders and congregations, the fascist state multiplies the bodies devoted to helping their members or persuading those who still hold back from believing in the benefits of the regime.

The primary role of the party is to take on this churchlike quality of the state by fulfilling this twin function of dynamic element and inspirational activity on behalf of the state.[65]

Fascism was perhaps the prototype for the political religions of the twentieth century.[66] Fascism was the first totalitarian movement of the twentieth century that

    a. Openly proclaimed that it was a political religion by asserting the primacy of faith in the activism of the individual and the masses, and explicitly appealing to the irrational as the energy for political mobilization in contrast with rationalistic ideologies;

    b. Brought myth-based thought to power by officially declaring that it was the only form of collective political culture suited to the masses, who are by their very nature incapable of any form of self-government;

    c. Worshipped the charismatic leader as the interpreter of the national conscience and main pillar of the totalitarian state;

    d. Laid down an obligatory code of ethical commandments for the citizen, and established a collective political liturgy to celebrate the sacralization of the state and the personality cult.

    Anyone who did not conform to the myths and rituals of the fascist religion and did not obey its commandments was outlawed by the national community.

## Nazi NeoPaganism

Nazism made its own contribution to the sacralization of politics through its beliefs in the rituals, and symbols of a religion based on blood and race, which immediately became the dominant and most visible features of the new German regime. The Nazi political religion found a particularly fertile ground in which to put down its roots in order to consolidate and develop a dense foliage of myths, rituals, and symbols.[67]

Because of its cultural tradition, Germany was perhaps the country that since the beginning of the eighteenth century had experienced the greatest ferment of philosophical, aesthetic, and political currents that treated human history as sacred or worshipped Man, society, or nation. Postwar Germany was teeming with sects, clubs, and sympathizers that mixed ancient Germanic myths and modern nationalism, and brought to life a tendentially pagan political mysticism that celebrated the cult of race as a manifestation or incarnation of an Aryan and Germanic God. Delio Cantimori, a young Italian historian who lived for some time in the Weimar Republic, observed the spread of these trends and in 1928 he wrote that "they do not want to be a genuine profession of religious faith in the confessional sense, but rather a political religiosity in the sense of something that can be accepted as the positive side of various tendencies and confessions, and in the acknowledgment of a divine meaning to history and life."[68]

The Nazi movement derived its own political religiosity from these movements, a religiosity that was founded on the deification of the Aryan race, the cult of blood, anti-Semitic hatred, and idolatry of Hitler.

The sacralization of politics became dominant and pervasive under Nazism and involved every aspect of German life in its dogmas, myths, rituals, and symbols. The Austrian historian Karl Polanyi wrote in 1935 that Nazism was a political religion and contained the very essence of fascism, because only in Germany had fascism "advanced to that decisive stage at which a political philosophy turns into a religion."[69] The political religion of Nazism, with the assistance of expert propagandistic direction, took the liturgical representation of the mass to new heights and culminated in the adoration of the Führer. In 1941 Raymond Aron, who lived in Germany toward the end of the Weimar Republic, described the fascination of Nazi ceremonies and rituals that Hitler celebrated with the participation of immense "human masses, in which individuals, spectators, and actors mixed together" in a "spectacle that was either warlike or peaceful but always impressive, and presented to them by the most extraordinary direction the world has ever known":

> Foreigners were left with the disturbing impression of a society in which every one of its members was either a worker or a soldier, and that those collective events were touched by some kind of religious fervor. Labor days, military festivals, and all the party congresses, typically of all national-socialist events, seemed like ceremonies of some barbaric cult, in which the triumphant community had both an active and a passive role: the Third Reich was worshipping itself.[70]

Foreign and hostile observers were able to sense an experience of the sacred during mass celebrations of the Nazi cult, as André François Poncet, the French ambassador in Berlin, demonstrated in this description of the May Day festival:

> As the sun went down, close-packed processions moved through the streets of Berlin in perfect order and in step. At the head of each, there were banners, fife-players and musical bands, and all these masses made their way to the appointed meeting place. It was like watching the entrance of the confraternities of choristers. They were all in the place assigned to them in the vast expanse of the airport. . . . A sea of red flags acted as the backcloth to the scene. On one side, a rostrum covered with numerous microphones rose up like the prow of a ship, beneath which flowed the swelling crowd. In the

foreground stood the units of the Reichswehr, and behind them a million men. The SA and SS kept this enormous gathering under strict control. The Nazi leaders appeared and one by one they were loudly cheered by the crowd. Bavarian peasants, miners and fishermen in their respective costumes, and deputations from Austria, Saar and Danzig climbed up onto the rostrum as honored guests of the Reich. Everywhere there prevailed an atmosphere of satisfaction, harmony and joy. There was nothing that reminds you of the coercion. . . .

At eight o'clock, there was a sudden commotion. Hitler appeared standing up in his motor car, with his arm stretched out, his face stiff and a little drawn. He was greeted with long shouts of jubilation that burst forth from thousands of throats. In the meantime, night had fallen. Floodlights switched on and these were placed at a considerable distance from each other so that the circles of bluish light they projected were broken up by areas of darkness. There was a sea of human beings in which here and there groups stood out as they were lit up by the rays of the floodlights. It was an extraordinary spectacle that was offered to this pulsating crowd that in one moment rippled beneath the floodlights and in another dropped away into the darkness.

After Goebbels's brief introductory speech, Hitler climbed up the rostrum. The floodlights were switched off, with the exception of those that enveloped the Führer in a radiant halo of light, so that he appeared to float on board a fabulous vessel riding the waves of the crowd. Silence worthy of a temple hushed the people. Hitler began to speak.[71]

Nazism, like fascism, did not openly declare war on the Christian churches. Indeed, its program asserted the freedom of all religious confessions that did not endanger the existence of the state and did not challenge the moral sentiment of the Germanic race, and proclaimed itself to uphold a "positive Christianity." Although he despised Christianity profoundly, Hitler did not encourage the currents in his party that explicitly wanted to conduct a religious war against Christianity and Catholicism in the name of a purely Aryan and Germanic national religion. However, all the ways in which Nazism conceived and practiced politics exalted its own features of a new religion, while mixing its political ideology with the beliefs, symbols, myths, and rituals of the ancient Germanic religion that had been revived and adapted as a form of new anti-Christian paganism.

## BOLSHEVISM LIKE ISLAM

We can look on the Bolshevik Revolution as another example of the sacralization of politics brought about by the Great War. It was fueled by Marxist eschatological passions and millenarian beliefs typical of the Russian tradition.

Bolshevism never defined itself as a religion, although there had been some Bolshevik leaders, such as Lunacharsky, who had been old exponents of the movement "God-building" and interpreted Marxism as a new religion. They argued that socialism had to become the religion of modern man, of God-Man and a humanity entirely free from the myth of transcendence and supernatural being. Their attempts to define bolshevism in this manner came up against Lenin's contempt and derision. Yet, Bolshevik Russia also quickly embarked on a process of sacralizing politics, which developed over the coming years through the dogmatization of ideology and the imposition of absolute power on behalf of communism, along with the establishment of a system of beliefs, rituals, symbols, and ceremonies that conferred sacredness on events and on leading figures connected with the Russian Revolution. A new calendar, new national holidays, new rituals, and new symbols were introduced to challenge the rituals of the Orthodox Church and eradicate ancient religious beliefs. These were to be replaced with a new atheistic faith in the socialist fatherland, which was in the vanguard of the triumph of reason, progress, and the liberation of humanity. But as occurred with all civil and political religions, the influence of religious tradition consciously or unconsciously penetrated and permeated bolshevism's mass politics either through imitation or spontaneous crossover. Immediately after his death in 1924, Lenin was declared immortal as a result of the declared immortality of his thought, and his body was embalmed and venerated like the saints of the Orthodox Church. The mythical and symbolical iconography of Soviet propaganda imitated the iconographic tradition of the Orthodox religion. Even universalist communism's new eschatological mythology absorbed the traditional currents of millenarianism and Russian nationalism, together with the myth of the Third Rome. It then combined these syncretically with materialist scientism, the idolatry of modernization, and proletarian internationalism. Thus Marxist atheism was transformed into the new religion of Russian bolshevism.[72]

Some observers of Soviet Russia realized this back in the early twenties. In 1920 Fritz Gerlich, a Catholic journalist and tenacious opponent of Hitler who died in a Dachau concentration camp in 1934, defined bolshevism as a millenarian movement.[73] For the Austrian writer René Fülöp-Miller, Russian bolshevism was the product of the revival of Russian chiliastic ideas and millenarian traditions, mixed with Marxist revolutionary messianism. Fülöp-Miller argued that, although it claims to be a science, "Bolshevik materialism is nothing more than a surrogate religion that offers humanity a new confession in place of the lost faith and aims to satisfy its eternal aspiration to be free from all evils with a new form more suited to the utilitarian spirit of our age."[74] By absorbing Russian millenarian traditions, bolshevism had become "the political embodiment of Russia's centuries-old hope for the advent of a millenary kingdom of the 'God-Man'; Lenin's doctrine ultimately comes down to the Russian Old Testament, and his followers are a group of sectarians."[75] Even Nikolai Berdyayev, the Christian philosopher who abandoned Russia after the establishment of the Bolshevik dictatorship, believed that Russian millenarianism had been grafted onto Marxism's revolutionary messianism, which it had exacerbated and transformed into a new religion. The socialist state and society, wrote Berdyayev in 1923, "belong to a confessional type that is sacred and not secular or profane." The socialist state "claims to be a sacred state blessed by the grace not of God but of the devil," and it takes on the semblance of a church and a theocracy, because it wishes to subject the whole man to its power, "not just his body, but also his soul":

> In a socialist state, there is a faith and a dominant set of beliefs, and those who embrace this dominant religion must be entitled to privileged rights. This state is not indifferent to faith, as in the case of the democratic liberal state, but establishes its truth and imposes it through force. Those who do not acknowledge the socialist faith must be placed in a similar situation to that of the Jews in ancient Christian theocratic societies.[76]

Other observers of bolshevism in the twenties compared it to Islam. Those who made this comparison did not necessarily start from anticommunist positions. One example was the philosopher Bertrand Russell, who declared in 1920 on his return from a trip to Russia that "Bolshevism is not merely a political doctrine; it is also a religion with elaborate doctrines and inspired scriptures."[77] When the philosopher started his journey, he was motivated by sympathy for the new revolutionary regime and asserted that "Bolshevism deserved the gratitude and admiration of all progressive part of mankind."[78] However, Russell judged the way Bolsheviks operated to be dangerous because it did not favor the creation of a "stable and desirable form of Socialism."[79] He expressed his most fundamental reservations over the religious nature of bolshevism.

> Bolshevism as a social phenomenon is to be reckoned as a religion, not as a normal political movement. . . . By a religion I mean a set of beliefs held as dogmas, dominating the conduct of life, going beyond or contrary to evidence, and inculcated by methods which are emotional or authoritarian, not intellectual. By this definition, Bolshevism is a religion. . . . Among religions, Bolshevism is to be reckoned with Mohammedanism rather than Christianity and Buddhism. Christianity and Buddhism are primarily personal religions, with mystical doctrines and a love of contemplation. Islam and Bolshevism are practical, social, unspiritual, concerned to win the empire of the world. Their founders would not have resisted the third of the temptations

in the wilderness. What Mohammedanism did for the Arabs, Bolshevism may do for the Russians. As Ali went down before the politicians who only rallied to the Prophet after his success, so the genuine communists may go down before those who are now rallying to the ranks of the Bolsheviks.[80]

Equally, John Maynard Keynes was not prejudiced against Russia when in 1925 he defined Leninism as a religion that promised the realization of a new order and the regeneration of humanity, and that was ready to demand any sacrifice, use any means, even of the most violent nature, in order to triumph without stopping in the face of material difficulties, mistakes, and tactical necessities. Keynes found that Leninism's religious nature was betrayed by the fundamental motives of seeking a new order and the regeneration of humanity.

> Like other new religions, Leninism derives its power not from the multitude but from a small minority of enthusiastic converts whose zeal and intoler-ance make each one the equal in strength of a hundred indifferentists. Like other new religions, it is led by those who can combine the new spirit, per-haps sincerely, with seeing a good deal more than their followers, politicians with at least an average dose of political cynicism, who can smile as well as frown, volatile experimentalists, released by religion from truth and mercy but not blinded to the facts and expediency, and open therefore to the charge (superficial and useless though it is where politicians, lay or ecclesiastical, are concerned) of hypocrisy. Like other new religions, it seems to take the color and gaiety and freedom out of everyday life and to offer a drab substi-tute in the square wooden faces of its devotees. Like other new religions, it persecutes without justice or pity those who actively resist it. Like other new religions, it is unscrupulous. Like other new religions, it is filled with mission-ary ardour and oecumenical ambitions. But to say that Leninism is the faith of a persecuting and propagating minority of fanatics who are led by hypo-crites is, after all, to say no more no less than that it *is* a religion and not merely a party, and Lenin a Mohamet and not a Bismarck.[81]

Bolshevism continued to profess its atheism and continued its fight against traditional religion with varying degrees of aggression. However, this did not prevent the increasingly intense sacralization of ideology, the party, and the Soviet state, while drawing heavily, as we have said, on the messianic myths and religious tradition of the Russian people. After 1924, all these elements came together in the myth of Lenin, Leninism, and the Communist Party as the creator of the Revolution, founder of the Soviet state, depositary of the doctrine, and elected vanguard of the proletariat.[82]

The sacralization of the party opened the way to the sacralization of Stalin when he became the supreme leader. After 1929, the political reli-gion of Russia mainly concentrated on the deification of Stalin, who until his death in 1953 dominated the party and Soviet system like a tyrannical and merciless deity. He was surrounded, however, by the spontaneous devotion of the people, whose sentiments of veneration and devotion for the new despot poured forth as they had previously done for the tsar over many centuries. In his memoirs, Ilya Ehrenburg, the Russian writer who had witnessed the personality cult of Stalin, wrote that it would be "more correct simply to use the word 'cult' in its original religious sense," because in the minds "of millions Stalin was transformed into a mythical demigod; all trembled as they said his name, believed that he alone could save the Soviet Union from invasion and collapse."[83]

The Soviet Marxist historian Roy A. Medvedev, who also experienced Stalinism, very effectively evoked the creation of this cult and its consequences for the Soviet system, such as the ruthless policy of terror that Stalin adopted in the thirties, when he exterminated the great majority of the political and military old guard of the Bolshevik Party along with millions of Russians. The Stalinist terror did not encounter any opposition or resistance from his party comrades, who were unmoved by the most iniquitous crimes, so much were they in the thrall of the captivating and terrifying power embodied by the despot in the Kremlin:

> The deification of Stalin left the party unable to control his actions and justified in advance everything connected with his name. The embodiment of all the achievements of socialism in his person tended to paralyze the political activism of the other leaders and of the party membership as a whole, preventing them from finding their own way in the welter of ongoing events, leading them to blind faith in Stalin. The cult of Stalin, following the logic of any cult, tended to transform the Communist Party into an ecclesiastical organization, producing a sharp distinction between ordinary people and leader-priests headed by their infallible pope. The gulf between the people and Stalin was not only deepened but idealized. The business of state in the Kremlin became as remote and incomprehensible for the unconsecrated as the affairs of the gods on Olympus.
>
> In the thirties and forties the social conscience of the people took on the elements of a religious psychology: illusions, autosuggestion, the inability to think critically, intolerance towards dissidents, and fanaticism. As Yuri Karyakin put it, a secular variant of religious consciousness arose in the Soviet Union. Perceptions of reality were distorted. It was difficult to believe the terrible crimes charged against the Old Bolsheviks, but it was even more difficult to think that Stalin was engaged in a monstrous provocation to destroy his former friends and comrades.
>
> The cult of Stalin's personality was accompanied by the belittling of everyone else, especially ordinary working people. Conformism, uniformity of behavior and thought, was implanted in the Soviet people. Serving socialism

was transformed into serving Stalin: it was not he who served the people but they who served him. His praise, his encouragement, his smile were considered the highest rewards.

For the sake of future beatitude, religious believers are expected to endure without complaint any misfortune in their earthly lives. Just as believers attribute everything good to God and everything bad to the devil, so everything good was attributed to Stalin and everything bad to the evil forces that Stalin himself was fighting. "Long live Stalin!" some officials shouted as they were taken out to be shot.

. . . .

This kind of religious outlook crippled the will even of those people who had stopped believing in Stalin and had begun to see where Stalin was taking the party. Why did Ordzonikidze kill himself rather than Stalin? Why was there not one real attempt to remove Stalin during twenty years of bloody crimes? Those who were capable of such an act were stopped not so much by fear of their lives as by fear of the social consequences, which could not be predicted in the conditions of the cult.[84]

The fideistic seductiveness that emanated from the Soviet experiment was not confined to Russia. During the thirties and particularly during the Second World War, faith in the communist religion embodied by the Soviet system spread around the world among humble workers and affluent intellectuals. One of the Finnish emigrants working in the mines of Minnesota recalled how they brightened up the squalor of their environment with meetings in which "the mentioning of the name of Lenin made the heart throb. . . . In mystic silence, almost in religious ecstasy, did we admire everything that came from Russia."[85] Harold Laski, an educated and sophisticated political theoretician and English labor party activist was captivated by the religious fascination of Stalinist communism, and in 1943 he argued that the Soviet Union "had found a new way of life in which faith might play the part supernatural creeds had played elsewhere."[86] "I think the Soviet Union has discovered the secret of vigour, and, therein, the means to that common faith which binds men together in Peace."[87] For this reason he was indulgent toward the cruel harshness of the Stalinist dictatorship, believing that this was the result of provisional political circumstances and also the authentic religious fervor that inspired bolshevism:

> We are dealing with men who have, rightly or wrongly, a conviction that is religious in its profundity that they are bringing the inevitable future to birth. . . . They believe that no sacrifices are too great for its attainment. . . . They believe that the only sin is weakness, that error is as profound a threat to victory as was heresy to the Christian of an earlier age. Their effort has for them all the elements of a crusade.[88]

Laski added that in order to understand Bolsheviks and their politics, you had to take into account the inner force that has driven great revolutionaries throughout history, such as Mohamed, Luther, Calvin, and Cromwell, for whom all things that endangered their concept of the revolution were mistaken and morally detestable. Laski compared the "spirit of bolshevism" to the radical and militant Puritanism of the 1600s and believed that there were "considerable similarities" between the Puritans and the Bolsheviks.

> No one who has seen a Bolshevik Congress at work but can fail to recognize there the historic hopes of the earlier [Puritan] movement; a meeting of the Praesidium at Moscow must have its psychological affinities with those Putney Debates of Cromwell's Ironsides of Cromwell . . . ; and the Bolshevik reliance upon their texts from Marx and Lenin and Stalin is identical with the Puritan dependence upon the citations from the Scriptures.[89]

Like the Puritans, the Bolsheviks felt they were the chosen and predestined precursors of a future preestablished order. They shared a fanatical faith in their own truth and its inevitable triumph, contempt for the normal behavior of human nature, hatred for half-measures, and the conviction that anyone who opposed their truth was an agent of the devil and must be immediately annihilated. The Bolsheviks were so convinced that they possessed the truth that on taking power they felt obliged to impose it, believing every deviation from the established doctrine to be a source of intellectual errors and consequently of deviant behavior. Tolerance of enemies was impossible for Bolsheviks, just as it had been impossible for Puritans to come to a compromise with Rome. "They have the truth, and they will die rather than fail to impose it."[90]

*Chapter 3*

# THE LEVIATHAN AS A CHURCH
## Totalitarianism and Political Religion

Humanity produces Bibles
and canons, tuberculosis
and tuberculin. It is democratic,
has many nobles and kinds,
and builds churches, against which
it builds universities; it transforms
convents into barracks,
but barracks are provided with
military chaplains.
—Robert Musil

### Totalitarianism: A Preliminary Definition

The sacralization of politics reached its highest point between the two World Wars in the new totalitarian regimes. It was in fact totalitarianism that led the sacralization of politics to display their full range of ideological and institutional features, by which totalitarian regimes resembled new churches devoted to propagandizing faith in absolute and unquestionable ideological truths, persecuting the unfaithful and worshipping sacralized human entities. It was because of totalitarianism that the sacralization of politics came to be perceived as a real danger to traditional religions and human destiny. This danger was attributed not only to the boundless material power exercised by totalitarian regimes but also to their insistence on invading and dominating every aspect of the public and private lives of those they ruled over, and the fascination that power inspired, leading to fervor, fanaticism, faith, and devotion in relation to secular entities physically embodied in the person of a leader transfigured into a living deity. As we shall see in this chapter and the next, the features totalitarian regimes shared with churches were considered by both opponents and supporters to be the expression of a genuinely religious component to be found in the very nature of these political movements.

It is impossible to understand the particular nature of the sacralization of politics introduced by bolshevism, fascism, and Nazism without first clarifying the nature and significance of totalitarianism as a new form of political domination that required the establishment of a political religion as an essential and fundamental component.

The definition of totalitarianism is the subject of much controversy. Scholars are not in agreement over either the essential elements of totalitarianism or the historical, cultural, ideological, and political phenomena to which this definition can be applied. Some believe that totalitarianism goes all the way back to Plato; others to Rousseau and Robespierre; some to Marx, Lenin, and Stalin; and still others to Mussolini and Hitler. Some believe that totalitarianism is now dead as a political phenomenon, along with totalitarian states, while others consider it to be a permanent threat inherent to modern mass society, lurking in fundamentalist political and religious movements or in the very structures of the technological organization of global civilization. There are also contentions over the application of the concept of totalitarianism to the states that were defined as such between the wars. For example, some argue that Fascism was not totalitarian, because it did not achieve the complete subordination of society, the state, bodies and consciences to the rule of the single party and the creed of its political religion. Others use the same argument to assert that Nazism and Stalinism were not truly totalitarian either.

Given the highly differing views on totalitarianism and the central importance of totalitarian religions to this study, it is appropriate to clarify the meaning in which the term is adopted here, with particular reference to communism, fascism, and Nazism.

By the term "totalitarianism" we mean an *experiment in political domination* implemented by a *revolutionary movement* that has been organized by a party with military discipline and an *all-absorbing concept of politics* aimed at the *monopoly of power*, which on taking power by legal or illegal means destroys or transforms the previous regime and builds a new state founded on a *single-party regime* with the principal objective of *conquering society*, that is, the subjugation, integration, and homogenization of the ruled on the basis of the *totally political nature of existence*, whether individual or collective, as interpreted by the categories, myths, and values of an institutionalized ideology in the form of a *political religion*, with the intention of molding individuals and masses through an *anthropological revolution*, in order to regenerate the essence of humanity and create a *new man* devoted body and soul to the realization of the revolutionary and imperialist projects of the totalitarian party, and thus a *new civilization* of a supranational nature.

From the start, the totalitarian experiment is the product of a revolutionary party that will not countenance the existence of other parties and ideologies and perceives the state as a means to achieve its plans for domination. The party, being solely responsible for the implementation of the totalitarian experiment, is equipped from the very beginning with a more or less developed system of beliefs, dogmas, myths, rituals, and symbols that interpret the meaning and purpose of collective existence in this world, and define good and evil exclusively in terms of the principles, values and objectives of the party and the purpose of their implementation.

The revolutionary party is the origin of the totalitarian regime, which is presented as a political system founded on the symbiosis between state and party and on a network of potentates governed by the principal exponents of the *aristocracy of command*, chosen in turn by the *leader of the party* who towers above the entire structure of the regime with his charismatic authority.

The totalitarian regime is a laboratory in which people experiment with an anthropological revolution to create a new type of human being. The main instruments for its implementation are

a. *Coercion*, imposed through violence, repression, and terror, which are considered the legitimate instruments for the affirmation, defense, and propagation of its ideology and political system;

b. *Demagogy*, accomplished through permanent and pervasive propaganda, the mobilization of enthusiasm, and the liturgical celebration of the cult of the party and of the leader;

c. *Totalitarian pedagogy*, carried out from above in accordance with ideal models for men and women established in conformity with the principles and values of palingenetic ideology;

d. *Discrimination against outsiders* through coercive measures that range from banishment from public life to the physical annihilation of all human beings who, because of their ideas, social status, or ethnicity are considered *inevitable enemies*, because they are outside the community of the elect and incompatible with the realization of the totalitarian experiment.

The fundamental features of the totalitarian experiment are

a. *Militarization of the party* through a rigidly hierarchical organization, with the style and mentality suited to an ethic of devotion and absolute discipline;

b. *Monistic concentration of power* within the single party and the person of the *charismatic leader*;

c. *Organization down to the grassroots of the masses* in order to involve men and women of every generation and to carry out the conquest of society, collective indoctrination, and the anthropological revolution;

d. *Sacralization of politics* with the establishment of a system of beliefs, myths, dogmas and commandments that invest the entirety of individual and collective existence through the imposition of rituals and festivals that permanently transform the collectivity into a *liturgical mass* for the political cult.

The party, the regime, the political religion, and anthropological revolution are essential elements of the totalitarian experiment and are complementary to one another, but it has to be made clear that the totalitarian nature of this experiment, as defined here, does not coincide separately with any of the elements that make it up or the methods by which it is implemented. By defining totalitarianism as an *experiment* rather than a *regime*, we mean to emphasize the interconnection between its fundamental constituent parts and the fact that totalitarianism is a *continuous process* that cannot be considered complete at any stage in its implementation. Totalitarianism consists, therefore, of a dynamic set of elements and their interconnection. This means that the concept of totalitarianism, as we have defined it, cannot be applied solely to a system of power and a method of government (i.e., a regime) but rather indicates in the widest possible sense a political process characterized by the *experimental voluntarism* of a revolutionary party, whose fundamental purpose is to act on the heterogeneous mass of the governed and transform it into a *harmonious collectivity* or, in other words, a *unitary and homogeneous political body* that is morally united by its faith in the totalitarian religion.

This definition of totalitarianism is a modified version of the reflections of those who since the twenties observed the formation of new political regimes founded and dominated by a single party with a fundamentalist ideology. These regimes displayed attitudes that immediately suggested comparisons with religious movements because of the ways in which they conceived, experienced, and practiced their politics.

Totalitarian states established systems of beliefs, myths, rituals, and symbols that deified their political structures and their rulers and imposed codes of commandments and obligatory behavior to which all citizens were required to conform. Political power was removed from the citizens' control and right of recall, equipped with an exclusive, irresponsible, and terroristic might surrounded by a halo of mystery and charisma and transfigured into a terrible and majestic force. Thus it assumed the semblance of a sacred entity. The totalitarian political religion demanded absolute and unconditional obedience and loyalty from the collectivity. The totalitarian state thus took on by its very nature the features and functions of a church dedicated to the worship of a secular entity. Anyone who did not share this faith in the political religion and did not practice its cult was considered an intractable enemy to be expelled from the community of believers. If necessary, the persecution of such people could be taken as far as their annihilation.

## Comparison of the Various Interpretations

The religious aspects of totalitarian movements and regimes were so manifest, invasive, and ponderous that it was impossible to ignore them or relegate them to the margins of any reflections on the nature of this new political phenomenon. No one who looks at the images of Europe between the wars could avoid being struck by the spectacle of adoring crowds before their leader, by the rituals, and symbols that became part of life in many countries, and by the aesthetics of organized masses moving to a regular beat under perfect direction. The purpose of all this effort was to extol and venerate sacred secular entities. It was clear to everyone that totalitarianism was primarily an unprecedented system of political domination founded on force and violence, and this was not even denied by the leaders and followers of totalitarian movements. Equally unprecedented in the history of modern political regimes was massive and extravagant deployment of myths, rituals, and symbols that made totalitarian movements look like religious movements. How then do we explain the presence of these religious features in the politics of regimes that already had solid and unassailable power based on armed force, but nevertheless appeared obsessed with being surrounded by eager crowds of adoring and combative believers?

The early impressionistic interpretations and descriptions of the religious aspects of totalitarian movements, which we examined in the previous chapter, were soon followed by more considered analysis and interpretation of their nature, meaning, and role within the systems of totalitarian power. The explanations provided more or less correspond to the principal interpretations of religious phenomena referred to in the first chapter.

For example, the historian Gaetano Salvemini provided an analysis in line with the *crowd manipulation* interpretation, when in 1932 he examined the personality cults, myths, rituals, and symbols of fascism, Nazism and communism, and their claims to possess absolute and indisputable truths:

> God occupies a very uncertain place in modern dictatorships. So far Pius XI has certified that only Mussolini has been "sent by divine providence." It is quite possible that one fine day Hitler will also receive similar certification from the Holy See. On the other hand, the unbeliever Stalin does not aspire to such approval. But then he has his own bible and source of infallible inspiration: *Das Kapital*.
>
> Whether or not they have the cornerstone of divine inspiration, all the dictators proclaim themselves infallible. "Mussolini is always right." The "elect few" chosen by the dictator from above are equally infallible.
>
> The dictator and his "elect few" are "the state." . . . He who is convinced that he possesses the secret to make mankind virtuous and happy, and finds himself at the head of a party that preaches his infallibility, must always be ready to kill. . . . The dictator says: "I am the truth, and the outcomes of my activities are always good," "either with me or against me," and "everything in the state, nothing outside the state, and nothing against the state." Anyone who opposes the state is an outlaw. . . . A system in which all decisions come down from above and the fundamental duty and virtue of each subject to

blind obedience is a system that is obliged to impose some degree of intellectual abdication on its followers. It must not therefore appeal to the intellect and logic, but rather to a sinister area that exists in the spirit of every man and women from which logic and intellect are excluded.

Dictators need myths, symbols, and ceremonies to regiment, excite, and terrify the multitude and suffocate their every attempt at independent thought. The Catholic Church's fantastic and grandiose ceremonies and mysterious rituals in a strange language are masterpieces of their genre, and fascists and communists copied these models when they appealed to the irrational instincts of the crowd in mass demonstrations.[1]

The explanation of Hitler's charismatic power put forward by the political scientist Franz Neumann in 1942 at least in part belonged to this type of interpretation. He argued, "if the genuinely religious phenomenon of charisma belongs to the sphere of the irrational, its parallel political manifestation is simply a stratagem for the establishment, conservation or reinforcement of power": "The supposed charismatic powers of modern leaders are instruments deliberately used to spread a sense of impotence and desperation amongst the people, to abolish equality and replace it with a hierarchy in which the leader and his group enjoy the prestige and benefits of the *numen.*"

However, Neumann did not deny that the masses' religious experience had its influence on the formation of the charismatic power and the fideistic relationship between the masses and the dictator. Nor did he question the sincerity of the millions of people who believed in the sacred nature of their leader. The German academic made clear that this did not occur for purely propagandistic reason, but also because of a "psychological process that is the basis for the human adoration of other humans." In order to explain this phenomenon, Neumann explicitly referred to the numinous interpretation:

As Rudolf Otto has shown, the state of mind and the emotions involved are those of an individual who feels himself overwhelmed by his own inefficacy and who is led to believe in the existence of a *Mysterium Tremendum.* The mystery creates awe, dread and fear. Man shudders before the demon or God's wrath. But his attitude is ambivalent—he is awed and fascinated. He experiences moments of extreme rapture during which he identifies himself with the holy.

This entirely irrational belief will arise in situations that the average man cannot grasp or understand rationally. It is not only anxiety that drives men to embrace superstition, but inability to understand the reasons of their helplessness, misery and degradation. In periods of civil strife, religious turmoil, profound social and economic upheavals productive of misery and distress, men are often unable, or deliberately rendered unable, to perceive the developmental laws that have brought about their condition. The least rational strata of society turn to leaders. Like primitive man, they look for a savior to fend off their misery and deliver them from destitution. There is always a factor of calculation, often on both sides. The leader uses and enhances the feeling of awe; the followers flock to him to attain their ends.[2]

Paul Tillich, the theologian and proponent of anticapitalist Christianity, put forward a religious explanation of the totalitarian state in 1934, which can be used as an example of the functionalist interpretations of the totalitarian religion as a response to the disintegration of society. He believed that fascism's and Nazism's sacralization of politics (and in part also that of communist Russia, where, however, he thought the totalitarian organization to be more transitory, even if more efficient than in Italy and Germany) was due to the need to reintegrate the masses into the national state, following a period of crisis and disintegration and to give them a new sense of unity and collective identity. This occurred through a new organization of the totalitarian state, with concentration of power, wider control of society, and the adoption of a worldview capable of involving the individual and the masses in a common faith:

> Such a world view is religious in character and finds expression in a myth. The more unconditional and more inclusive the claims of the state are, the more fundamental and powerful must be the myth, which is the foundation of such claims. . . . When the totalitarian tendencies are more powerful, new myths are required in order to provide the basis for the struggle and for reconstruction. . . . This is the totalitarian state, born out of insecurity of historical existence during the epoch of late capitalism and designed, through national concentration, to create security and reintegration. . . . It has received mystic consecration and stands, not merely as the earthly representative of God, as Hegel conceived it, but actually as God on earth.[3]

It was more common for interpretations to attribute the origins of totalitarian religions to the need for a faith on the part of the masses, whom demagogues like Mussolini and Hitler were able to satisfy by using their charismatic skills, organizational force, and modern propaganda techniques. The fideistic interpretation was responsible mainly for the fruitful analysis of totalitarianism as a religion, in combination with reflections on the crisis of Western civilization after the Great War and the decline of rationalism and individualism in the face of the continuous flow of irrational collective beliefs, which had accompanied the expansion of mass society and favored the prevalence of mythical thought in politics. The need for security, certainty, and faith, which is deeply ingrained in mass psychology, had been heightened by the devastating and traumatic experiences to which the masses had been exposed since the outbreak of the European conflict. These experiences multiplied at an accelerated rate over an extremely short period of time through the postwar revolutionary unrest and the subsequent ruinous effects of the economic and social crisis of capitalism at the end of the twenties. The masses reacted against this sense of decadence and insecurity by attempting to satisfy their desire for faith, certainty, and security by placing their hopes, devotion, and obedience in those who were able to provide them with the beliefs, myths, and symbols of a new religion.

## THE MASSES, FAITH, AND MYTH

"Today political passions have attained a *universality* never before known," observed the writer Julien Benda in 1927.[4] The principal result of these political passions, which the French intellectual defined as "secular religions," was to degrade the individual, who had become the worshipper of a collective body transfigured into a sacred power through the fanatical exaltation of its own will to power multiplied by cohesion of the mass. The individual, Benda stated, "confers a mystical personality on the whole of which he feels himself to be a member, and he worships it in a religious manner, which ultimately is nothing more than the deification of his own passion and he considerably increases its power." The most powerful of these political passions was nationalism as a mass ideology, a "plebeian form of patriotism." Thus, "The national passions, owing to the fact that they are now exerted by plebeian minds, assume the character of mysticism, of religious adoration almost unknown in the practical minds of the great nobles. It is unnecessary to add that this makes these passions deeper and stronger." However, this religiosity of national passion did not only spring from the plebeian mind:

> Let me add that this mystical adoration of the nation is not only to be explained by the nature of those who adore, but also by the changes which have taken place in the adored object. There is first of all the spectacle of the military force and organization of modern states, which is something far more imposing than of old. And when these states are seen to make war for an indefinite period after they have no more men, and go on subsisting for long years after they have no more money, it is easy to understand why a man who has some tincture of religion in his mind may be led to believe that these states are of an essence different from that of ordinary natural beings.[5]

The faith of the masses, as an important factor in the genesis and success of totalitarian movements, occupied a central place in the majority of studies of the dictatorships that sprang up after the First World War.

politics in movements that constituted a "political community": "the life of men within the political community cannot be restricted to the sphere of the profane" in relation to matters of organization and power, because it is "also within the field of religious order, and knowledge of a political situation is incomplete on a crucial point if it does not cover the community's religious forces and the symbols through which those forces find expression."[26]

Voegelin placed the question of political religion in a historic context that lasted millennia, within which the novelty and specificity of political religions ended up being diluted by the general phenomenon of the sacralization of political power that covered both the cult of the Pharaoh and the totalitarian religions of the twentieth century.

## FANATICISM AND BUREAUCRACY

During the same period, Raymond Aron adopted a different approach to identify the nature and the meaning of political religion under totalitarian regimes. He mainly dealt with this subject in three articles published in 1939, 1941, and 1944, in which he seems to be unaware of contemporary studies that also dealt with it. Nevertheless, in some points his analysis echoed terms and concepts that had already been formulated by others.

In 1939 Aron wrote that ours is an "era of political religions": men struggle against one another not only because of their conflicting interests, but also because of "rival metaphysical interpretations or, more correctly, dogmas" because "they need their actions and sacrifices to be justified by an absolute value." Political religions, which sprang from this need, appeared to remedy the danger of disintegration of the national community as a result of divisions and internal struggles. "As long as the nation is divided, it will be impotent. A single doctrine adapted in all its crudeness to the needs of the masses, which combines strength with faith, attempts to re-create the indispensable sense of community" in order to shore up national unity. But he commented that so far the totalitarian regimes "have only succeeded in producing a caricature of a truly unified civilization" because neither Marxism nor racism provided "the equivalent of Catholicism in medieval society: too many people and too many spiritual niceties escaped them."[27]

However, for Aron this did not constitute an objection that invalidated the fundamental significance of political religion in the development and affirmation of totalitarianism. As he developed his ideas during the Second World War, Aron came to insist upon the mythical and religious aspects in order to explain the success totalitarian movements had achieved among the masses. He came up with a new interpretation of the connection between religion and totalitarianism that took into account the various ideological, cultural, organizational and institutional features within a coherent explanatory framework. Within this framework, political religion was considered an integral part of the totalitarian system, in that it was a modern form of tyranny that as a result of its own intrinsic needs combined genuine enthusiasm and religious fanaticism with demagogic cynicism and the most unprincipled and brutal political realism. Nazism put the fascination of *myth* and the efficiency of *organization* at the service of its will to power. The great celebrations of the Nazi religion in Nuremberg, which were the result of fanatical enthusiasm and bureaucratic efficiency, were a tangible symbol of the combination of rationalism and irrationalism that Aron considered to be the original and essential core of totalitarianism.

Fanaticism and bureaucracy: this was the formula that Aron adopted in 1941 to explain the nature of Nazism, the example of a political religion that studied in greatest depth and which he considered at that time to be the most complete form of totalitarian regime.[28] The potency of Nazism consisted in its ability to join together the strength of bureaucratic rationalization, which had swollen beyond measure with the unconditional expansion of totalitarian power, and the strength of collective irrationalism, which was encapsulated in the myths, symbols, and rituals of a new religion. Nazism had effectively engendered a new faith in the German masses who had been devastated by the crisis and rekindled a sense on national communion along with the security of an efficient and powerful state. Pride in that sense of national communion was achieved through a mystical union with the Führer and total obedience to his unconditional authority:

> An enemy was pointed out to these men who were so eager to act, fight, and march together. The enemy was the cause of all evils on which they could offload the store of hate and resentment that is always available to the unhappy masses. A prophet is found on which to focus all the wealth of trust and fervor held in the hearts of men. A small number of simple social principles are put forward to respond to the immediate demands and profound aspirations of the collectivity: primacy of the general interest, work and justice for all, and so on. That is how a political religion is born.[29]

Collective fanaticism, which was cultivated through the myths and rituals of political religion, was a fundamental feature of national-socialist politics, even though, Aron pointed out, it coexisted with the political cynicism of those who held power, who exploited it for their own ambitions. The fanaticism was also necessary to the totalitarian system as a corrective to bureaucratic rationalization and for maintaining the movement's dynamism, the communitarian enthusiasm of the masses, and the spirit of aggression in relation to the new imperial conquests. Political movements such as Nazism were always threatened by a return to the banality of daily life, so fanaticism had to challenge this threat and "enliven men in peace as in war." "Fanaticism gave a purpose and a sense to rationalized existence and communitarian hopes; it makes the sacrifices for the nation and future bearable; it pushes the young barbarians to the conquest of the old world."[30]

Although Aron acknowledged political religion to be an essential element of totalitarianism, he did not fully resolve the problem, and his definition of its nature and functions was substantially an instrumental and vaguely *crowd manipulation* one. His lack of satisfaction was evident from the question with which he opened his most methodical essay, which was published in 1944 and devoted to the phenomenon of secular religion, the term he now used to define "the doctrines that have taken the place of the vanished faith in contemporary minds and posit humanity's salvation in this world, but in a distant future under a type of social order yet to be created."[31] He wondered whether it was legitimate to talk of religion in these cases (i.e., in the absence of a transcendent or at least sacred object to which prayer and love could be directed)? Aron admitted that from a Christian point of view, secular religions could only be defined as such in the sense of a surrogate religion or a caricature of one. But he was inclined to accept the legitimacy of the term "religion," based on the more extensive definition of the religious phenomenon proposed by Gustave Le Bon and referred to without mention of the author. This interpreted "religion"—and therefore secular religions, too—as any manifestation of a fideistic sentiment that expressed itself through devotion, dedication, and fanaticism to the service of a cause or any entity that became the motive and supreme end of existence. He observed that it was now clearly the case that secular religions, like traditional religious beliefs in the eras of their greatest imperiousness and universal spread, had the ability to move minds to devotion, intransigence, and unconditional fanaticism.[32] Starting from this premise, Aron developed the concept of secular religion that clarified its specific features, whose essential points are summarized below.

Secular religions are doctrines that establish the final cause in relation to which good and evil are defined. If "religion has the function of establishing the highest values that give direction to human existence, how can we deny that the political doctrines of our times have a religious essence?" They are religions of collective salvation that do not acknowledge that anything is superior to the objective of their movement in terms of dignity and authority. All people and all things are subordinate to the achievement of this objective, and the measure of their value, even their spiritual value, is conditional on their usefulness to the realization of this final cause. The activist of a secular religion, without the slightest qualms to his conscience, makes use of all means, however horrible, because the end to be achieved always justifies and sanctifies intolerance and violence. Here we find the common foundation of secular religions and the origin of their ruthlessly Machiavellian behavior. Aron observes that it would be ridiculous to criticize secular religions for "creating intolerance and spreading war": after all, "the religions of salvation were no less intolerant in the eras in which they held undisputed sway over people's souls. They were harsh in the name of purity, and they pursued heretics with ferocity, never hesitating to triumph by putting to fire and sword."[33]

Structurally secular religions shared certain features with traditional religions: they provide a global interpretation of the world (or at least of the historical world), and they explain the meaning of the evils that torment humanity by looking into the distant future and perceiving the purpose of all these terrible trials. They also provide a foretaste of that future community of humanity delivered from its suffering. This is attained through the fraternal communion of the party, which compensates immediately for the sacrifices required by removing the individual "from the solitude of the soul-less mass and a life without hope."[34]

Aron's analysis of secular religions in his essay of 1944 contains some significant innovations. It breaks with the previous instrumental and *crowd manipulation* interpretation and reflects on other aspects, motivations, and functions concerning the origins and nature of secular religions. Aron had already highlighted the connection between collective fideism, demagogic cynicism, and bureaucratic rationalization, which constituted the truly modern feature of totalitarian regimes. Now he emphasized that the formation of secular religions also originated from the existential needs of modern man, who was disoriented, bewildered, and isolated in the world of bureaucratic and anonymous modernity, and was at the mercy of overwhelming forces that had torn down the traditional pillars of faith and authority. When viewed in this context, totalitarian religions acquired a rational justification as surrogates or replacements for faith and authority and as pseudoreligions that filled the void left in the consciousness by failure of ancient certainties and traditional religions. Modernity had undermined beliefs and institutions that had lasted millennia and which integrated the individual into a community. This created masses made up of millions of disoriented and uncertain individuals, "prisoners," Aron wrote, "of a monotonous trade, lost in the urban multitude" and desperate for a faith, a community, and some direction in life. Totalitarian religions could therefore appear to promise a solution to the crisis of modern man. In these reflections, Aron echoed the debate on the crisis of civilization that during the thirties had taken on the somber tones of apocalyptic pessimism, arising from a sense of imminent catastrophes about to strike "a demented world," as the Dutch historian Johan Huizinga defined it in 1935.[35] It was a world in which everything that had appeared sacred and dependable was now faltering or in the throes of a prolonged death. The German philosopher Karl Jaspers, writing in 1931, claimed the physiognomy of the era was

> that of an *insecure man* and it manifests itself in the rebellion of opposites in the desperation of nihilism, the impotent confusion of the dissatisfied mass, and the directionless search that never finds peace at any stage and rejects the need for conciliation. "God does not exist" is the shout that rises from the masses. When God loses his value, so does human life, which can be extinguished without any scruples, given that it no longer has any significance.[36]

According to Aron, secular religions in an era of tremendous upheavals fulfill the masses' need for direction, certainty, and leadership by offering it a system of beliefs capable of providing an explanation for existential problems by relating them to a single formula. Secular religions guaranteed isolated and marginalized individuals "participation in a spiritual community" while acting as a new principle for legitimizing authoritarian power, embodied in the person of the leader:

> The crowds that furiously acclaim the false prophets betray the intensity of the aspirations they direct toward the empty heavens. As Bernanos says, the tragedy is not that Hitler presents himself as a god or is taken for one, but that there are millions of people so desperate that they are willing to believe that he is. Every economic or political crisis that disrupts the masses delivers them up again to the twin temptations of desperation and enthusiasm.[37]

Thus a new order was "founded on the ascendancy of a secular religion, the brotherhood of the faithful to the same cult," and the prestige of a leader in whom the masses acknowledged their savior and the realization of their aspirations.

> Men are tired of obeying "officials" and faceless, nameless authority: the hero has suddenly arisen from the anonymity of rational organizations as a reaction. Men are tired of submitting to an order they do not understand and which, through a lack of moral inspiration, has been degraded to coercion or fatalism: the hope of salvation transfigures this order by restoring its spiritual meaning. Both aspirations tend to come together: the collective beliefs create prophets, and the potentates invent their religions. Even if the image of the earthly paradise fades, there is still the primitive doctrine of the man of providence.[38]

In this situation, the cynicism of the totalitarian tyrants finds fertile ground on which to sow the salvation myths of their political religions, and the necessary consensus of desperate people, which is then transformed into the fuel for their machinery of power. The central argument in Aron's analysis is that in mass society the irrational and the mythical became a formidable political force for collective mobilization, because they conferred the suggestive power of a new religion onto totalitarian regimes. That power derived from the fanaticism of believers who wished to conquer and transform the world by conquering and transforming consciences. They were therefore determined to take possession of human bodies and minds by regimenting them in rigid organizations that absorbed individuals into the mass and molded them according to the needs of the new secular deities. To achieve their ends, totalitarian religions have at their disposal the machinery of the modern state, all the instruments provided by modern technology, and another useful resource: the faith placed by the masses in their idol. As far back as 1935, while attending a conference on the ideology and reality of Nazism, Aron attributed great importance to the fideistic attraction of the Hitlerite movement for the German masses, particularly the youth. Driven "by a collective faith of a religious nature," they followed "a prophet who proclaimed the Third Reich" and promised a stronger and more prosperous future for the new Germany:

> For the youth, this religious fervor corresponded to an ethic and a concept of life. German youth was typified by a spirit of comradeship, common struggle, devotion to the leader, desire for heroism, contempt for the bourgeois lifestyle, and direct involvement in the community, and all these sentiments were spreading throughout the Hitlerite movement. Joining the party did not so much mean accepting a program or adhering to certain ideas, as swearing loyalty to a leader and participating in a struggle.[39]

## THE RELIGIOUS ESSENCE OF TOTALITARIANISM

During the period that Aron was defining the concept of secular religion in London as a refugee from Nazi-occupied France, the German intellectual Waldemar Gurian was in exile in the United States and independently developing the concept of political religion as a typology of totalitarianism and a system of power dominated by a newly formed elite organized hierarchically in a single party subject to a leader and united by an absolute belief in its own mission. Gurian wrote in 1939 that the totalitarian elite replaced the social or traditional legitimization of the old ruling class with the new formula of a political religion. But apart from justifying the power of the single party, the political religion had the twin roles of consecrating the primacy of its authority as the sole source of the law, and of molding public opinion from above so as to make it favorable to the regime. A particular characteristic of the totalitarian state that differed from other forms of absolutism was an intolerance of merely "passive exterior acceptance of authority" because totalitarianism considers "complete interior assent is necessary":

> The political religion of the totalitarian state is different from the political religion in the absolutistic regime by being not only the worship of one person or dynasty, but at the same time the worship of the mass represented by the leading elite and the leader. . . . The totalitarian state knows the individual only as an instrument of the state, as a completely submerged part of the national or social community and as a mouthpiece of the political religion.[40]

Totalitarian religions are based on "unquestioning obedience to the leader on the one hand, and cynical amoralism on the other," which is deliberately used to engender fervor among the masses and transform them into an active force for the dominant group's ambitions and power politics: "The totalitarian state based upon this political religion has despised the masses much more than did the old absolutist state. The old state considered the masses as passive instruments: totalitarian states attempt to hypnotize them into positive enthusiasm."[41]

Thus Gurian, like Aron, also thought that political religions were the creation of calculated political self-interest and were one of the demagogic instruments of totalitarian power. However, it was precisely the originality of this power in relation to traditional forms of absolutism and of dictatorship that led Gurian to believe that the problem of political religions could not be resolved through the *crowd manipulation* interpretation. When examined more closely, it became clear that totalitarian religions, far from being an ancillary tool, were the very essence of totalitarianism. In other words, totalitarian states did not have recourse to political religions for purely demagogic reasons, but because it was in their nature to be motivated by political religions. It was a genuine impulse to invade the field that had previously been the exclusive domain of traditional religions. By appropriating the right to define the meaning and the final cause of existence, the totalitarian state was obliged to occupy the religious dimension, because it claimed to be "not only the 'societas perfecta' in its order, but the 'societas perfecta' in the absolute sense. The state (or the movement bearing the state) is the present God; the racial substance of the people or the national myth or the classless society decide exclusively what the common good is."[42] Gurian concluded that totalitarian religions interpret the New Testament precept "render therefore unto Caesar the things which be Caesar's, and unto God the things which be God's" to their own exclusive advantage: "The totalitarian Caesar decides what can be given to God. God is no longer the aim of the political unity but its means. . . . The society is not reflecting God; God is the reflection of the society. The totalitarian regime adores the god produced by itself. Thus, in the last instance, if it uses the name of God, it adores its own image deifying itself."[43]

The political religion, Gurian asserted in 1944, "is not only necessary for utilitarian purposes, but is also considered the expression of a true, just and absolute order"; totalitarian "movements which emphasized *absolute* unity between politics and religion, and transformed politics into something all-embracing and absolute, the ultimate end of human existence."[44] In 1952, Gurian completely abandoned the *crowd manipulation* interpretation of political religions: to interpret the latter purely as "an instrument for establishing a political system in which the state concentrates as much power in its hands as it can" would prevent us from understanding the real importance of political religions in the twentieth century.[45] "These political religions, the various forms of totalitarianism, do not only aspire to create a strong state, but also to control and transform man and society completely." In this way, Gurian eventually came to identify totalitarianism and political religion with each other, in the sense that he considered totalitarianism itself to be a religious phenomenon:

> The totalitarian movements that have arisen after the First World War are basically religious movements. Their aim is not only to change political and social institutions, but also to remodel the nature of man and society. They claim to possess the true and obligatory knowledge of the meaning of life and its end. They forcefully argue that they are founded on doctrines that describe and determine in a total and complete manner the existence and activity of man and society. It does not matter if these doctrines are presented as the sole correct expression of scientific knowledge of society and the law of historical development, as in the case of the Bolshevik-Marxist variant of totalitarianism, or if they claim to justify the rule of the master race and express the myth destined to prevail in the twentieth century, as the Nazi asserts. The claim to hold the doctrine of the truth is the fundamental characteristic of totalitarian movements. They are intolerant. Their aim is to eradicate all other doctrines and philosophies. They do not tolerate any limitations on their demands and power. Totalitarian movements do not conceive of dimensions of life outside or beyond their control. They cannot accept that other doctrines or institutions have the right to remain independent, or have a dignity and validity in themselves. The fact that they accept that for a certain period they accept the existence of other groups and doctrines according to the exigencies of power, does not mean that they have renounced their purpose of complete domination and the elimination of all other doctrines.

Interpretations of totalitarianism as a political phenomenon that attempts to invade the field of traditional religions, motivated by a religious impulse, became increasingly common since the late twenties. The

originality of totalitarian political mystiques, according to Louis Rougier, was the "radical negation of the distinction between the spiritual
and the temporal," which had been Christianity's essential contribution
to Western civilization. The totalitarian state claimed that it could "regenerate the soul as well as the body, and put both body and spirit in
uniform." It desired "the passive obedience of the body and the joyous
support of the soul," and consequently it considered agnosticism to be
a crime.[46] This was the principle innovation of totalitarian dictatorship
in relation to dictatorships of the past. As the English historian Alfred
Cobban explained in a valuable study of the phenomenon of dictatorship
that was published in 1939, the latter were techniques of domination
that did not seek ideological legitimization, whereas in the case of the
former, there is a "real spiritual principle" acting behind the party, the
secret police, and the terror. "The new totalitarian dictatorship is powerful not because it rules men's bodies, but because it controls their minds.
Its essential aim is, in fact, . . . , is the identification of Church and
State."[47] According to Cobban, it is through its religious aspect that "totalitarian dictatorship reaches its highest point. Here its sway ends, for
it has become coextensive with human life. Totalitarianism takes the
spiritual discipline of a religious order and imposes it on forty or sixty
or a hundred million people. Its aim is a nation of Jesuits, serving not
the Vicar of Christ, but the *Führer*."[48]

At the end of the thirties, secular religion had become an established
theme in the interpretation of totalitarian regimes, and indeed was one
of the principal areas in which different forms of totalitarianism were
compared. Frederik Voigt equated Marxism and Nazism, which he considered to be different versions of "modern Messianism," the former rationalistic and the latter irrational, but both united by the myth of the
final struggle and the necessary catastrophe to free the world from Evil
and ensure the definitive triumph of Good:

> We have referred to Marxism and National Socialism as secular religions.
> They are not opposites, but are fundamentally akin, in a religious as well
> as a secular sense. Both are messianic and socialistic. Both reject Christian
> knowledge that all are under sin and both see in good and evil principles of
> class and race. Both are despotic in their methods and their mentality. Both
> have enthroned the modern Caesar, collective man, the implacable enemy of
> the individual soul. Both would render unto Caesar the things which are
> God's. Both would make man master of his own destiny, establish the King-
> dom of Heaven in this world.[49]

Political religion was seen to have an important role in the comparative
analysis of totalitarian states. Indeed, it appears in first place among the
constituent elements of totalitarianism at a symposium on totalitarian

states that was held in Philadelphia in November 1939 and organized by the American Philosophical Society.[50] Using an effective image in his introductory lecture, Fritz Morstein Marx, a professor of political science, defined totalitarian ideology as "the secular religion of the Leviathan as a Church."[51] As such, the totalitarian Leviathan could adopt different tactics toward the churches. It could play for time and agree compromises, but its ultimate aim was always the conquest of the whole person:

> The secular Leviathan as a Church, by its very nature, tends to affirm the universality of its absolutes. When faced with tangible obstacles, it can for some time prove acquiescent, but it is however driven to pursue the affirmation of its absolutes as soon as resistance gives way. As it is engaged in a sacred mission, it is incapable of respecting the demarcation line between persuasion and brute force.

The irrepressible vocation of totalitarian states to shatter all restraints, the millenarian aspirations of their secular religion, and their fanatical self-belief all found fertile ground in the situation of "tragic insecurity of 'mass-man,' that in Italy, just as in Germany and Russia, has been aggravated by moral and material upheavals of the World War and its consequences." The new secular religion could not have taken power "if it were not for the fact that it meets human needs that had not been met elsewhere."[52] Carlton J. H. Hayes, an American historian and the greatest scholar of nationalism as a religion at the time, was of the same opinion. With the decline of traditional Christian faith among the Western masses, a religious vacuum had been created that the masses felt they had to fill with a new faith, and the totalitarian movements provided them with this new faith. For this reason, it would have been a mistake to neglect "the essentially religious element that they contain and the essentially religious fascination that they exercise. It is the guise of the high priest of new and ardent religions that contemporary dictators address the masses. And it is with the enthusiasm and fanaticism of novices that the masses respond to the appeal of dictators."[53]

The political scientist Sigmund Neumann also assigned an essential role to political religion in the interpretation of totalitarianism. He was the author of the first systematic comparative study of totalitarian states, which was published in 1942 in the United States, where he was in exile. Taking the example of the Fascist Party, he observed that

> the inner driving forces behind the modern dictatorial party are no doubt closely connected with this spiritual, one may almost say semi-ecclesiastical, character. The party is an assertor of faith, a faith that permeates all aspects of human destiny and reaches into the region of the absolute. Its totalitarian nature inevitably turns the party in a religious order, in a theocracy. . . . The

reality of the Fascist party can be well described by this religious character. The party has its hierarchy, its rituals, its dogmas, its seminaries. It offers spiritual rewards and punishments. It prosecutes its mission also by administrating material pain or pleasure. Fanaticism becomes the most significant feature of the zealous followers; heretics have to be converted or they will be burnt. To this end churches have always needed their militant orders and their missionaries. Institutions of propaganda were created to propagate the faith. Persuasion, stimulation, charitable works, public worship, and commemoration of saints and martyrs are consequential techniques of this new religious sect.[54]

In this manner, the totalitarian party itself becomes a church that wants to claim the souls of its supporters. This is why totalitarianism was destined to come into conflict with traditional religions: "Modern dictatorships are "political religions" (inner worldly religions, to be sure). In fact, their very survival depends on their final victory over religion. Because religion represents the supreme challenge to totalitarian rule, religious forces may be the last protection against totalitarian claims."[55]

Many analyses of totalitarianism during the period between the wars concluded with predictions of a conflict between political religions and Christian religions, because, according to the general opinion of these interpreters, totalitarian religions could not have renounced the imposition by every means of their will and their unlimited dominion over the bodies and souls of their subjects, while justifying and exalting hate, violence, and criminality against their enemies as a holy crusade to free the world from Evil. "Engaged in a sacred mission, totalitarianism cannot respect the demarcation line between persuasion and brute force. Its torture chambers are sanctified just like its temples."[56]

## Chapter 4

# THE INVASION OF THE IDOLS
*Christians against Totalitarian Religions*

> Idolatry not only refers to false pagan worship. It remains a constant temptation to faith. Idolatry consists in divinizing what is not God. Man commits idolatry whenever he honors and reveres a creature in place of God, whether this be gods or demons (for example, satanism), power, pleasure, race, ancestors, the state, money, etc.
> —Catechism of the Catholic Church

### IDOLATRIES OF MODERNITY

For those who believed in the religion of Christ, the triumph of political ideologies, movements, and regimes that deified secular entities and party leaders was a grave and dangerous return to paganism, which threatened the future of Christianity with the spread of a "collective idolatry," as Luigi Sturzo, a Catholic priest and the founder of the Italian Popular Party, defined it in 1933:

> But why should we be surprised? Is it perhaps not the case that there are more idols and more idolatry in modern times and among Christian and civilized peoples? They may not be called Jove or Moloch, but our idols have more seductive names: they are called Nation, State, Liberty, Authority, Republic, Monarchy, Race, and Class. While incense and hieratic or rather occultist rituals are not offered up to them, there is another much more significant incense used, that of infinite praise, and there is no shortage of civil rituals, which often take on religious forms.
>
> It is true that modern idolatries are secularized religions, but they are not without sanctuaries, altars, and victims. Since the development of the cult of the Goddess of Reason, modern idolatries in moments of particular fervor feel nostalgia for the ancient idolatries and the need to imitate their rituals of worship.
>
> But what they particularly need are victims. Today the number of victims sacrificed to these cruel gods in civil and conventional wars is far greater than at the time of Iphigenia. They can be counted in thousands and in millions.[1]

In 1937 the French pastor Elie Gounelle, who edited *Revue du Christianisme Social*, wrote about the revival of idols that wanted to destroy Christianity:

All the dead gods, which were thought to have been permanently buried in their crimson shrouds, have been reawakened and have risen up again. It has been a great invasion of idols, which have entered the field to drive out all forms of Christianity and to attack the disunited and disoriented Church of Christ with the aim of finishing off the Religion of the Spirit.

The mystical dogmas of Class, Race, Blood, Nation, Force, and War are everywhere replacing the mystical dogma of the Gospel that can bring salvation; they are doing so in public opinion, in the press, in political parties, and in politics in general.

The central viewpoint for these problems is not so much the economy as politics, but it is even more spiritual than it is political. The worst of the pagan dangers that rises up before the conscience of the churches is no longer the specter of evil (which, in any case, has triumphed everywhere and in all fields) but is instead the totalitarian state.[2]

We find the same perception of the uncontrolled expansion of idolatry in an Italian Catholic journal. Father Giulio Bevilacqua, writing at the beginning of 1940, described an apocalyptic war waged by the modern gods against the true God for the domination of humanity:

The soul of modern man has become a *pantheon* of *gods* incensed with the only jealous *God* who does not consent to share altars and adoration, and against other *gods* who struggle for primacy over the prostrate crowd of worshippers. This struggle of everything against everyone and this immense and divided kingdom, in which the biological condition of life has been accepted, contain one point on which all are in agreement: their loathing for Christ and He who said: "No servant can serve two masters: for either he will hate the one, and love the other; or else he will hold to the one, and despise the other."

The apostle of the modern world must become aware of a tragic and demeaning reality: the century of the scientific analysis, exact observation, concrete achievement, and boundless daring is an idolatrous century. New cults, new liturgies, new acts of faith, new symbols, new priesthoods, new inquisitions against past ones fade into insignificance, new wars of religion and above all new incarnations in which it is no longer the *Logos* that becomes flesh in order to sanctify the flesh, but intelligence, will, and the soul that abases itself in blood so as to bring forth a life that consists of nothing but instinct, violence, and madness.[3]

The protagonists of this chapter, Catholic and the Protestant believers and scholars of religious phenomena, thought very deeply about totalitarian religions, and for them they were a source of great anxiety and even anguish. They were aware that it was not just a theoretical question but an intense and tragic reality of new powers that were rising up with terrible majesty and the attractions of a new religion.

Perhaps because they were more sensitive to perceptions of the sacred in all its fascinating and terrifying manifestations, Catholics and Protestants were able to understand and to sense the religious meaning of totalitarianism, and its threat to Christianity and human destiny, precisely because of its religious essence. Leaving aside the ethical evaluation of the phenomenon, their reflections constitute an important theoretical contribution. In the examples that we will examine, the analysis of totalitarianism is undoubtedly filtered through a believer's consciousness of a certain religion, which is obliged to see other religions, particularly civil and political religions, as "false" religions or, to use the terms they usually adopt, manifestations of paganism and idolatry. However, the anguish they experience in relation to the new political religions demonstrates that they actually perceived them as tragic revelations of the sacred nature of a power that could challenge the very existence of Christianity in the future. Totalitarian states deified the new "numinous reality of the collective entity, to which it assigned all the properties of a transcendent being, and did not even have any scruples over burning incense before its altars," as the Jesuit priest Antonio Messineo wrote in 1943. He was the principal academic contributor to *Civiltà cattolica* on the question of the "secular religion of the nation," as he himself defined it.[4]

For believers in Christ, of course, totalitarian religions were pseudo-religions, replacement religions, or in other words "false" religions, because they negated the "true" God and the "true" faith. Messineo, almost repeating the *crowd manipulation* theory, considered them to be the product of the "bad habit, which had been widespread for some time, of transferring sacred terminology to the profane, so as to surround the implementation of social duties with a certain aura of religiosity," excite "people's minds with fervor," and drive them to action by offering them "a kind of human faith that not infrequently takes on the forms of a genuine surrogate for religion."[5] In this manner, the Jesuit observed, "politics is transformed into a secular religion, which is so demanding that it requires the whole person and even prevents individuals from using their reason." It inspires in them a "mythical faith," which is "an instinctive, blind, and passionate abandon, a total dedication of the will in the pursuit of particular historical goals, whose intelligence has not even been tested by reason, and an immersion of man into the currents of political life to be buffeted by natural, unconscious, and mechanical forces."[6] Politics, as a secular religion, thus attempts to satisfy the need for faith, which is inherent to human beings by offering them "human surrogates of God."

For example, Messineo cited the "mythical concept of nation," which tends to "instill a certain religious inspiration in the cult of the nation, and this comes close to, and often becomes confused with, the religious inspiration that is exclusively due to the Supreme Being."[7]

> The substitute God has been discovered in the nation, which is idealized and personified as an autonomous, absolute, and sovereign being that transcends its parts as the final cause for human life and its reason for existence. In this way, nationalism is converted into a secular religion, whose divinity is the nation, whose insignia are its flags, and whose altars are the memorials to its heroes. It is a religion that has its own faith, its own unquestionable dogmas, its own Commandments, its own martyrs, and its own extravagant festivals.[8]

Although he considered the phenomenon to be a "false religiosity," this Jesuit priest was fully aware of the seriousness of the issue for "true religiosity" and sensed the impending "danger of a veritable overturning of the hierarchy of values," which was intrinsic to a concept of politics that "tends to transpose the absolute into the contingent, by humanizing the divine and sanctifying the human" through a "mythical faith" that "places greater demands than a genuinely religious faith."[9]

## THE STATE AS A CHURCH

For Christians, the religious problem of totalitarianism was primarily the question of a state that wished to control all aspects of human life, and for this reason was inevitably driven into conflict with the churches, either to destroy them or transform them into instruments of its rule. But the ambitions of totalitarian states went even further because they wanted to be a religion and a church, and were therefore intrinsically incompatible with the Christian religion and inevitably hostile to its independence. "If you consider the totalitarian principle in itself as an historical force with its own laws," observed the Catholic philosopher Jacques Maritain in 1936, "it becomes clear that the principle contains an intrinsic aversion to Christian order, an aversion that is rendered ineffective only inasmuch as totalitarianism is genuinely opposed by religion." While totalitarianism, in the case of fascism, did not attempt to destroy religion as communism was attempting to do, it did aim "to take it over and practically take possession of people's consciences." For this reason, totalitarianism was a much more serious danger than any previous case of interference by the state in church affairs. Since the times of Constantine, temporal power had attempted "to utilize the Christian religion and distract it from its own purposes," but, Maritain warned, "we must not fool ourselves: there is a gulf between these disorders and perversions, however serious they may have been, and the all-consuming absolutism that today asserts itself and demands the entire individual for the temporal community or the state":

> Political totalitarianism wishes in every case that the state become the absolutely sovereign reality and the absolutely sovereign ruler of people's temporal lives, and therefore of the acts of conscience that such lives imply—"everything within the state, nothing against the state, and nothing outside the state"—and it wishes to be alone in shaping the "soul within the soul" and the energies of the soul as it leads its earthly life, which is the only life that concerns it. As a result of inevitable logical requirements, it will therefore demand that the spiritual—at least where it encounters the temporal and affects the conduct of "civil life" and civilized order—be integrated, in people's consciousness, into the state and the spirit of the people in their service.[10]

Viewed in this way, the power of totalitarian states was increasing out of all proportion, and such states were transforming themselves into sacred, majestic, beguiling, and terrifying powers, as described by Adolf Keller, the director of the Ecumenical Seminary of Geneva:

> The State is a mythical divinity which, like God, has the right and might to lay a totalitarian claim on its subjects, to impose upon them a new philosophy, a new faith; to organize the conscience and thinking of its children. . . . The state in this myth acts like a superhuman giant, claiming not only obedience, but confidence and faith such as only a personality has the right to expect. . . . This personifying tendency of the myth finds its strongest expression in the mysterious personal relationship of millions with a leader. A mystical personalism has got hold of the whole political and social imagination of great peoples. The leader, the *Duce* is the personified nation, a superman, a messiah, a saviour.[11]

*Civiltà cattolica*, the semiofficial organ of the Holy See, described the sacredness of totalitarian states in similar terms: "The state is being transformed into an obscure, intangible, and tyrannical deity: a Moloch that devours men by suckling them to her ample breasts. Before this manifestation of the divine in the world, the human being disappears, subjective rights come to nothing, and objective law fades away."[12]

When investigating the origins of this phenomenon, an important role was attributed to genuinely political factors such as force and material power, which naturally appeared more evident and decisive, but the interpretation of the meaning of totalitarian idolatries transcended the specifically political dimension, because the totalitarian state was not only a terrible material power, as had never occurred in the past, but also a power capable of exercising a seductive fascination over the masses by presenting itself as a movement based on beliefs, faith, and salvation as an alternative to the Christian religion.

Catholics and Protestants shared the belief that the advent of totalitarian states was not a temporary phenomenon concerning political events of the postwar period, but rather the culmination of a long process and the product of the secularization and expansion of state power in modern society, which had forced the churches either to retreat into the private sphere or to conform to the myths and politics of secular states. The Great War, political revolutions, and the economic crisis had extended the state's authority and control over society through centralization and planning to the point that it became possible to conceive politics in a totalitarian manner. According to the Catholic historian Christopher Dawson, the "essential principal of the Totalitarian State was, in fact, asserted by Liberalism before Fascism was ever heard of."[13] This principle had its roots in the expansionist tendency of the modern state, which had asserted itself after the fragmentation of Christian unity, when temporal power had achieved the primacy of its sovereignty over the church, and it therefore started to extend its control over every aspect of life. Totalitarianism had taken "organized secularism" to its extreme consequences by dissolving parliamentary democracy, which was an obstacle to the complete affirmation of statist absolutism. It did so by imposing the dictatorship of a single party organized like a religious order.

Protestants put forward a similar interpretation of the origins of the totalitarian state, and considered totalitarianism to be the consequence of a long series of challenges, attacks and interference on the part of the secular state and directed against the church, in order to deprive the church of its control over society while extending the state's power over all aspects of human life. Willem A. Visser't Hooft, who was a Dutch exponent of the ecumenical movement Life and Work as well as general secretary of the World Federation of Christian Students, wrote in 1937: "Liberal, socialist and more recently totalitarian parties and governments tried to eliminate the influence of Christianity in the fields of politics, social services and education, and were to a large extent successful in doing so, because church members were not always alive to their responsibilities." In many countries, the church was "confronted with the problem of its attitude to the powerful new political ideologies, which are all more or less totalitarian, and therefore attempt to use the church for secular ends. The European Churches are thus forced to realization of the fact that the era in which Europe was officially Christian is over."[14] In the new Europe, Christian churches had to meet the challenge of regimes that rejected the value of the individual, attacked the freedom of churches, and aimed to merge temporal power and spiritual power under the aegis of the state, thereby claiming responsibility for controlling, educating, and transforming human beings in accordance with a wholly political concept of the meaning and purpose of existence. As Joseph H. Oldham, an Anglican theologian and another authoritative exponent of the ecumenical movement, observed in 1935, by so doing the state claimed for itself the nature and functions of a church. A state that claims to dominate man in the totality of his being, that rejects the independence of religion, culture, education, and the family within their own spheres, that attempts to impose a particular philosophy of life on all its citizens, and that wishes to create a certain kind of man through its organization of information and public education in accordance with its concept of the meaning and purpose of the human existence "is not only a state but also a Church" and professes a concept of life that, although "it cannot properly be called a religion," is however "a substitute for religion and becomes its powerful rival."[15]

Oldham was one of the principal organizers of the ecumenical conference that was held in Oxford from 12 to 26 July 1937. The conference proceedings are one of the most significant demonstrations of the attitude of Christian churches to the advent of the totalitarian state-church. Four hundred members from various Christian confessions all over the world took part in the conference. The only missing representations were the Catholic Church, because it was not part of the ecumenical movement, and the delegation from the Evangelical Church of Germany, which was unable to take part. The subject of the conference was the role of Christian churches in society and in relation to the state. This subject had been chosen by the ecumenical movement in 1934, just after the advent of Nazi power and the beginning of the religious struggle in Germany between the regime and the churches that did not agree to conform to racist ideology. These dramatic events had forced Christian churches to take notice of states that, as the Archbishop of Canterbury said in his introductory speech, claimed "to dominate the nation and direct its life, its thought and its action. This claim certainly comes into conflict with Christianity and its human personality to a greater or lesser extent."[16]

The conference above all had the purpose of defining the attitude of Christian churches "toward the rapid progress of secular and pagan trends that manifest themselves principally in the national and political life of the entire world."[17] The motions put forward at the conference were resolute declarations of antitotalitarianism, which were unanimously approved. It asserted that the mission of the churches was "to create a community founded on divine love," to respect the state "as the guarantor of order, justice and civil liberty," and "to serve the nation and the State by proclaiming the will of God as the supreme standard to which all human wills must be subject and all human conduct must conform."

However, the declaration added that they strongly opposed "the growing de-Christianization of society" and the "widespread tendency of the State to control the totality of human life in all its individual and social aspects, combined with the tendency to attribute absolute value to the State itself, to the national community, to the dominating class or to the prevailing cultural form." The Christian churches had a duty to criticize a state that neglected its tasks of upholding "the standards of justice set forth in the Word of God" and a duty of disobedience "only if obedience would be clearly contrary to the command of God." They also had the duty of "permeating the public life with the spirit of Christ."[18] The motion on "the Church, the Nation and the State in their relations with education" was also approved unanimously. The church, it was asserted, has to protest against any state monopoly over education and must reclaim the freedom to carry out its mission by organizing youth, preparing and training its leaders, and opposing "any deification of the nation or the state."[19]

The ecumenical conference ended its proceedings with a message to all Christian churches in the world in which it stressed once again that the duty of Christians in the face of a totalitarian state was to remain faithful to their mission, to defend the liberty of the church, and to oppose "contemporary paganism," racism, and imperialism. "Against racial pride and race-antagonism," came the message, "the Church must set its face implacably as rebellion against God." "But national egotism tending to the suppression of other nationalities or of minorities is, no less than individual egotism, a sin against the Creator of all peoples and races. The deification of nation, race, or class or of political or cultural ideals, is idolatry and can only lead to increasing division and disaster."[20]

The reflections and conclusions of the Oxford conference were summarized and systematically reworked by the Swedish pastor Nils Ehrenström who explicitly referred to the arguments of Dawson, Visser't Hooft, and Oldham when he traced the origins of totalitarianism to the expansionist tendencies of the modern state and their need to incorporate all aspects of life and society. Moreover, totalitarian tendencies were inherent in all contemporary states, even in countries with strong liberal traditions, and were in part due to needs imposed on contemporary states by a "process of disintegration and reconstruction" that had afflicted modern society and demanded guidance and direction. This had increased planning measures that made greater state control inevitable. The expansion of the state was also due to proliferation of the functions that it was taking on and which had previously been carried out by other institutions. However, the Swedish pastor made clear that the birth of the totalitarian state was not a mere consequence of this tendency because it also presupposed a qualitative change in circumstances:

This great extension of State control accompanies, and is at least in part the result of a qualitative change in the nature of the State itself, and in man's understanding of its purpose. A State which behaves as though it were potentially omnicompetent usurps in practice, even if not in theory, the divine attribute of omnipotence. Whether the State claims to be an earthly absolute, or whether as an executive agent it shares in the glory of a particular class or culture or race, its expansion is no longer due simply to social and national necessities, but it becomes a divine imperative which desires to claim man and society exclusively for itself. The expanding State tends to develop symptoms of totalitarianism. It becomes aggressive and ambitious. In fresh outbursts of tyranny, caprice, and brutality, of a widespread depreciation of human life—phenomena which are increasing to a terrible extent—demoniac features of the State are emerging which constitute a grave menace to Christians and to mankind as a whole.[21]

Given this situation, those taking part in the conference were in general agreement that Christian churches were bound to come into conflict with totalitarian states.

## THE TOTALITARIAN THREAT

This conviction that conflict exists between Christianity and totalitarian states was shared by some exponents of Catholic culture, such as Dawson, who believed that the very existence of the traditional religions was at stake. He felt that they were threatened not only by totalitarian states but also by what he called "Liberal Humanitarianism." In 1934 he wrote:

> Today the conflict is a deeper and wider one. It goes to the very roots of life and affects every aspect of human thought and action. One might even say that the very existence of religion is at stake, were it not that there are some who hold that religion is no longer to be identified with Christianity and the other historical religions but is finding a new social expression in the movements that are creating the new state: Communism, Nazism and Liberal Humanitarianism. . . . The coming conflict is not one between religion and secular civilization but rather between "the God-religious and the social-religious"—in other words between the worship of God and the cult of the state or of the race or of humanity.[22]

French Catholics also thought that conflict between Christianity and totalitarianism was inevitable, as the writer Denis De Rougemont argued in 1937:

> Everyone knows or at least senses what is meant by the *totalitarian threat*, whether it be fascist or soviet: it is the "regimentation" of our lives and all

aspects of our lives, both spiritual and material, in the service of the deified state. . . . The new state wishes to be worshipped, if not yet in religious forms, then at least in forms that contradict the Ten Commandments and the duty of Christian love. Conflict is inevitable: will it be enough to allow ourselves to be persecuted? . . . Any passive waiting-game, however courageous, becomes complicity in this *particular case*.[23]

The Semaines sociale de France, an event organized by the Catholic Church, took up the question of the totalitarian threat, and a great deal of attention was paid to the religious aspects of totalitarianism. A lecture on the Soviet state, which came under the general subject of "Political Society and Christian Thought" during the "Semaine sociale" of 1933, concluded with these considerations: "The communist state can be unhesitatingly categorized as one of the great social phenomena that come under heading of religions."[24] On that occasion, Paul Cuche, a professor of law, dwelled upon the fascist concept of the nation and the state, and he defined it as an exact application of Durkheim's doctrine, because it personified the national collectivity by transforming it into the object of a "mystical and religious cult. Here then the nation sanctified. . . . Here we find before us this being endowed with a superior life, this Leviathan made up of individual atoms."[25]

During the "Semaine sociale" of 1937, the subject of the totalitarian state was thoroughly examined in a lecture by Colonel André Roullet on the question of the person in totalitarian regimes. Roullet prioritized "the sanctification of the state and the religious cult of the leader" in his definition of the constituent elements of totalitarianism, which were then followed by the dictatorship of a party, which in a totalitarian state claims all prerogatives and powers for itself, the transformation of society into a rigidly conformist aggregate, where a person is simply part of the whole as in an anthill, and the imperialist drive that is inherent in the very logic of the system and which militarized the nation by transforming it into the unquestioning instrument of the state and the leader for the pursuit of expansionist and power-hungry objectives.[26] Totalitarian states would never accept the internal presence of the "rival authority of a spiritual state" because it wanted the whole individual for itself, and given that man "is a religious animal," totalitarian states had claimed for themselves "a religious power of seduction and spiritual dominion" in order "to captivate consciences and beguile spirits":

> This aspect of false religion in totalitarian systems is expressed through their ideals, dogmas, morality, and concept of life, and all the more clearly the further away they are from Catholicism. Party grandiloquence has a religious accent. Propaganda is animated by religious fervor. There are no ceremonies, speeches, or rituals that do not have religious tone.

The idolatry of the state finds its most visible manifestation in the almost divine cult of the man who created it. The sentiment of respect and affection, to which all heads of state can normally aspire, here takes on the features of ardent devotion, which is carefully cultivated by propaganda and imposed by all the means that power has at its disposal. The dictator possesses the attributes of omnipotence and infallibility. There is no power above his power either in heaven or on earth. The police and the armed forces are his secular arm, his eye that peers into people's hearts, and the thunderbolt that strikes. Infallibility is the condition of such power, because it would lose its prestige if it were capable of making mistakes. Hence the press, the walls covered with inscriptions, and the dictator's own voice ceaselessly proclaim that he "is always right."[27]

Roullet recognized that totalitarianism encountered limits to the realization of its ambitions—"not everything is totalitarian in a totalitarian regime"—but this did not provide him with any comfort as to the gravity of the totalitarian threat, which came not only from the brute force of totalitarianism, but also from its ability to satisfy the masses' need for faith through the "mystic of force, race, blood, the people, the earth, the dictatorship of the proletariat, or the party," which offered "the illusion of a kind of Messianism." Totalitarianism appeared to be endowed with an "unconscious and collective force, a mixture of ideology and sentiment that imposes itself like a sort of revelation and takes possession of the heart and the will,"[28] by using all the instruments of propaganda and organization. Totalitarian states attempt to mold this elusive inner world with all the means at their disposal, and principally "the seizure of children away from their families, the direction of the intellectual and moral culture, the mechanized obsession with propaganda and the exploitation of the mass psychology electrified by an emotional shock,"[29] by seducing the crowds with a sense of the boundless, colossal, and titanic nature of the "totalitarian intoxication"[30] and involving them in "a collective spell and a contagious rapture,"[31] which made it possible for the leader to mobilize all the resources of the nation under his command. A state conceived and created in such a manner, which worships the collectivity and dehumanizes the individual, constituted a mortal danger to Christians. It presented them with the option of "a new submissive and animal-like order or a human order enlightened by the divine reflection of the person. We have to choose. But we have to realize that for civilization this is a matter of life and death."[32]

In the "Semaine sociale" of 1939, Father Joseph Delos, a law professor, again took up the question of how in relation to social classes within totalitarian regimes, the totalitarian state wishes to concentrate the whole of society under its physical and moral control so as to transform it into a close-knit, disciplined, hierarchical, and militarized organization subject to the absolute command of its leader, in which the "political soldier" replaces the citizen.[33] At the end of his lecture, Delos evoked the threat of the totalitarian state and described it in its essential features of sacredness as a majestic, captivating, and terrifying power:

> There is something grandiose in the spectacle of this revolution guided by an iron fist to transform a mass society and reconstruct it according to a new model that is both modern and archaic, a model such as the West has not seen for centuries. But it is also terrifying. A powerful and disciplined organization that goes against freedom of the human individual has been imposed on an exceptionally numerous, hardworking, and gifted people, and has isolated it from other peoples with its doctrine of the chosen race. This has imprisoned the people behind the threefold barrier of economic autarchy, political hegemony and racial pride. Internally, it has disaccustomed a people to freedom, a people who have the greater need of education now that they have proved themselves less master of themselves, because it has established a disciplinarian social order that conflicts with the free nature of man. You do not need to be a prophet to consider this organization to be short-lived in its current form, and this transience surrounds the future in an aura of uncertainty that increases concerns currently created by this regime among the friends of liberty and peace.[34]

## RELIGIONS OF THE ANTICHRIST

Assessments of the danger and its gravity, and predictions as to the inevitability of conflict between Christianity and totalitarianism were influenced not only by the attitude of totalitarian states toward Christian churches, but also by the interpretation of the specific content of their political religions and their effect on the success of totalitarian movements, which were capable of evoking faith and devotion and exciting the enthusiasm of the masses with exaltation of national power and the promise of a better world. "One of the characteristic features of our time," states one of the papers to the Oxford conference, "is the response made by youth to the appeal of political leaders who offer them a part in the building of a nation."[35] The sacralization of politics, with its symbols, myths, and rituals, involved the masses in continuous experiences of collective euphoria, which were facilitated by an aptitude for meticulous stage management. But the seductive powers of totalitarianism were not simply the result of skillful propaganda. The aspect of totalitarian movements that most struck Christians was their fanaticism and willful assertion of their faith by any means, however brutal or ruthless. This presented traditional religious believers with many problems when it came to understanding the nature, origins, and meaning of this phenomenon, by which a state became a church, a political movement took on religious forms, and the masses worshiped mortals as though there were earthly deities.

Catholics and Protestants had no doubts that totalitarian religions, albeit "false" ones, were manifestations of a genuine faith and were dangerous precisely for this reason. From this point of view, the case of communism provoked greater interest, given that it was a movement that professed atheism and, in spite of this, had taken on the characteristics of a religion and a church. It had incorporated the attitudes and mentality of the Russian people's religious tradition into its own materialist ideology.

Because it was atheist and committed to actively opposing any religious belief by every possible means, Soviet communism naturally seemed to Christians of every church to be the most avowed and formidable adversary. "Amongst the forces hostile to Christianity," Berdyayev wrote in 1933, "doubtless the most powerful and threatening in the world is Communism."[36]

> And as a religion, as a doctrine of salvation, as a discipline for the human spirit, it clashes cruelly with the Christian faith and conscience. Hence comes the fanaticism of communism, its intolerance of all religion, of any other system of thought; hence come its anti-religious propaganda and its anti-religious persecution. This is inherent, not in the economics and politics of communism, but in its religious nature.[37]

Soviet communism, according to the Russian philosopher, had derived its religious essence from the materialist messianism of Marxism and the Christian messianism of the profoundly religious Russian soul, and fused these together in proletarian universalism, which was a "caricature of Christian universalism and the Christian Church."[38] Nevertheless it was powerful and effective as a system of beliefs and could instill faith and enthusiasm in the masses. Precisely for this reason, the communist religion could have been a greater danger to Christianity than fascism and Nazism. The greater threat resulted from the universalistic ideology of Soviet communism, which turned it into a direct challenge to Christianity on its own ground, because its message of salvation for all humanity foretold the advent of a new society of free and equal individuals in a more just world freed from the evil generated by the existence of private property and the division of society into classes: in other words, a paradise to be created on this earth. According to Keller, "elements of a positive religious faith penetrated unconsciously into the Bolshevik antireligious movement, and transformed the scientific social system of Western Marxism into a 'secular religion,' a 'land without God,' but with religious fervour and religious symbols. . . . Leninism is a camouflaged secular religion, a Messianism without a Messiah."[39]

As well as by messianism that derived from the Marxist vision of history, the formation of this secular religion was largely assisted by the religious sentiment of the Russian people and the revolutionary tradition of populism, which joined together in bolshevism. It was a mixture of antireligious nihilism and millenarian mysticism. This explains the ambivalent nature of the secular religion of the Soviet state, which appeared to be steeped with typically religious fervor and faith in its Promethean ambitions to create a new civilization, while at the same time being fanatically antireligious in its hate of the church and traditional religions.[40] "From the perspective of atheism and materialism, is it not the case that a great religious phenomenon is now occurring in Russia?" asked the Dominican Joseph-André Ducattillon in his study of communist and Christian doctrines. Communism, he wrote, "is a phenomenon of passion, and one of the most formidable, not only in our own era, but undoubtedly in the whole of history."[41]

> Thanks to this heroic passion, a handful of men were able to transform that enormous, monstrous and amorphous mass, that human magma to which we attach the label of Russia (a sixth of the inhabited world), into the citadel of communism, and for almost twenty years they have kept the whole thing regimented and domesticated. Moreover, this same passion has had its repercussions in the furthest reaches of the world. There is not a single country that has not recorded them, causing terror among some and frenzied hopes among others. . . . Precisely because of this passionate side, communism becomes mystical. . . . Fascism, Hitlerism, nationalism and religion itself all contain passionate and mystical elements of some kind. This is the explanation for communism's extraordinary dynamism, its irresistible fascination, and the no less passionate aversion. Hence its titanic greatness, its gravity, its tragedy and its global force, but also its weakness.[42]

In the Western world, English Protestants who believed in the revolutionary role of socialist Christianity could not evade the fascination of the Soviet experience and communism as a message of human salvation, and they hoped to enter into a dialogue with Soviet communism and establish an understanding based on a shared opposition to capitalist society. Some of these Protestants considered communism itself to be a new religion that had affinities with Christianity. This group included the majority of the contributors to a volume on Christianity and social revolution, published in England in 1935, to which Soviet philosophers also contributed. These Soviet contributors did not in any way soften their profession of atheism or distance themselves from the concept of communism as a science based on reality.[43] In spite of this, socialist Christian hopes of an understanding were sustained by the successes of Soviet Russia, which was progressing with the construction of a new social order, albeit with brutal methods, and was disproving the catastrophic predictions of its enemies. The extraordinary creative energy and faith in the future displayed by communists seemed to prove that they were indeed animated by a genuine religious energy. "There is in their movement," wrote the professor of theology at Cambridge, Charles E. Raven, in the introduction, "the authentic exaltation, the generosity, the self-sacrifice of a religion. Indeed, whatever their philosophy, these folk have found a faith to live by, or, what is perhaps more important, a cause to die for."[44] A social and revolutionary Christianity could not ignore this new religion, which displayed many of the characteristics of the eschatological and apocalyptical tradition of early Christianity, and indeed had to recognize that communism was the heir to Christianity and probably would not be able to remain tied to its profession of atheism and antireligious prejudices, precisely because of its religious nature.[45] The Christian religion had to join up with the communist religion in the common commitment to social revolution to prevent the imminent catastrophe of the capitalist society. "The apocalyptic crisis has descended upon our age, not prematurely as in the time of Jesus, but in the fullness of time. . . . The new Christ is an insurgent Proletariat, the uprisen people of God, and the Church which fails to do Him reverence must be cast forth into the outer darkness. The Day of the Lord is at hand," announced John Lewis, professor of social philosophy at Cambridge.[46]

Other writers did not share the same enthusiasm for communism, but were equally convinced of its religious nature. Another contributor, who used the pseudonym Bruno Maier, claimed that, in spite its declared atheism, bolshevism had "entered a religious phase. Nowadays, it has its God, its Holy Scriptures, its Church, its dogma, its inquisition and its heretics."[47] The very affirmation of the dictatorship of the proletariat as the supreme principle for moral discrimination is an expression of "the Chiliastic enthusiasm of the Bolshevist religion."[48] For the American theologian Reinhold Niebuhr, Soviet communism was "a political idealism with religious overtones,"[49] a new "politically oriented religion," because although "communism is avowedly irreligious, its significant attitudes are religious."[50] However, like the Marxism to which it refers, Soviet communism was an "inadequate religion," "due to its effort to solve the total human problem in political terms," by means of a strategy made up of simplistic and dogmatic formulas applied with fanaticism and brute force. The fanaticism and brutality of communism were the inevitable consequence of the "sanctification of the peculiar insights and of a particular class." Besides, Niebuhr observed, the "worst cruelties and tyrannies in political history always result when religion and politics are thus unwholesomely compounded and absolute significance is claimed for the relative values of a particular social group."[51] In spite of its inadequacy as a religion, communism appeared to offer an effective alternative of hope and faith in a period of epoch-making crisis marked by the decay of capitalist society. Niebuhr speculated that for this reason communism could perhaps "conquer Christianity and become the dominant religion of our industrial civilization." He added that the new communist order, having been built on fanaticism and brutality, would in any case be a "return to barbarism" for the Western world.[52]

The interpretation of Soviet communism as a religious phenomenon, in which Marxist eschatology mixed with the Russian millenarian tradition, was most widespread in European Catholic culture. Maritain defined communism as a religion that was unaware that it was one, because it professed an atheism that was in reality itself "a religious and metaphysical position."[53]

> Considered in its spirit and principles, communism as it exists—particularly the communism of the Soviet republics—is a complete system of doctrines and life, which claims to reveal the meaning of existence to Man, responds to all the fundamental questions posed by life, and manifests an unequaled power to encapsulate totalitarianism. It is a religion and one of the more imperious of religions. It is certain that it has been called upon to replace all the other religions. It is an atheist religion whose dogma is dialectical materialism, and whose ethical and social expression is communism as a way of life . . . in reality faith in the communist revolution presupposes a complete universe of faith and religion on which to build itself. But this universe is so natural for communists that they do not bother to clarify it to themselves. Moreover, they do not think of this religion and this faith as a religion, because they are atheists, nor do they think of them as a faith, because they are presented as a scientific expression. Thus, even though they have no sense of communism being a religion, it is in fact a religion. The perfect religious believer prays so well that he is unaware of praying. Communism is so profoundly and so essentially a religion—albeit an earthly one—that it ignores the fact that it is a religion.[54]

The Catholic writer Henri Daniel-Rops was convinced that communism was a "new religion." He asserted in 1937 that communism "is nothing if not a religious movement, which proposes a new concept of man and an explanation of his destiny. At this level, and solely at this level, it comes face to face with Christianity. In the struggle that pits one against the other, there is a great deal more than the interests of class or cast at stake. The very meaning of our lives is at stake."[55]

*La Civiltà Cattolica* also had no doubts about the genuine faith that animated Soviet communism, and in 1941 it described communism as a dogmatic and fideistic concept, in which the religious tradition that had permeated "the national life of the old Russia," mixed with an ideology that "consisted of a real and fanatical dogmatism founded on the doctrines of communist theoreticians."

> There is no doubt that Soviet leaders are so imbued with dogmatism that they do not debate. The persecuted faith in God has been replaced with blind faith in the "quaternity" Marx-Engels-Lenin-Stalin. There is something incredible about the cult that is officially directed toward this quadruple god of the USSR. If something has changed in their assertions, that is exclusively due to Stalin, the sole authorized interpreter of communist doctrine.
>
> The worst accusation you can make against *tovarich* is that of not having sufficient command of the doctrine of the quadruple god, or of not accepting it in its entirety. In such a case, he is declared an "enemy of the people." This faith has in practice many similarities to a religious cult, confirming once again the saying of Tertullian: *genus incredulorum credulum.*[56]

Another Italian Catholic magazine asserted in November 1942 that the victory of bolshevism in Russia, at the time of the Civil War, was to be attributed to the "faith" of the reds rather than force of arms, terror, and propaganda.

> In the great duel between revolution and counter-revolution the reds won because they had more faith: they believe fanatically in *one* ideology, and acted in *one* direction under *one* discipline. Every faith is a force, and can obtain anything from men. The mountains move, and blood is spilled.
>
> This is the secret persuader used by the whole Soviet regime from 1917 until today.[57]

Whereas the atheism and antireligious politics of Soviet communism clearly revealed its anti-Christian nature, the mark of the fascist and Nazi religious policy was equivocation and ambiguity toward Christianity, and it was not openly anti-Christian. Indeed, both Mussolini and Hitler did not believe it politically useful to declare a war of religion against the churches. They did not support those within their regimes who were more determinedly hostile to Christianity, and they preferred instead to adopt an opportunist tactic that alternated between conciliatory and intransigent tones, but still aimed to exploit Christianity to strengthen their regimes.

After Hitler took power, the threat to Christianity posed by Nazism appeared as serious to many Christians as that of Soviet communism. However, the ambiguity of Hitler's religious policies, which did not openly encourage the theoreticians of racist neopaganism, led some observers, although hostile to Nazism, to have doubts over whether National Socialism could be identified with racist neopaganism. One example was the Catholic historian Mario Bendiscioli, who in 1937 claimed that it was too early to make this connection, because it clashed with "official documents not yet revealed, and with the conservative features of the religious policy of Hitler's government."[58] In reality, there were strong and compelling neopagan and anti-Christian currents in the Nazi regime, or at the very least, ones that were favorable to the establishment of a German national Christianity founded on the cult of the national God and an Aryan Christ of pure race. The persecution of Protestants and Catholics who did not conform to Nazi dogmas became so widespread that all remaining doubts as to the effectively anti-Christian nature of the Nazi religion faded away.

Even before Hitler took power, the religious and anti-Christian nature of Nazism had drawn the attention of Catholic culture. Nazism "is something much broader than a simple political movement; it is a philosophy that attempts to provide an answer to all the problems of life," wrote Anton Hilckman in 1932. He was a conservative philosopher who during that period conducted a campaign against the Nazi threat, and in 1935 he ended up in a concentration campo, where he remained until the end of the war. Hilckman considered Nazism to be an "irreligious religion" and a "political 'religion,' because there are many irreligious religions in our times, a *Weltanschauung* that puts politics at the center and at the heart of all things," and given that "the irreligions that reject the supernatural belong to the dominion of the history of religions, Nazism in the future will possibly be of more interest to historians of religions than to political historians. It really is a new religion that rises up against the existing religions. It would be no exaggeration when it is said that Hitlerism wishes to introduce a new religion founded on an atheist philosophy."[59]

The dogma of this "religion or, we should perhaps say, replacement or surrogate for religion," was the "deification of the Nordic or Germanic race," which became "the essential value, the absolute value, to which all else is subject" through the power of the state. This was tantamount to saying that "the state per se is deified" as "the visible and tangible instrument of this preservation of the sanctified race." The racist dogma was peculiar to Nazism, but it was necessary to remember, according to Hilckman, that it was not an isolated phenomenon, because the deification of the race was only one of the many manifestations of the modern "irreligious religions" that deified purely human entities by putting them in the place of God.

The central reality of the national-socialist religion *is not God, and is therefore man*, not as an individual, but as a member of a race. The ultimate and absolute yardstick is race. If you consider the essence of modern irreligions to be the negation of the supernatural, the excessive exaltation of the human, if you observe the continuous and persistent conflicts over the last few centuries between religion (i.e., the cult of a supernatural God) on the one hand, and the idea of the purely human and the cult of humanity on the other, then *racisme* constitutes the clearest of the possible forms of deification of the human. In any event, it is a-Christian, anti-Christian, pagan, humanist in the particular sense that we want to attribute to this word, and naturalist. You can deify the individual (egotistical individualism) and you can deify humanity (humanism); the religious *racisme* of social-nationalists is a third aspect of this generalized theophobia.[60]

As it was *deification of the human,* Nazism could have been seen as "a German equivalent of Russian bolshevism" by which "the economic value is absolute and the measure of everything," given that both Nazism and bolshevism were "specific cases of vast generalized heresies that are the great malady of our century: values that are unjustly exalted or false values that are considered an absolute good." This Catholic writer lucidly described the essential elements of the sacralization of politics applied by totalitarian movements with specific reference to the case of Nazism.

For Nazism, all values are a function of politics. Nazism is perhaps the most extreme case of state socialism and statolatry: the state is everything and individuals have no inherent value: that is the gospel openly professed by Hitler's followers. You could talk of a cult and worship of the state. The state is the source of every right and every duty. It is the absolute and total negation of every natural and divine right. The national-socialists do not conceal this pagan statolatry: the omnipotence of the sanctified state is the first article of the Hitlerite credo. It is not hard to find the roots of this inhuman concept of politics.[61]

Hilckman qualified this argument by pointing out that Hitlerites "did not worship the state per se, the state above all parties or the state as the embodiment of the entire Nation, but only *their* state." They were therefore the "fiercest enemies" of the state that acknowledges the equality of rights of all its citizens before the law: "*their* state, the state they wish to create and their *drittes Reich,* must be the *complete identification of the state with their party.*" What is more, national-socialists were hostile to the fundamental principles and values of Christianity. Hilckman concluded that just as it was not difficult to predict the fate of the parliamentary state after the Hitlerite movement took power, it was possible to predict without having to be a prophet "that Hitlerism once in power would launch a new and more terrible *Kultur Kampf*" against the church, which "will be judged dangerous to the dissemination of the idea of the omnipotence of the state" and will be considered "the great center of resistance to introduction of the new heresy of neo-Wodenism called the German National Church."

Protestants and Catholics became considerably more interested in the religious characteristics of Nazism once Hitler was in power. Opponents of Nazism published specific studies that analyzed the origins and content of its racist religion and the ways in which it attempted to spread throughout Germany in opposition to the Christian churches.[62] The *Revue des deux mondes* published numerous articles denouncing "the innate anti-Christianity of the Nazi doctrine," as Robert d'Harcourt defined it. Nazism wished to provide "humanity with a new gospel and a new religion" by taking over the mission previously reserved for the church, that of wholly imbuing and molding the totality of man. "This is not just a question of political propaganda, but also of spiritual assimilation and replacement of the church's role, because it openly demands the annexation of the soul" by an "integral national and ersatz mystical dogma of religious faith."[63] The Nazi regime did not declare that it wanted to suppress the churches, but it could not tolerate a plurality of religious confessions. The unification of the churches under the supreme law of the nation was "the manifest aspiration of totalitarian Hitlerism" because for Nazism the confessional division of Germany was "an intolerable scandal."[64] Even though the Hitlerite government did not appear openly to support exponents of neopaganism and a Germanic national religion, and for political reasons refused to recognize officially the new Germanic anti-Christian religion, the substantial agreement between these and the Nazi ideology was entirely evident. Nazism itself, its program and above all its leader, commented the Swiss writer Albert Béguin, occupied "a privileged position in the sanctuary of the new religion," which explicitly identified itself with Hitlerism.[65] Following the commencement of hostilities in 1939, the British association Friends of Europe published many pamphlets that documented the religious struggle in Germany and demonstrated the anti-Christian essence of the Nazi religion. "The Nazi religion of Race and the State, and the cult of a national God contradict all Christian concepts," according to the preface to one of the first of these pamphlets.[66]

Fascism's attitude toward Christianity appears to have been more ambiguous, and the policy of concordat seemed to be in the tradition of the authoritarian confessional state that is deferential to the church and traditional religion. Mussolini's policy on religion was considered an example of either prudent realism or vulgar opportunism, according to one's point of view. But for those who looked beyond the superficial official declarations and the formal relations between the regime and the Vatican, there could be no doubt about the non-Christian or anti-Christian essence of fascist totalitarianism, precisely because it was totalitarianism, and the fascist regime's policy of concordat was considered opportunistic, contingent, and unstable. Ruth Kenyon argued in 1935 that fascism was a militant nationalism that exalted the national state as a supreme being by putting it in the place of God: the totalitarianism of the fascist state was, therefore, essentially inimical to Christianity.[67] Keller considered fascism to be one of the enemies of Christianity, and the concordat between the regime and the church to be an opportunistic maneuver on the part of Il Duce, one that left the way open to future conflicts.[68] Maritain defined fascism as "a totalitarianism restrained by Catholicism: we are in the presence here of one of those reciprocal curbs on two opposing forces, which has its advantages and disadvantages," as can be seen from the different development of relations between the state and the church in Italy and in Germany, because in Germany the acknowledged space in public life for the works and institutions of the church and for its ministry of the faith has become increasingly restricted, while in Italy it has remained very great, "in spite of the ethic of the state which, with its pagan virtues, puts pressure on religion and extracts from it only those concessions that it is strictly obliged to concede."[69] Marcel Prélot observed in 1936 that, in spite of the concordat, increasingly there were conditions of a latent conflict between Catholicism and fascism as a result of its statolatry. Nevertheless he did not think likely that an autonomous national church or a new paganism could be born in Italy, as some fascist exponents would have wanted, given the Catholic tradition of the population and Rome's particular role as the capital of Christianity.[70]

By the end of the thirties the similarities between communism, fascism, Nazism as totalitarian states, and political religions appeared to be more significant and serious for the future of Christianity than the differences of ideology, political organization, and social transformation, which were indeed substantial. The anguished sense of imminent catastrophe, which would have endangered the very existence of Christianity and humanity, left little room for analysis of the differences between political religions and their different attitudes and behavior toward the churches. Their threat was their shared desire to replace the religion of Christ—or at least subordinate it to their own aims—with religion of State, Race, or Proletariat, whose final goal was to remold human beings in accordance with their politicized principles and values. Protestants did not hesitate to attribute an apocalyptic meaning to this phenomenon, and to identify totalitarianism with the advent of the Antichrist prophesized in the Book of Revelation, nor did they do so in a purely metaphoric manner. The political religions were the religions of the Antichrist. Totalitarianism was the most formidable enemy Christianity had ever encountered, an enemy that had presented itself as a new religion of salvation and power and was supposed to create paradise on this earth. It challenged the religion of Christ to mortal combat, in which the very destiny of human civilization was at stake. "The totalitarian state, whether of the left or the right, is Antichrist, both a revolution and a religion," Roger Lloyd, the Canon of Winchester, asserted unreservedly in 1938. Only the force of a revolutionary religion like Christianity would have been capable of challenging it, fighting it, and defeating it. Totalitarianism was "fundamentally anti-Christian" and for this reason it was comparable to the Antichrist of the Apocalypse. Like the Antichrist, the totalitarian state appeared in a beguiling and seductive guise and presented itself as a new and powerful religion of salvation. It fought against Christ and his church by taking on his image, deceiving the people, leading them astray, distancing them from the true faith, and instilling in them the faith in the divinity of the Antichrist, whose ultimate aim is to destroy the forces of God by replacing God. The final battle of Armageddon was inevitable and imminent: "That the Totalitarian State, in both its Communist and Fascist forms, embodies a way of life and an attitude of mind which is emphatically destructive of Christianity is clear."[71]

## THE CHURCH OF ROME AGAINST STATOLATRY

In Catholic Italy, reflections on totalitarianism concentrated mainly on its characteristics of a political religion in the case of bolshevism, Nazism, and fascism, although only the first two were explicitly condemned. In relation to the latter, however, the church and the majority of Italian Catholics adopted a more cautious approach, which was heavily influenced by the policy of concordat and the ambivalent attitudes of fascism itself, which swung between formal homage to the church of Rome and ostentation of its own political religiosity that exalted the absolute and indisputable power of the state and the nation and wished to monopolize the education of new generations and bring them up in the cult of fascism and Il Duce. The church, however, did not remain silent or reticent in the face of totalitarian fascism and, although it did not explicitly mention fascism in its condemnation of the totalitarian state, the Italian regime was indirectly brought to mind every time the Holy See and the Catholic press condemned the deification of nation, race, and class. However, it should be made clear that the church's opposition to totalitarianism was not motivated by its general aversion to antidemocratic principles. Indeed, in relation to the totalitarian state, the church demanded its own liberty and the liberty of its believers above all to obey the leader of their church, but not the legal and political liberties of citizens that had resulted from democratic and national revolutions.

The church of Pius XI was not averse to the legitimization and religious consecration of an authoritarian state that recognized the spiritual primacy of Roman Catholicism, respected the prerogatives of the church in society and in relation to the state, and shared with the church an aversion to movements that exalted a secular concept of politics and the state. In fact, the church then perceived such antimodernist and Catholic authoritarianism as a not inconsiderable tool for use in the Catholic reconquest of secularized society and in halting the advance of political modernity, which had its anti-Catholic origins in the French Revolution. This explains its favorable attitudes to dictatorial governments such as the regimes of Salazar in Portugal, Dollfuss in Austria, and Franco in Spain, which were willing instruments or appeared to be willing instruments in the implementation of a Catholic restoration. The same occurred in relation to the fascist regime, even though relations between the church and fascism were troubled by tensions and conflicts, which always arose from the desire of the fascist state to remain true to its "religious" ambitions in molding the consciences of the coming generations.

The attitude of the church toward totalitarianism, the reason for its hostility, and the arguments for its condemnation concerned a "theoretical system or practical method and direction that give the state unlimited or all but unlimited power over the individual in isolation and in association so as to deprive him of all or part of his natural rights."[72] This was the definition provided by Angelo Brucculeri, a Jesuit priest and one of the foremost Catholic scholars of totalitarianism when writing for *La Civiltà cattolica* in 1938.

Totalitarianism, he explained, is a form of "pan-statism" or "state pantheism" that in the past was the preferred system of government of the Greeks and Romans, as a result of the "profoundly theocratic soul of the ancient city," in which "society, the fatherland, and sovereignty were worshipped [and thus] their powers and rights were irresistibly inflated beyond measure." The state could not only dispose of an individual's goods and person as it wished, but "thought and belief on religious matters also had to bear the state's stamp of approval, [and] the conscience had no right to make itself felt."[73] Christianity, which had radically modified the concept of the state and sovereignty by asserting the total autonomy and primacy of religion, was challenged over the centuries by "remnants of a recurring paganism, which during periods of crisis renewed their assaults on the Christian ideal," such as the despotism that "consolidated itself after the Protestant religious revolution," absolute monarchy, Caesaropapism, and lastly modern totalitarianism. According to this Jesuit priest, the latter and most recent version of "pan-statism" originated from the "lethal humanism" of the Renaissance, which revived the ideals and costumes of pagan life and was further developed through the progressive subordination of the individual to politics in the works of Machiavelli, Hobbes, Rousseau, and ultimately Hegel, who went beyond "the pagan concept of state divinity" and argued that "the state is actually God Himself, and as such does not and cannot have any limitations on its powers."[74] In Italy, this "equally vacuous and insane dogmatism"[75] had been disseminated by Giovanni Gentile and the school of idealism, "which glories in touching the very bottom of the statolatry aberration."[76] In this way, Italians arrived at totalitarianism by following the current of "intemperate nationalism, which is an aberrant manifestation of patriotism and a return to trite and implacably exclusivist pagan forms."

> This fanatical nationalism perceives nothing—not a prime cause, not a natu-ral law, not a universal community—outside or above the national being. The nation, an absolute entity, rises up as a colossal Leviathan above every-thing and everybody, so that everything and everybody can be sacrificed: individuals, families, classes, religions, and autonomies of any kind. This irrational concept of the national collectivity turns out sooner or later to be a source of disorder, precisely because it repudiates (or ignores) the ethi-cal limitations of a superior law, and precisely because it has no law other than itself, no motive other than its own egotism and no ideal other than its own interests.[77]

The same had occurred with bolshevism in Russia, where the demand that an entire generation be subjected to "an immense tragedy" in order "to provide the country with the most advanced industrial infrastructure from one moment to the next" had transformed "the state into the most rapacious and inhuman Leviathan that history has ever known."[78] Soviet communism also derived from Hegel, and Lenin's system, which was founded on the "principles of a essentially politicized morality," "led to an oppressive centralism not very dissimilar from the one Plato dreamed of."

> Capital and private property are therefore suppressed, given that both give rise to those social inequalities that disturb the tranquility of the state. The family is suppressed through the extreme facility given to divorce, particu-larly in the early period. Personal rights are suppressed, not excluding the right to life, which must be truncated in those who are loyal to the revolution. Education becomes the exclusive right of the community. All citizens are transformed into wage-earners and employees of a single universal corpora-tion, whose only option is chaos and the most brutal oppression humanity has ever experienced.[79]

For Brucculeri, totalitarianism substantially originated from the de-mand to transform the political function into a moral one, to give "the state the ability to penetrate the innermost recesses of the conscience and guide its attitudes."

This gives rise to the flowering of supposed mystical dogmas throughout history, by which concrete political formations are not only provided with inspiration and religious embellishments, but also tend to impose a cult of and an absolute subordination to authority. When we say absolute, we mean the subordination that should be given to God. It is believed that a surrogate for religion can be created from political factors. In other words, it is believed that politics can expand to occupy the whole wide horizon of religiosity.

It is self-evident that politics of this kind sees no point in the survival of religion; indeed, it finds religion embarrassing and harmful, if it is a religion that is unwilling to bow before and submit to ceasaropapism.[80]

For the Church of Rome, then, the essence of totalitarianism was the politicization of morality and deification of the state or, as it was commonly referred to, *statolatry*. In reality, the Church of Rome used this term not only to describe totalitarian states, but all secular concepts of politics that assert the separation of the state from the church and the primacy of state sovereignty. Back in the nineteenth century, the Catholic Church was already accusing liberalism of an idolatrous concept of the state, because it wished to remove human beings from teachings of the church so as to subordinate them to its will. The accusation of idolatry was also directed against "exaggerated" nationalism that put forward a fundamentalist concept of the nation as a sanctified secular entity. In 1915, *La Civiltà cattolica* condemned the currents of the new imperialist nationalism, because it proclaimed the absolute primacy of the nation and the state over citizens. This meant that nationalists had exacerbated the principles of liberalism by adding "the concepts of paganism, imperialism, conflict, and 'egoism' or, in other words, Greek and Roman statolatry," thus turning back history "by twenty centuries, and simply dressing up those errors in modern form."[81] The reason for this was that "nationalism, like ancient paganism, will mistakenly demand the sacrifice of the individual to the illusion the State-God, and will return to barbarism whereby human life has no value, the individual counts for nothing, the family does not exist, and the state is everything."[82] The Catholic periodical went on to say that these nationalists were also a threat to the church because "by almost deifying the state and exalting the nation and its greatness as a supreme ideal, they tend to impose this same cult (of *statolatry*) onto the religious society that is the church. In other words, they want it to be subordinate to the state" by denying it "in practice, both a social existence and any liberty or right, so that it is at the beck and call of the sovereign state."[83]

The experience of the Great War, the aggravation of nationalist pressures, and the overriding expansion of state control of society could only increase the alarming threat of a "secular religion" that deified the power and authority of the state. This was precisely the expression that Luigi Sturzo used in December 1918 to define what he considered to be the principal cause of the World War.

> With the collapse of Germany a profound crisis was revealed in its absurd practice of perceiving the state in pantheistic terms that subordinate everything to its force. The inner and the outer world, man and his reason for existence, social forces, and human relations are all subject to the deification of force and absolute power, which replace the great values of justice and grand designs of the spirit.
>
> This pantheist concept has penetrated all the liberal and democratic civilized nations to a greater or lesser extent, and the prevailing beliefs of the philosophy of public law. Those nations that have challenged most fiercely the religious purposes of the church have negated every collective spiritual problem and substituted them with a new secular religion of the absolute sovereign state, which has become a domineering and binding force, a moral norm and law, an irrepressible power, and sole synthesis of the collective will.[84]

After the war and particularly from the late twenties, papal speeches and encyclicals officially developed the concept of statolatry, which was generally used, along with the concept of paganism or neopaganism, to define totalitarian politics. At the end of the celebrations of Holy Year in 1925, Pope Pius XI referred to examples of anticlerical policies in various states from Mexico to Czechoslovakia, and condemned both liberalism and socialism. He accused them of implementing in different ways a "political concept that, by treating society and the state as ends in themselves, easily and indeed fatally leads toward the sacrifice and stifling of individual and particular rights, with a no less disastrous outcome, as can readily be imagined."[85] A year later, Pius XI condemned the nationalist movement Action Française, because it professed a doctrine that "put politics before Religion and made the latter subservient to the former,"[86] and he stressed that a political concept that "treats the state as the end, and the citizen or man as the means, thus monopolizing and absorbing everything into the state" was in no way compatible with the Catholic religion.[87] This same condemnation was repeated in relation to liberalism, democracy, socialism, and bolshevism. All these movements, asserted the Jesuit magazine in 1927, were states produced by the "havoc affecting ideas and the behavior of modern people resulting from revolution, that tyrannical centralizer and then constant exponent of dictatorship and despotism under the name of liberty, fraternity, and equality, as we have seen in the Napoleonic era and then throughout modern 'parliamentarianism.' "[88] Liberalism and socialism converged "in proclaiming the omnipotence or deification of the state, albeit under different names and in accordance with various systems," reaching the point of "declaring the triumph of the State-God."[89]

In the following years, the condemnation of statolatry was reiterated by the pope with increasing vigor, culminating in 1937 with the encyclicals against Nazi racism and atheist communism, which were published almost simultaneously. In the encyclical *Mit brennender Sorge* (14 March 1937), the pope condemned the racist and pantheistic concept that "identified God with the universe, materializing God in the world and deifying the world in God," raising up earthly values, such as the race or the people, "to the supreme law of everything, even religious values, and worshipping them with an idolatrous cult" of "a national God and a national religion" in the "insane attempt to imprison God, the Creator of the world and king and legislator of the peoples within the confines of a single race."[90] The pope also exhorted Catholics to be "particularly vigilant, when religious notions are emptied of their genuine content and applied to profane meanings,"[91] as was occurring with words like "revelation," "faith," "immortality," "baptism," and "incarnation," and to be ready to react when "the torch of faith is torn from this living temple of God and replaced by a false surrogate faith that has nothing in common with the faith of the Cross."[92]

As for communism, Pius XI in his encyclical *Divini Redemptoris Promissio* (19 March 1937) condemned not only atheism and the antireligious campaign, but also warned against the insidious deception that hid within it "in a more accentuated manner than in any other similar movement in the past," and that deception was "the idea of a false redemption": "A pseudo-ideal of justice, equality, and fraternity in labor pervades all its doctrines and all its actions, filling them with a false mysticism, which entices the crowds with false promises and fires them up with contagious enthusiasm, especially in times like these when a flawed distribution of earthly goods has resulted in an unusual degree of poverty."[93]

Pius XI never explicitly condemned fascism, as he did in the case of communism and Nazi racism, but there was no shortage in some circumstances of explicit declarations against aspects of fascist policy that directly invaded areas that the church considered its own preserve, such as the Catholic education of the younger generation. Pius XI had already demonstrated his aversion "to the state that wishes to absorb and swallow up the individual and the family in order to diminish them, and to the state that wishes to raise up conquerors to go in search of conquest," in a speech to the pupils of a Catholic college on 14 May 1929, shortly after signing the Lateran Pacts.[94] A few months later, the pope expressed his dislike of "exaggerated and false nationalism" in his encyclical *Divini Illius Magistri*, which was published on 31 December. He also condemned those who "dare to argue that children belong to the state more than they belong to their families, and that the state has an absolute right of education." He considered "groundless" the argument that "man is born a citizen, and therefore belongs primarily to the state, without reflecting that before being a citizen, a person must exist, and that existence comes not from the state but from the parents."[95] The most explicit and harsh protest was expressed in 1931, when the regime unleashed its campaign against the organization Azione cattolica. In his encyclical *Non abbiamo bisogno* (29 June 1931) Pius XI openly condemned fascist "religiosity":

> We have in fact seen in action a religiosity that rebels against the instructions of the superior Religious Authority and it imposes or encourages nonobservance. It is a religiosity that becomes persecution and the attempted ruination of all that the Supreme Leader of the Religion is well known to value and hold most dear. It is a religiosity that indulges or allows itself to indulge in the excesses of verbal and actual insults against the Person of the Father of all the faithful to the point of shouting "down with" and calling for his death: a veritable initiation in patricide. Such religiosity can in no way be reconciled with Catholic doctrine and practice, but is as far away from both as is imaginable. . . . The concept of a state that would have the younger generations belong to it entirely and without exception from birth until adulthood cannot be reconciled with either Catholic doctrine or the natural right of the family. The demand that the Church and the Pope must restrict themselves to the outer practices of Religion (Mass and the Sacraments) and that the rest of education belongs entirely to the state cannot be reconciled with Catholic doctrine, as far as Catholics are concerned.[96]

Pius XI was unequivocal in his denunciation of the fascist state's desire to "monopolize youth entirely, from very early childhood to adulthood to the complete and exclusive advantage of a party and a regime, on the basis of an ideology that explicitly chooses an authentic pagan statolatry, which is no less in conflict with the rights of families than it is with the supernatural rights of the Church."[97]

In the following years, the pope did not direct any such harsh and explicit attacks on the "fascist religiosity." In the case of fascism, there was nothing equivalent to the condemnations of atheist communism and Nazi racism, although up until his death Pius XI remained anxious about the arrogant invasiveness of fascist totalitarianism in fields that he considered to be the exclusive dominion of the church's spiritual power. In Pius XI's so-called hidden encyclical, *Humani Generis Unitas*,[98] which attacked the totalitarianism of nation, race, and class and was written in 1938 but not promulgated, the allusions to fascist totalitarianism appear every time the text refers to the nation as one of the entities deified by totalitarian states:

Here inflexible doctrinarians proclaim the unity of the nation as an absolute value, over there a rabble-rouser rouses the spirit by launching intoxicating appeals to the Unity of the Race, while Eastern Europe offers the entire world the promise of renewing humanity through the Unity of the Proletariat, a promise that is steeped in terror and blood.

On top of the often incompatible requirements of these different collectivities of nation, Race, and Class, there are additional obligations imposed by a genuinely political community in the name of unity of the state.[99]

Vatican circles probably did not always perceive the gravity of fascist statolatry or look on it with any great apprehension, possibly because they considered the manifestations of fascist "religiosity" to be marginal and external features restricted to the inner circles of the regime, and not significant enough to undermine the pressing reasons for cooperation and agreement between Catholicism and fascism on many questions. In its deeds and practical outcomes, fascist "religiosity" was certainly not as dangerous as Nazi paganism or communist atheism. The danger of anti-Christian and anti-Catholic political religiosity appeared to be averted by the Concordat, the church's authoritarian sympathies for the regime which had resolved the Roman question and restored observance of the Catholic religion, their shared aversion for such enemies as liberalism, socialism, communism, and individualistic and hedonistic modernity, trust in Mussolini's pragmatism, which included public repudiations of a religious war between church and state, the mutual interest of the regime and the Vatican in not exacerbating any tensions or conflict, and the fascism of many Catholics and Catholicism of many fascists. The same factors also seemed to constitute an effective curb on fascist totalitarianism and any desire to follow the example of Nazism and Soviet communism. An eloquent exponent of this line was the Franciscan priest Agostino Gemelli, who founded the Catholic University. When commenting on the encyclical on atheist communism, he praised "Italy's Christian mission in the world" and the fascist crusade against communism, the "Barabbas of today, and the Antichrist of our century." He saw before him "a magnificent road that our country shall be called upon to travel to provide humanity with a lesson, a road along which we shall journey expeditiously in order that Christian doctrine shall inspire our actions."

Our country is uniquely pacified and well ordered thanks to the intuitions of a Leader of a kind that we lacked for a long time, and is singularly unified around the Seat of St. Peter by physical proximity and the bond of the Concordat. It could therefore be a living example of a people cured of the communist madness that infiltrated it after the War, and could proceed unhesitatingly with the most monumental task of our history, which is to achieve the moral and material well-being of the entire people.[100]

Other Catholics, such as Brucculeri, attempted to exorcise the presence of fascist totalitarianism by arguing that this neologism, although coined in Italy, did not denote in the case of fascism "the actual absorption of the individual" into "state pantheism" as had occurred in Germany and Russia. To demonstrate this, Brucculeri quoted Il Duce's assertion that "the individual in the fascist state is not nullified but rather multiplied. . . . The fascist state organizes the nation, but leaves sufficient margins of maneuver to the individual."[101]

However, these arguments did not allay the fears and anxieties of those Italian Catholics who did not believe in the possibility of a lasting reconciliation between Catholicism and fascism, which had never renounced its totalitarian ambitions or the cult of its political religion through myths and rituals.

## THE MALIGNANT SNARE OF CONCORDATS

Following the advent of Mussolini's government, and while the church courted the new leader and sought an accommodation with him through practical concessions, some antifascist Catholics warned that fascism was pursuing the ideal of a "national church, of the church *as a function* of the state, and therefore of a church subject to the state," as claimed on 23 July 1923 by Francesco Luigi Ferrari, an exponent of the left on the Italian Popular Party who was forced to leave Italy.[102] Another exponent of the Popular Party, Igino Giordani, had complained of the fundamentally anti-Christian nature of what he called "fascist totalitarianism" as far back as 1924.[103] He claimed that it praised Catholicism only in order to subjugate it to its "fascist religion," another expression that he coined. He saw fascist totalitarianism as the "ultimate consequence of the Protestantism, rationalism, and philosophical liberalism, the various stages in the progressive fragmentation of spiritual unity and therefore social cohesion, to which the theory of fascism is bolted on as its most aggravated form."[104] The intention was to foment a "religiosity centered around the God-State, who destroys natural freedoms and the rights of family and class, which Catholicism upholds as essential to its doctrine."[105] Fascism wished to involve the church in a new experiment in "caesaropapism with fanciful hopes of overwhelming and controlling all manifestations of religious worship and all the church's obligations,"[106] thus exacerbating the tendency of the modern state "to go beyond its own functions and invade those of the church."[107] The "fascist religion" was all the more dangerous precisely because of the evil intentions behind its formal deference to the Catholic religion:

Hence the Catholic motif regularly pops up in the framework of the "fascist religion." The church was to be the third point that marked out the fascist triangle on which the dictatorship was built: Monarchy-Capitalism-Church with Il Duce at its center. . . . Because of its totalitarian, egocentric and all-encompassing spirit, [fascism] cannot tolerate independent and uncontrolled forces outside its jealously guarded enclosure. It resents the church as it proceeds along its clear and peaceful road to eternity. The church too has to conspire in the fascist revolution, the fascist era, the parades, the bragging and Il Duce's inflated reputation: either for me or against me. The ban on political activities by priests means that they cannot engage in politics outside fascism. When they wear the black shirt, when they hold forth from the podium at "national" meetings, when they take part in village fairs, when they toll the bells for local fascist bosses, and when they take out party membership in the grassy meeting place of a sunny village, well then they provide the rituals of the fatherland with a moving grandiloquence. In these cases, they join the ranks and absolve a mission worthy of the thousands of eyes watching the "Italian experiment." They are either down in the squares with the fascists or holed up in the vestry refusing to take notice of what happens outside, where for political reasons and pretexts it is permissible to cheat, barter, and fight. A priest must take no notice of beatings, arson, and even murder. He must be content with commending the souls of obsessively devout women and muttering a few lines from the Prayer Book. In other words, either you join in or you are reduced to an ineffectual nothingness.[108]

Sturzo was one of the first Catholic antifascists to be exiled by Mussolini's dictatorship. In the context of Italian Catholic culture, Sturzo was in all probability the keenest observer of the totalitarian phenomenon during the thirties, and he had doubts that it fully included fascism. It should be remembered that he was one of the first to use the term "totalitarian" to define the peculiarly domineering spirit of fascism, which desired to control every aspect of life. By the end of 1923, Sturzo had written that "the prevailing trend is the *totalitarian* transformation of each and every moral, cultural, political, and religious force into this new concept: 'the fascist.' Given that neither minds nor consciences can be transformed, it is inevitable that heads are bowed and knees are bent by the use of external force."[109] Three years later in a study on Italy and fascism published in exile, he was again one of the first to compare the fascist dictatorship with the Bolshevik one, and to identify "the similarities" in their totalitarian concept of power.[110] Fascism, observed Sturzo, had taken the centralized state, "the scourge that corrupted the continental state," to its ultimate conclusion: a "Leviathan that subsumes every other force and becomes the expression of a pervasive political pantheism. Man as a free individual is no longer the purpose of the state and society. Instead the purpose of man is the state: the deification of the state (now called the nation) is complete."[111]

The concept of deification of the state became central to Sturzo's interpretation of totalitarianism in the thirties, and he paid particular attention to the new aspects of the sacralization and deification of politics in relation to previous ways in which the state had been treated as something divine. As a symbol of power, Sturzo wrote in 1932, the state "is an old God who has been modernized" and "from time to time, some of the many kings, emperors, and leaders put in an appearance and even in this day and age claim (whether or not they have an aura of magnificence) to represent the sanctity of the state which they, as it were, personify and manifest." When this occurs, "signs of an actual religion" manifest themselves around the "new and visible divine reality" of a leader, and these signs are "the incense of the adulation, the rituals of bowing and giving Roman salutes, blind obedience, unconditional trust, and unconscious praise. There is no shortage of victims chosen from those infidels and heretics who refuse to believe in the divinity."[112] However, Sturzo did not believe the cult of the leader to be an innovation of the totalitarian sacralization of politics or even to be the most fundamental of its features. The "divinization of political power was not necessarily linked to the personality of a man of genius: it can be found in the most rationalistic of centuries, even when the anonymous figure of the state replaces the personality of the leader."[113] The secular religion of totalitarianism, therefore, cannot be reduced to the personality cult, nor does it originate from the personality cult, but was rather the embodiment of modern phenomenon of collective idolatry, which gave rise to all the "secularized religions," as he called them in 1933:

The preconditions for idolatry are that the idol has more power than man and that this power derives from absoluteness. It does not matter if there is more than one idol; indeed it is in the nature of idolatry that it increases the number of idols, because it is in them that man attempts to rediscover the means to make up for the deficiencies of the individual through a symbol of the collective force. Idolatry is collective rather than individual. It is the *totem* of primitive society, and the symbol of the clan, the tribe, the race, or the nation. Hence the individual's duty to sacrifice himself as though to the principle itself of social vitality.

If you apply these elements to Russian bolshevism, German Nazism, and Italian fascism, you will find the idolatrous motivations contained within their essence and affirmation as *totalitarian* systems.

Why the surprise that Lenin's tomb is today the object of pilgrimages, veneration, and religious exaltation? The logic of bolshevism drives its leaders to declare open war on every religion, because every religion today—in our civilization—is Christian and can only allow for the one true God.

Hitler's Germans do not go as far as openly fighting against Christianity, as they would encounter fierce resistance. However, they use insidious means to fight it, as they attack the universal principle of the children of God and human brotherhood outside the confines of race and nation. The Nazi gospel is the race, the purity of Aryan race, which is the foundation of their mystical religion. . . . Today victims are sacrificed to the German race, in the midst of hymns of adoration and revelry.

Fascism does not escape this idolatry. For some time Catholics have been complaining of the use of theological terms and rituals to exalt fascists and fascist festivals. On several occasions, orators, journalists, and ministers have let slip the word *god*, attributing it to Mussolini, and the word *godhead* when speaking of Italy.[114]

According to Sturzo, totalitarian systems were therefore in many ways the consequence and cause of the deification of politics. This, in turn, was the consequence and specific manifestation of modern collective idolatry, which also occurred in "countries with secular democracies," where "there was no shortage of similar attitudes toward the Goddess of Reason, the state's immortal principles or secular nature, and suchlike." But in these countries, "those who do not believe in these principles can fight them without anyone harming them," whereas "in those other most unfortunate countries, any criticism of Mussolini, Hitler, or Italy is punished by the strictest of laws and would render any imprudent critic unacceptable to human society," and the victim of a spirit of intolerance resulting from "the idolatrous aura that surrounds the men who represent the absolute principle of class (Russia), race (Germany), and nation (Italy)."

Sturzo reworked the reflections on the totalitarian state that first appeared in an article in 1936 and published them in his more systematic work *Politics and Morality* in 1938.[115] He developed them within a structured interpretative framework, in which the deification of politics occupied a central place as an essential part of the very nature of totalitarianism. Sturzo carried out a comparative study of Bolshevik Russia, fascist Italy, and Nazi Germany, the "three great totalitarian states of differing natures, but all three of a national type and founded on administrative and political centralization, militarism, the monopoly of education and a closed economy."[116] They shared a basic concept of politics that considered individuals to be "neither citizens or subjects, but merely members of a group, as units within an inflexible collectivity whose moral acts were subsidiary to the requirements of the state. The individual person is lost and absorbed into pan-collectivity, and labeled with the symbolic names of nation, class, or race."[117] Consequently, totalitarian states "suppress political freedom and diminish personal freedom through state interfer-

ence in ways of thinking and in the field of morality and religion." The
totalitarian state was induced "by its very nature" to "break through
the boundaries previously adhered to," and in so doing, it triggered the
religious essence of totalitarianism, which conferred sacredness on the
state and those who embodied it. It aimed to dominate and mold individual minds and consciences by monopolizing collective education, organizing culture, and involving the masses in a permanent mobilization
through rituals and symbols:

> Everyone must have faith in the new state and learn to love it. There can be
> no voice of opposition, no voice of dissidence. It is not enough to practice
> emotional conformity; what is required is complete moral and intellectual
> submissiveness, trusting enthusiasm, and the mystical fervor of a religion.
> Bolshevism, fascism, and Nazism are and must be religions. School on its
> own is not enough to create such a mood; other complementary means have
> to be added, such as state books, standardized state newspapers, cinema,
> radio, sport, scholastic associations, and prizes, all of which are not only
> controlled but directed toward a single purpose: the cult of the totalitarian
> state under the banner of nation, race, or class.
>
> To gain this unanimous consensus and stimulate this collective spirit of
> veneration, the entire life of society is continuously mobilized for parades,
> festivals, processions, plebiscites, and sporting events that touch the imagina-
> tion, mind, and emotions of the population.

In this complex ritualistic and symbolic structure, the personality cult
fulfills an important function, because the leader embodies and manifests
the religious essence of the secular entity by identifying it with the physical
person, whether living or mummified.

> The cult of the state, class, or race would be too general without the presence
> of the man, the hero and the demigod. Lenin now has an imposing mauso-
> leum and he has become a secular Mohamed for the Russians. Mussolini
> and Hitler, being still alive, are protected by a swarm of policemen and body-
> guards. They behave and speak in such a manner as to capture the crowd's
> imagination and play upon their senses. Their bodies are sacred and their
> words are the words of prophets. Hitler passes between two dense ranks of
> guards, who march at some distance from him so that he emerges between
> them and takes on an air of dreaminess with eyes raised to the heavens and
> his open hands stretched out before him like a savior. Mussolini has invented
> an almost magical ritual: he has the crowd call for him for a period of vari-
> able length. They shout "duce! duce! duce!" with increasing insistence to the
> point of paroxysm. It becomes a murmur and progressively becomes louder
> until there are throbbing cries of "duce! duce! duce!" Finally he appears
> before the crowd to be greeted with a storm of applause.[118]

The centralization of power, police repression, monopoly over consciences, and personality cults are essential constituent elements of the
totalitarian state, and they gravitate toward the more or less rapid elimi-
nation of every sphere of autonomy for the human personality. Sturzo
emphasized in another work written in 1938 that the "essential nature of
totalitarianism is such that it is made impossible for the citizen to remain
outside the system once it has been established, because totalitarian politics penetrates all aspects of life: family, culture, religion, economics, and
outer behavior."[119] There was no room for autonomy of the individual
in the indissoluble symbiosis that was thus established between political
absolutism and totalitarian religion, unless it was an arbitrary and temporary concession by the state. For this reason, Sturzo had no illusions about
a policy of conciliation and the repeated compromises between fascism
and the Vatican.

> It is said that Italy is in a favorable moral and religious condition under
> fascism. You have to distrust a situation in which favors and persecutions
> depend solely on the will of a single man. When the favors abound, con-
> sciences lose their vigor, and resistance risks becoming less forceful at the
> time it is needed. You could draw up a long list of the abuses of power for
> which no one objected by asserting the principle of moral boundaries. When
> it came to the militarization of youth—at the age of six boys must be enrolled
> in the *Figli della lupa* and at the age of eight they have to receive premilitary
> training (see the laws of 31 December 1934 and 11 April 1938)—there was
> no criticism, no protest, and no reservations.

The most worrying aspect of totalitarian states is the education in violence, the
blessing bestowed on the principle of supremacy of force over law and of power
over morality, and above all the instruction in hating one's adversary, despising
his personal rights, and holding his very life in contempt. At the beginning this
evil spirit, which has been unleashed on the world by leaders in the name of the
state's authority, encountered only weak opposition from Catholics, and very
soon that opposition disappeared altogether.[120]

Sturzo deplored the Italian Catholics who displayed such an indulgent
acquiescence toward fascist totalitarian politics by underestimating the
seriousness of the situation and minimizing the consequences, such as
racism and anti-Semitism. He was not at all convinced that fascism was
free from the totalitarian disorder or from the anti-Christian impulses
triggered in Germany and Russia, although he did acknowledge that the
Italian situation was not comparable with the German one, because in
Italy there was no "open and unremitting persecution of Christianity."
However, "in Italy there is a continuous appropriation of the soul of
youth by fascism, which amounts to enlargement of political dominion
in all fields at the expense of the spiritual and religious dominion,

hoarding of people's intelligences, and subjugation to its will. It is asphyx-iation by slow and continuous poisoning."[121] According to Sturzo, there was therefore no policy of compromise capable of canceling the "incom-patibility between Christianity and the totalitarian state," which was based on "sociopolitical monism," "most evident in the logical premises of totalitarianism which in practice are translated into the mystical exal-tation of a superhuman principle: the *absolute* nature of class, nation or race."[122]

For Sturzo, totalitarian systems were therefore essentially secular reli-gions and embodiments of a *"collective mystical dogma* that negated Christian moral values," because as far as that dogma is concerned, "ev-erything is sanctified (in the widest sense of the term) by an end that justi-fies every means, even the most unacceptable means, for the good of the country, the future of the race or the demand for the rights of the down-trodden. . . . Whoever makes a god of nation, state, class, party, or race can never love his neighbor unless he subjects him to these entities, which are then turned from means into ends."[123]

From this point of view, the problem of totalitarian religions for Catho-lics, like Protestants, was fundamentally a religious problem, because it concerned religious phenomena, albeit ones that Brucculeri had defined as "religions orchestrated by Man."[124] Using cautious language that avoided any direct reference to fascism but did not make his meaning unclear to a careful reader, Brucculeri point out in 1940 that there had already been an era, such as pagan antiquity, in which religions "had become so corrupt and degenerate that they obscured civilization and were cut off from it," thus losing "its individuality, its separate existence and its specific and select activity, as it was entirely assimilated into the state, with which it had a relationship not so much of symbiosis as of identical existence. The religion became not a simple auxiliary element, but the identification of civilization with this or that social group into which it was absorbed."[125] Christianity had reacted against this degrada-tion of religion by asserting its independence and paying the price in mar-tyrdom so as to free humankind "from the stony all-powerful majesty of the state." Christianity, wrote the Jesuit Brucculeri, "produced an ideal that surpassed the city and the fatherland," thus guaranteeing "a special set of rights" for the individual and "a sphere of action beyond any inter-ference from social authority."

> Sadly a tribute in blood was required to defend this Christian attainment. Christianity did not shirk this heroic duty, and let rivers of blood flow from its veins.
>
> The first magnificent appearance of the new man, of man reborn, was called the Martyr.[126]

These words were written in January 1940, when the war had already commenced. The evocation of the figure of the martyr as the "new man" or "man reborn" reveals the mood in which the European Christian conscience witnessed the triumphal advance of a totalitarian state driven by a fanatical anti-Christian religion that wished to regenerate humanity with fire and sword and to create a new man who devoted body and soul to his state and his race.

## THE APOCALYPSE OF MODERNITY

Through this tragic prediction of a new era of martyrdom, Catholic culture showed that it too could not avoid an apocalyptic interpretation of totalitarianism, even though the Church of Rome had always been reluctant to encourage messianic hopes or millenarian fears. However, when faced with such powerful and formidable enemies as communism, Nazism, and even fascism (in spite of the latter's more devious attitude toward the church), the evocation of apocalyptic prophecy and reference to its imagery came spontaneously to mind as the most appropriate expression of the profound anguish, fear, and perhaps even terror that tormented Catholic consciences in the late thirties. The advance of the new political religions appeared relentless. In the case of communism, the use of the apocalyptic metaphor was instinctive and inevitable: "The Antichrist of our century is called the blandishment of communism," asserted Agostino Gemelli in 1937. "We can easily say that communism is so much the opposite of Christianity and the Christian concept and practice of life that it truly represents the embodiment of the Antichrist in the twentieth century, or, to put it another way, of the Barabbas of our times."[127] The identification of communism with the Antichrist of the twentieth century, because of its atheist ideology that sanctified man and wished to destroy Christianity, was soon accompanied by a similar perception of Nazism, because of its profoundly and radically anti-Christian essence, which in reality made it an ally of the communist Antichrist in its fight to the death against Christianity. The church was faced with a twin red and brown Antichrist, based on a shared and implacable hatred of the religion of Christ. Messineo wrote in 1937:

> The atheist materialism of the red international and the neopaganism of brown Nazism are today working in close alliance on the systematic destruction of Christian and European civilization, and they both foster and encourage in their followers an implacable hatred against the church, which they consider to be the strongest fortification they need to bring down and overcome in order to implement their insane plans to build a new pseudo-civiliza-

tion on foundations other than those laid down by Jesus Christ and strenuously defended by his representatives on earth.[128]

Now that any illusions of a possible avoidance of conflicts between the church and Nazism had faded, Nazism revealed its true nature as an anti-Christian movement to Italian Catholics, a movement that brought together various currents with a common aim of annihilating "not only the Catholic religion, but also Christianity in all its doctrines, forms, and confessions," because Nazism laid claim to be a new religion founded on principles and values radically opposed to the Christian and Catholic ones.

> Nazism was presented to the German people and imposed upon them not only as a political revolution, but more especially as a totalitarian concept of the world based on the principle of racism, which invests and informs everything and determines ideal attitudes and practical behavior. This is an uncompromising concept that wishes to invade not only the political field but also the religious one, and tends to manifest itself in the form of a racist totalitarian state using every means at its disposal; it is a Moloch that devours all the rights of the human person and sets itself up as the sole obligatory religion for those who have Aryan blood. . . . As a result, the central reality and the absolute value in Nazi perceptions is not God but man, and not the transcendent being but the divine immanent in blood and race. The individual is subordinate to this absolute value, which is the measure and rule of every reality, because the individual is a transient phenomenon in which his race is expressed through its perpetual act of renewal. Given that the divine is identified with race, and race does not operate by itself but through the German human type, who bears the most genuine elements of Aryan blood, the visible deity that every German must honor and serve with absolute devotion is the leader of the nation, his Fuehrer. We thus come to idolatry of the human in the form it took during the period of the crudest paganism, with the apotheosis of living man. . . . There can be no doubt therefore that the essence of the struggle we are now waging in Germany is religious and not political.

The prefiguration of a terrifying apocalyptic scene, in which the final and inevitable battle between political religions and the religion of Christ would take place, brought Protestant and Catholic interpretations closer together. Both foresaw a new war that was about to ravage the world again. It also brought them together in the attempt to understand the profound human and spiritual reasons at the root of these new anti-Christian religions. Protestants and Catholics agreed, for instance, that the totalitarian state was a result of the separation between church and state and the state's demand to take on the tasks and functions of the church and extend its presence, influence, and actions to every aspect of life in society. The sequence of historical events that had marked out the overweening growth of the modern state, itself enormously accelerated by the Great War, had prepared the way for the advent of the totalitarian state, which had taken the logic of the primacy of state sovereignty over man and society to its ultimate conclusion in terms of political perceptions and political practice.

However, this explanation of the origin and nature of totalitarianism concerned only its external features: the effective power, the organization, the management of the state apparatus, and the control of relations between rulers and the ruled. As we have seen, many Protestants and Catholics agreed that in this area there was no substantial and radical genetic difference between the liberal secular state and the totalitarian secular state, whether communist or fascist. According to the Protestant and Catholic viewpoint, such states, in spite of their not inconsiderable differences, were the result of the same process that started with the birth of political modernity and the assertion of man's ability to shape his own destiny by himself without reference to the spiritual teachings of an established religion. The origins of totalitarian religions had to be sought not only in political motivations but also more deeply in the origins of their spiritual motivations, namely in the altered perception of mankind that occurred with the advent of modernity, when man wanted to become master of his own destiny and no longer felt dependent on God. Indeed, man's ambition was then to become a god himself. The consequences were revolutions, wars, massacres, the breakdown of society, and the crisis of modern man, who was overwhelmed by the forces he had unleashed and was now unable to keep under control.

It was asserted at the Oxford Conference that faith in the power of man to control his own destiny had resulted in social breakdown and unending conflict.[129] Industrialization and urbanization had destroyed the basis for community and spiritual bonds, thus provoking a perpetual diaspora of rootless individuals who crowded together in a collective and anonymous mass. Modern man was restless, directionless, and constantly at war with himself and with everyone else. Humanity was sick because he was made by God for God and was now going against his own nature by attempting to live without God.[130]

The adventure of modernity had witnessed the appearance of new religions and idols, which modern man has set up on altars so as to worship himself and to gratify his need for faith, direction, and harmony in an increasingly fractured, fragmented, and dynamic world that is dominated and devastated by impersonal but also tempestuous forces that drag along human beings in their wake, the very human beings who fool themselves that they can control such forces. The liberty acquired by modern man is nothing more than the opportunity to be transformed once more into a slave by sacrificing one's person to the power of great anonymous organizations. The ambition to become master of one's own destiny and be similar to God entailed the worship of new masters and new idols.

Basing himself on Berdyayev's critique of modernity, Nils Ehrenström traced the distant origins of totalitarianism to the Renaissance and the Enlightenment. Spiritually they were the cradle of that absolute and self-sufficient humanity that through a historical irony "has gradually become the slave of the political projection of its own apostasy, namely, the absolute and totalitarian State."[131] Modern man, echoed the Catholics of the Semaines sociales de France, "is a fallen god who no longer recalls the heavens. Having lost all memory of his origins, he has also lost the secret of his nature, pride in his destiny and his titles of nobility. Stripped of all that makes him a person, he agrees to be reduced to something similar to an animal. Deprived of his essential vigor which resides in the spirit, he seeks out the indiscriminate power of the mass."[132]

In 1938, Giulio Bevilacqua observed that modern man is always in search of God because he obsessed with the absolute, and "he seeks him more feverishly in some current atheistic movements. . . . He seeks him in his anxiety to build ridiculous earthly paradises; he seeks him in the childish game of grandstanding, which is nothing more than an attempt to rebuild the sacred in a world that has desecrated everything; he seeks him in fanciful liturgies that surround the idol made of mud; but he does seek him." Bevilacqua added modern man "goes from 'one false god to another in search of the true God' " and this was a profound psychological sign "of our times that produce idols out of words and out of living beings" and of an "anguished era in which the army of the godless advances like an unstoppable lava flow."[133]

According to the assessment of Protestants and Catholics alike, the original human roots of totalitarianism were to be found in the spiritual processes that led to the development of secularization, modernization, and mass politics. The more recent conditions that favored its eventual appearance were the crisis of modern man and the breakdown of society, which was overwhelmed by the violent impact of modernization that aimed to create the Kingdom of God here on earth by disposing of God altogether. Then the devastations and revolutions caused by the Great War stimulated the growth of the seeds left by these processes and led to the birth and triumph of political religions. Then at the end of the thirties, Protestant and Catholic views of what lay in store for humankind became apocalyptic, because the crisis of modernity, itself inherently catastrophic, had created a situation of irrevocable conflict between concepts of life and humankind that were diametrically opposed, irreconcilable, and destined for a final struggle. According to Igino Giordani, this struggle had already commenced: "Today we are all engaged in a religious war," he wrote in 1938, "the greatest religious war that ever tested the faith of the children of God." It was the final phase of an "immense and complex insurrection against God," in which "the Ancient Adversary, Satan, is taking part with new forces."[134]

The reference to the devil's responsibility in the creation of totalitarian religions was not a rhetorical hyperbole, but was entirely consistent with the apocalyptic vision of modernity evoked by Protestants and Catholics in the face of the triumph of totalitarian regimes at the beginning of the forties, when the war of religion had also become a world war. An Italian Catholic writer considered the birth of new religions "the latest trick of the devil." The devil "presented himself as the founder of religion" so as to participate in the "restless and troubled modern world" which believes it can "resolve the question of faith outside Christianity." Hence the stream of various humanist faiths, forms of mysticism, and deification of man, society, nation, race, and blood that ended up in the attempt "to provide irreligion with the pathos and religious fascination of revolutionary emancipation by presenting militant and intolerant atheism as a faith."[135] Faced with the reality of totalitarian religions, the Protestant theologian Nathaniel Micklem went so far as to argue in 1939 that all political problems were ultimately theological ones. No political theory could affect a human being profoundly, if not backed up by religious endorsement. Therefore, even democracy needed a religious basis and to fight for the salvation of Christian civilization if it was to be effective.[136]

Many Protestant scholars evoked the Apocalypse in their interpretations of totalitarianism. For example, Adolf Keller wondered whether, in the light of the apocalyptic prophecy, bolshevism's war against Christianity and the very presence in the world of such an immense and demonic power should not be considered the apparition of the Enemy, the Antichrist, and the Beast emerging from the abyss, whose imminent arrival had been announced by Russian philosophers such as Leontyev and Soloviov.[137] Even John Lewis, who supported an understanding between socialist Christianity and Bolshevik communism, believed that humankind had already entered the period of the Apocalypse predicted in the New Testament, and the coming of the son of God was not far off, but the Antichrist, who in his view was identified solely with fascism and Nazism, while communism, cleansed of its atheism, was counted among the forces of Good that would destroy the forces of Evil in the final battle of Armageddon.[138]

Ultimately the problem of totalitarianism for Protestants and Catholics was an essentially religious one, entirely caused and influenced by the arrogant behavior of political movements. As new religions, these movements claimed that they could define the meaning and the final cause of existence for the individual and for the masses, and that it lay under the complete control of a single party. However they were defined—idolatry, false religion, pseudo-religion, or surrogate for faith—totalitarian religions were movements of a religious nature, if for no other reason than their status as "the latest trick of the devil."

*Chapter 5*

# TOWARD THE THIRD MILLENNIUM

*The Sacralization of Politics in States Both New and Old*

As it is impossible to distinguish between false prophets
and true ones, it is best to be suspicious of them all. It is
better to give up on revealed truths, even when they
inspire us with their splendor and simplicity, and even
when we find them convenient because they come free
of any charge. It is better to make do with more modest
and less exciting truths, the ones that you acquire slowly,
laboriously, and without any short-cuts through study,
discussion, and reasoning, the ones that can be subjected
to verification and demonstration.
—Primo Levi

## A WAR OF RELIGION

The Second World War was fought and experienced by the allies as a war
of religion that would decide the fate of humankind. "Victory for us
means victory for religion,"[1] President Roosevelt declared in his State of
the Union address to Congress on 2 January 1942:

> Our enemies are guided by brutal cynicism, by unholy contempt for the
> human race. We are inspired by a faith which goes back through all the years
> to the first chapter of the Book of Genesis: "God created man in His own
> image."
>     We on our side are striving to be true to that divine heritage. We are fight-
> ing, as our fathers have fought, to uphold the doctrine that all men are equal
> in the sight of God. Those on the other side are striving to destroy this deep
> belief and to create a world in their own image—a world of tyranny and
> cruelty and serfdom.[2]

The causes of the war were national ambitions, conflicts of power, and
imperial rivalries, but something much more serious and decisive was at
stake for the whole of humankind: the survival of a civilization founded
on Christian and liberal values or the advent of a new pagan and secular
barbarism, founded on the primacy of force, on the inequality of men,
nations, and races, and on totalitarian idolatry:

Western countries—Gerhard Leibholz told a conference held in Oxford in 1942—are actually fighting the present war for universal principles, ideas and values. This is why the present conflict has been compared to a kind of crusade, or to a holy war, or to a war of religion. . . . This is why this conflict has been described again and again as a struggle between good and evil.[3]

Benedetto Croce wrote in 1943 that the allied powers were united by "a bond that differed from and was superior to any political treaty, armistice, or act of surrender, because it is a promise of a moral and religious nature that we accept in the spirit of religion."[4] Croce also defined the spirit that animated those fighting against fascism and Nazism as "religious." The philosopher believed that the war was the result of the spiritual and moral crisis of European conscience overcome by the idols of nationalism, imperialism, activism, and irrationalism, which had imposed a cult of violence and power. Fascism and Nazism therefore had to be fought not by force of arms but also with renewed and strengthened faith in the universal and humanitarian ideals that were the common heritage of both Christianity and liberalism. The philosopher joined the latter two together and reconciled them with each other. He claimed the title of "Christians" also for liberals,[5] as they were both engaged in the defense of the progress that commenced with the Christian revolution and continued toward "a humanity united in love and pain and in the search of the sublime."[6]

The interpretation of the war as a religious drama was echoed in the words of Simone Weil when she wrote in 1943 shortly before her death in London, where she had escaped to safety:

> If we had understood that this war would be a religious drama, it would have been possible many years ago to foresee which nations would be the protagonists and which the victims. The nations that did not live by religion could only be passive victims. This was the case of almost all of Europe. But Germany lives by idolatry. Russia lives by another idolatry; it is perhaps possible that beneath this idolatry there still persist the remains of a rejected past. Even though England has been eaten away by this century's diseases, there is such historical continuity in this country and such living power in its traditions that some of its roots still draw nourishment from a past imbued with a mystic light.[7]

Raymond Aron, another citizen of France who had escaped to London during the Second World War, felt the need at the time to reflect on the phenomenon of totalitarian religions, which had proved capable of inspiring "fighting ardor, devotion, and heroism in hundreds of thousands of young people."[8] The advent of fascism and Nazism was also the consequence of the lack of trust in democracy and the cynicism that had morally undermined democratic societies. Aron warned that democracies now had to learn how to keep alive in citizens "patriotic impulses, . . . the ability to make sacrifices for the common cause, courage and discipline in action," virtues "without which the survival of any collectivity is under threat."[9] The war was "a fight to the death: for nations it was a matter of either surviving or perishing,"[10] and therefore all moral forces were required alongside the material ones. "To defeat the national-socialist legions it is not enough to counter one tank with another; you also need to challenge one idea with another," so as to inspire the defenders of liberty with "an equally ardent faith as the one that drives the mercenaries of tyranny to the conquest of the world."[11] At the same time, Johan Huizinga, who lived in isolation, virtually a prisoner of the Germans in Holland, reflected on the catastrophe of western civilization, and, shortly before dying, he came to the conclusion that "in order to continue to live in an ordered community people had to rediscover an awareness of the metaphysical foundation of their existence, if and insofar as this awareness has been lost."[12] The Dutch historian's arguments were shared in England by Harold Laski, who asserted that the most important historical task imposed by the war on the Allies was the "recovery of a common faith" to combat irrationalism, nationalism, and imperialism in the future.[13] Yet the English academic, unlike Croce, did not assign the task of recovering the lost faith to Christianity, a faith that he considered to be "something like the civil religion which Rousseau recommended as the unifying cement of state-organization,"[14] but rather to Russian communism. As we have seen, he was convinced of its religious nature, and he argued that only the Soviet Union "had found a new way of faith in life,"[15] following the deep failure of existing values that unleashed the barbaric forces of fascism and Nazism.

The struggle of the Western democracies allied with Stalinist Russia ended in victory. The political religions of fascism and Nazism, destroyed by the definitive collapse of their regimes, disappeared from the political scene. The collective memory perceived them as irredeemably cursed and considered them responsible for the horrors of persecution, war, and systematic massacres. But the sacralization of politics, which had given rise to them, did not end there. During the last five decades of the century, religions of politics flourished around the entire planet and produced many varied results, some of which proved lasting and others much less so. It was occasionally accompanied by new explosions of fanaticism and fundamentalism, which created still more victims by the million, who were sacrificed in order that sacralized political entities could triumph.

With the Cold War came a new conflict between opposing concepts of the world, which concerned the meaning, the principles, and the fundamental values of individual and collective existence. From the late forties

until the fall of the Soviet Union in 1991, the Western democracie
to confront the challenge of communism, which, although an ally c_
the war against Nazism, was now considered their most formidable
enemy. The communist religion spread its presence over the entire planet
through the expansion of the Soviet empire in Eastern Europe, the creation of communist movements in every country, and the advent of new
communist regimes in Asia and Latin America. Between the late forties
and the mid-sixties, the sacralization of politics also found the new states
brought about by the end of colonialism to be favorable ground in which
to put down roots. The new rulers made many attempts to establish
systems of beliefs, myths, rituals, and symbols to legitimize their authority, integrate the masses into the state, and inculcate a national consciousness and a common identity for the purpose of creating loyal and rever-
ential citizens.

## COMMUNIST DEIFICATIONS

As a political religion, communism triumphantly entered the second half
of the twentieth century reinvigorated by the prestige the Soviet Union
had gained through its victory over Nazism and its rise to the status of
superpower.[16] As it reproduced itself in various national versions all
based on Marxism-Leninism, communism spread around the world taking with it cynical attitudes based on brute force and ruthlessness. However, it also had the fascination of a doctrine that seemed to be simultaneously a science, a faith, and a political power that promised liberation,
emancipation, and equality to all peoples of this world. "Humanitarian
and terrorist, idealistic and cynical, millenarian and Machiavellian, dogmatic and scientific, communion of the masses and conspiracy of the
elites, war now and peace later: this is the communist doctrine. It attracts
and repulses, seduces, and horrifies: even those who resist its spell end
up being fascinated by it."[17] Aron wrote those words in the early fifties
as he deepened his understanding of communism as a secular religion.[18]
He added that communists were "an extreme example of ambivalent
experiences: humanitarianism that accepts terror, terror that claims to
be the incarnation of the humanitarian will, oligarchy that invokes the
masses, and masses that believe they constitute an elite. This is a very
particular religious experience, which is founded on a secular belief."[19]
The religious nature of communist activism, which was based on faith
and devotion, was confirmed by intellectuals such as Arthur Koestler
and Ignazio Silone, who had become disillusioned with communism after
the experience of Stalinism.[20]

The denunciation of Stalin's crimes did not, however, prove to be an obstacle to this fascination with communism. During the following decades and up to the end of the seventies, communism was a religion of the intellectuals and the masses, it made many converts among all peoples and races, and it inflamed the new generations who rebelled from within the capitalist world and found communist revolutions of the Third World to be a source that renewed their faith in revolution. Mao's China, Castro's and "Che" Guevara's Cuba, and Ho Chi Min's Vietnam became the new beacons of enlightenment for Western intellectuals who, disillusioned with the experience of actual socialism in the countries of Eastern Europe, were now fascinated by new socialist experiments in the regeneration of society and the creation of "new man." Meanwhile, they continued in the exuberance of their faith to ignore or deny the costs of such experiments in terms of suffering and human lives, just as they had previously done in relation to Stalinism before it was officially condemned. They considered violence and brutality to be necessary measures that were sanctified by the nobility and grandeur of the ends they wished to achieve.[21]

The sacralization of politics became an essential aspect of all the communist regimes that arose during the Cold War and copied the Soviet model. Of course, variants were produced in each country according to the prevailing conditions at the time of taking power, the roles of particular leaders, and relations with the Soviet Union. In spite of the oft-repeated professions of internationalist faith, the new communist religions took on strikingly nationalistic connotations, and their spread around the world was accompanied by disagreements and conflicts that ended up in heresies, schisms, and excommunications, as in the case of Russia and China. These two countries divided over rivalry for power and ideological conflicts concerning the correct interpretation of Marxism-Leninism, and they then competed for the leadership of world communism.

In spite of the different historical experiences, the common features of the new political religions are quite clear. All the communist regimes established a compulsory system of beliefs, myths, rituals, and symbols that exalted the primacy of the party as the sole and unchallenged depositary of power. They all dogmatized their ideology as an absolute and unquestionable truth. They all glorified the socialist homeland and imposed a code of commandments that affected every aspect of existence. They all safeguarded their monopoly of power and truth through a police state and hard-line ideological orthodoxy backed up by constant surveillance and persecution, which enormously increased the number of human lives sacrificed for the triumph of communism. Finally, they all used the sacralization of politics with the ultimate aim of carrying out an anthropological revolution that would transform the population and create a "new man."

In 1958 Walter Ulbricht, the leader of the communist regime in East Germany, issued the "Ten Commandments of Socialist Morality," which were to inform the life of the "new socialist man," a virtuous and model citizen wholly committed to his socialist fatherland.[22] After seizing power in 1959 and converting to Marxism, Fidel Castro also undertook to mold a "new man," a militant dedicated to achieving the Cuban version of socialism by exalting Cuba's socialist mission in the triumph of the world revolution.[23] The theoretical magazine *Cuba socialista* asserted in 1964 that all educational efforts should aim at "training a new type of intellectual, socialist, and activist conscious of the formidable tasks of his time."[24] Cuban communism's new man was imagined as a "member of an egalitarian society who acted in the interests of the whole community to the full extent of his abilities."[25]

Artificiality and spontaneity came together in the formation of the new communist religions and influenced the socialization of the new system of beliefs, myths, rituals, and commandments imposed by the regime, just as they influenced the religious traditions of the majority of the population, something that sat rather oddly with the regime's profession of atheism. The reference to the traditional religion is an important one because, as had already occurred in the Soviet Union, the new communist countries, particularly in Asia, found that traditional religious beliefs heavily influenced the way in which the new political religion was perceived and received by the masses. There was a syncretic process of fusion between communism and traditional religion in the majority of the new regimes, particularly through deification of the leader, who embodied the values and commandments of the new political ideology and whose image was shrouded in sanctity partly through popular religious beliefs.

In Russia, "the personality cult" was publicly condemned by Khrushchev in 1956 following Stalin's death. Five years later, the dictator's embalmed body was removed from Lenin's mausoleum and was buried in the Kremlin Wall next to the remains of other leaders of the regime, but Soviet citizens and communist activists from all parts of the world continued to file past the mummy of Lenin with religious reverence. The sacralization of politics in Russia did not end once the Stalinist cult had been discarded. Particularly during the Brezhnev era (1964–1982), the regime campaigned systematically to establish and spread new myths and rituals of both a political and a civic nature in order to revitalize the sacralization of communist power and accelerate the creation of *homo sovieticus*. During this phase, praise was lavished on Russian nationalism and Soviet patriotism by glorifying the events, the victims, and the combatants of the Second World War, called the Great Patriotic War. The sacralization of politics even survived during the Gorbachev era (1985–1991), and only came to an end with the breakup of the communist regime, when an iconoclastic frenzy brought down the statues and monuments raised to glorify the demigods of the Soviet empire. Only Lenin's embalmed body was saved, and it still lies in the mausoleum in Red Square.[26]

Once abolished in Russia, personality cults became one of the fundamental features of the sacralization of politics in other communist regimes, which applied the Stalinist model and often surpassed it in the megalomania of deification. The establishment of the cult of the leader was not everywhere immediate following the conquest of power and depended on several factors concerning the presence of a charismatic personality, power struggles between the regime's leaders, and the attitudes of the masses. In Cuba, for example, the myth and cult of Castro, *Jefe Máximo*, originated from his leading role in the revolutionary struggle for power and his genuine popularity among the masses.[27] In other cases, the cult of the leader resulted from the affirmation of absolute power by a dominant personality, who succeeded in prevailing over his rivals within the new regime, and crowned his victory with his own consecration as the unchallenged leader and living myth. This is what occurred in Romania, where Nicolae Ceausescu, who lacked any charismatic quality, introduced a personality cult a few years after achieving the highest position in the regime's hierarchy following the death of its founder, Gheorghiu-Dej. In 1974 Ceausescu proclaimed himself *Conducător* and concentrated absolute power in the hands of his family. He established a political religion founded on communism and nationalism, and his very public independence from the Soviet Union won him popular consensus for a certain period. From then until his fall in 1989, Ceausescu governed the country as a despot, falling prey to an increasingly unrestrained fever of self-exaltation and megalomania.[28]

It appears that the Romanian dictator was first suggested the idea of a "personality cult" by a visit to North Korea where he was stunned by the spectacular cult of Kim Il-Sung.[29] The latter was a communist activist educated in Russia who took part in the war of liberation from the Japanese with Stalin's support. As founder and dictator of the communist regime in North Korea since 1948, Kim Il-Sung adopted the Stalinist model to set up a personality cult after eliminating his rivals. Since the sixties, he put a great deal of effort into establishing a political religion founded on the deification of his person and the sanctification of his thought, the *Juche* doctrine ("rely upon one's own forces"), which was a mixture of Marxism, Leninism, and nationalism imposed upon the entire population through terror, propaganda, and a pervasive and grassroots system of indoctrination.

Isolated from the rest of the world, North Korea was transformed into a totalitarian laboratory that defined itself as the "hermit kingdom." Its communist warriors fought against imperialism under the orders of the

"Great Helmsman" and committed themselves to the realization of socialism and the forging of the collectivized personality of the socialist "new man," in accordance with the doctrine of the "Great Leader." Forty thousand study centers were established in villages, factories, schools, production cooperatives, and the armed forces throughout the country to teach the doctrine of Kim Il-Sungism, and a state apparatus permanently engaged in symbolic and ritual works implemented the deification of Kim Il-Sung, who was glorified as the "Savior of the Nation," "the Nation's Sun," "Father of the people," and "Genius of all humankind."

On his death in 1994, Kim Il-Sung was immortalized by embalmment and his body was placed in a great mausoleum to be worshipped. Since 1997, the official calendar of North Korea has counted the years since 1911, the year in which Kim Il-Sung was conceived, and the birthday of the "Nation's Sun," 12 April 1912, is the most sacred of the regime's national holidays. Mangyondae, his birthplace, is venerated as the sacred heart of the nation. Gigantic statues were erected both before and after his death to immortalize the image of the "Great Helmsman," which every North Korean must carry on him as a sacred icon. Museums, sculptures, paintings, and poems represent his life as a mythical epic of heroic deeds leading to the liberation of Korea from the Japanese and the realization of socialism. "All his activities," one can read in a recent official biography, "were directed toward the realization of his plan to build a communist paradise."[30] "Our Father is Marshall Kim Il-Sung, our home is the Party, we are all true brothers and we are the happiest people in the world": these are the words sung by children brought up in this totalitarian laboratory. The Kim Il-Sung religion added racial superiority to the mixture of communism and nationalism, and it exalted Korea as an "ethnically homogeneous nation."[31] Kim-Il-Sungism was declared to be an immortal doctrine not only for the Korean people but for the entire world.[32] His mission of universal "enlightenment" was celebrated symbolically with a gigantic tower in the center of Pyongyang, which is 150 meters high and topped with a 20-meter light in the shape of a flame to signify the spread of Kim Il-Sung's doctrine around the world. A compulsory textbook, *Kim Il-Sung, Great Man of the Century*, concocts fanciful statistics on the spread of the Juche doctrine:

> Today, there are university courses on Juche ideas in many countries. . . .
> Some one hundred have more than 400 institutions, organizations, and
> streets named after Kim Il-Sung and his secretary Kim Jong-Il. Their portraits
> hang in many homes around the world. Thus, the rays of the *Juche* tower
> have touched the hearts of innumerable people, increasing the mass of his
> followers. . . . Every year the works [of Kim Il-Sung] are translated and pub
> lished in numerous languages in more than a hundred countries, with print

runs of tens or hundreds of millions of copies. . . . Just as you cannot hide the sun with the palm of your hand, so nothing can stop the spread of truth. The same happens with *Juche* ideas. *Juche* ideas, the source of life that revitalizes the spirit of all peoples wherever they live, are considered by humanity to be the truth of all truths.[33]

The deification of Kim Il-Sung was passed on to the son Kim Jong-Il, the appointed successor in the first communist dynasty. Since 1982 his birthday has been celebrated as a national holiday. After the death of the "Great Leader," who had been proclaimed President for Eternity, the son inherited absolute power and was venerated in the regime's liturgy as "the Sun of the XXI Century," a living perpetuation of his father with whom he was identified: "Kim Il-Sung lives among us. Kim Il-Sung is Kim Jong-Il, and Kim Jong-Il is Kim Il-Sung" is a current slogan in the Korean liturgy. It is no coincidence that the slogan evokes the Christian identification of father and son. Kim Il-Sung persecuted traditional religions and destroyed their institutions and temples, but traces of the Christian tradition are evident in the myths and rituals of his political religion. A French journalist, who pretended to be a tourist, was one of the very few foreign visitors to the country in 2000 and has observed that in North Korea "the Christian liturgy appears to have merged into the political model, whose sole morality is that of the state."[34]

> The similarity between this pagan liturgy and Catholic and Protestant rituals is quite surprising. The analogy is something of a caricature: Kim-the-father is immortal, and Kim-the-son is the bearer of good tidings in this country defined as a "paradise on earth." But there is also something palpable about it: the endless gigantic painted panels like icons, statues like those found in churches, slogans like the commandments, rituals of purification, the sacred scriptures of the "Great Leader," and above all his "testament" on reunification, which is treated as a Bible. The official propaganda associates this "sacred task" of reunification of the two Koreas with the promise of a future free from all evils. The comparison with Christianity is by no means an extravagant one. Korea as a whole was the country in Asia that was most heavily Christianized after the eighteenth century, apart from the Philippines. . . . Christianity was the principal factor in the modernization in Korea, where missionaries set up thousands of schools and infirmaries.[35]

Even today, while hunger, famine, and epidemics resulting from an uninterrupted series of failed economic experiments have caused the death of hundreds of thousands of Koreans, the regime governed by "Sun of the Twenty-First Century" is glorified by its inhabitants as an earthly paradise.

## THE "HUMAN SUN"

Kim Il-Sung probably used both Mao and Stalin as models to inspire a political cult based on the deification of his person, given the many similarities between the political religions. There are also clear analogies between the Chinese communist religion and Stalinism, especially in the transition from the sacralization of the party to the deification of the leader, but equally there are clear differences. While in Russia this transition went through an intermediate stage, represented by the establishment of the cult of Lenin and Leninism, which was the premise for establishment of the cult of Stalin and Stalinism, in China both before and after taking power, Mao and Maoism always had a predominant role, although not always an unchallenged one.

The sacralization of the Chinese Communist Party went back to the time of the Long March (1935–1949) and manifested itself in the very way activism was perceived, namely as the result of a ritual process of initiation, character improvement, and "reforming thought," which created a new human being and a "good communist" who devoted himself completely to his party and fully identified with its ideology and politics.[36] Within the party, Mao, who was already legendary and messianic because of the heroic Long March, was invested with charismatic authority as leader of the revolution, president of the party, and the greatest theoretician of Marxism-Leninism.[37] In 1945, at the Seventh Congress of the Chinese Communist Party, Mao was proclaimed the greatest revolutionary in Chinese history, and his thoughts were canonized in the party statutes as the supreme theoretical guide for Chinese communists. After 1949, his glorification continued apace as he was attributed with mythical and messianic qualities—"Mao-sun," "Mao is the star of salvation," "Mao is China's helmsman." However, this glorification was not yet matched with absolute personal power. There was in fact strong resistance from within the party to Mao's claim to be considered the unchallenged and infallible leader. In 1956, following the denunciation of Stalinism, the Chinese Communist Party held its eighth congress at the behest of Liu Shaoqi and Deng Xiaoping. It condemned the personality cult and argued in favor of collective leadership. Deng, who was the party's general secretary, declared "love for the leader is essentially an expression of love for the interests of the Party, the class, and the people, not the deification of an individual."[38] The congress decided to remove the reference to Mao's thought as the ideological guide to Chinese communism, while continuing to pay formal homage to his person. But two years later, Mao decided to declare war on his rivals and argued that a personality cult can be "good," if understood not as blind obedience but as reverence toward a personality who represents the truth. The reason, he explained, was that "the question at issue is not whether or not there should be a cult of the individual, but whether or not the individual concerned represents the truth. If he does, then he should be revered." Marx, Engels, Lenin, and in part even Stalin were individuals who, in this sense, merited eternal reverence.[39]

The sacralization of politics in communist China thus became a factor and a symptom of Mao's struggle against his adversaries within the party to achieve absolute power. He had been marginalized as a result of the failure of his policy known as the "Great Leap Forward" (1958–1961), which aimed to introduce socialism to the countryside and cost the lives of 20 or perhaps even 30 million Chinese. As Mao recovered power, there was a parallel increase in the glorification of his thought as an absolute truth and the sanctification of his person as a living demigod. In 1960 an Italian journalist called Virgilio Lilli visited communist China and described it as "both an immense battlefield and a huge church." The Chinese were dominated by "a religion that can be reduced to blind obedience to the Communist Party"[40] and the deification of Mao.

> For the Chinese masses, Mao Tse-Tung is a saint who already has something of the divine about him. The Central Committee of the Communist Party is now a supernatural power very similar to divine power. The revolutionary leaders, ministers, members of the Central Committee, generals, etc. are personalities in a living religious iconography that has its own supernatural, indisputable, and cultish dynamic. For mystical and ritualistic reasons, the world in which today's Chinese move from dormitory to refectory, from ordinary school to political school, from workshop to field, from kindergarten to military barracks, is a sacred one in which the redemption of mankind is being fulfilled from above, from the ideological heavens. Contrary to what occurs in our Western societies (in which earthly and heavenly matters are kept well apart), in the world of the communist Chinese, man already finds himself within a revealed paradise, a paradise of matter, machines, stomachs, salaries, and compulsory work, where he awaits only to be perfected. It is a world in which he has been privileged to be placed by the revolution. . . .
>
> Compared with the capitalistic world, communist China is a mystical and liturgical phenomenon and an endless religious service. It is an enormous church in which every workbench is an altar, every piece of iron an incense-burner, and every product a sacred image, whether it is an iron pipe, a brick, a roll of cloth, a pencil, a tin container, or a tool.[41]

Mao attributed a fundamental role in the implementation of his policies to the deification of his person. When the American journalist Edgar Snow, who had known Mao on the Long March and had become an admirer, visited China in 1965, he was perplexed to find "an immoderate glorification of Mao Tse-tung": "Giant portraits of him now hung in the streets, busts were in every chamber, his books and photographs were everywhere on display to the exclusion of others. In the four-hour revolutionary pageant of dance and song, "The East is Red," Mao was the only hero."[42] Snow questioned Mao about this, and he "stated that there was a need for more personality cult in order to stimulate the masses to dismantle the anti-Mao party bureaucracy."[43] A year later, now determined to impose his absolute power on the party, Mao launched the "Grand Proletarian Cultural Revolution" with the support of the army. He appealed to the masses over the heads of the party bureaucracy and mobilized young people and students in the Red Guard militias against their old leaders. From the very beginning, the myth and cult of Mao were the engine driving the Cultural Revolution, as a Chinese sociologist was able to witness:

> Beginning in the summer of 1966, the streets of Beijing were filled with banners with such slogans as "Long live Chairman Mao" and "Be ready to die in defense of Chairman Mao." The songs children sang were reminiscent of Western hymns in praise of Jesus. One song proclaimed, "My love for my parents is great, but greater still is my love for Chairman Mao." Another said, "We think of you every minute, Respected Chairman Mao."
>
> Mao was glorified as "the Red Sun," "the Great Teacher," "the Great Leader," "the Great Commander," "the Great Steersman," and significantly "the Messiah of Working People." Catching a glimpse of him in public left observers with unforgettable memories, and many were reduced to tears by the experience. The masses would spend the night in the street if they knew Mao's route the next morning would take him past them. When Mao finally appeared, the people would jump, shout, cry out, and wave the "Little Red Book" in agonies of joy. This experience of ecstasy is not unlike the uncontrolled outpourings of emotion that sometimes accompany religious revivals in the West.[44]

Cinema and theater celebrated Mao's glory by evoking the heroic story of the Long March, the War of Liberation, and the conquest of communist China, which thus transformed spectacle into ritual. A Soviet student who frequented Peking University at the time compared the presentation of the film *Red Sun*, which described events in the War of Liberation, to a pagan rite of collective ecstasy.

> Before the screening, there was an amateur show introduced by a choir that sang compositions in praise of Mao. There followed a ballet on the war between the Vietnamese and the Yankees. The apotheosis was a group of dancers and a chorus who sung the praises of the Great Leader of the Chinese People. . . .

As the dancers started to sing their praises of the Leader, they turned toward an enormous portrait of Mao that dominated the background framed by large red flags. The Leader's face stood out against the red canvas and radiated a golden light. The dancers lifted their arms toward this human sun and kneeled down before him in small groups in artistic poses. The choir lifted the general enthusiasm and electrified the dancers in a frenzied crescendo.

I felt like fainting in the middle of all those people intent upon their collective worship. In this delirious spectacle there was much of the ancient pagan cults. The only thing missing was human sacrifice. The collective ecstasy so palpably expressed by the collective and youthful grace of the performers brought to mind the worship of the sun, thunder, and fire, the submission to heavenly will, and shamanic rituals.[45]

The image of the "Great Helmsman" was everywhere: in homes, workplaces, schools, public buildings, streets, and squares. Mao, who disliked mixing with the crowd, offered his person for adoration by the masses as a modern reincarnation of the ancient Chinese emperor venerated as the Son of the Heavens, by appearing at the top of the Gate of Heavenly Peace before the immense Tienanmen Square filled with a great sea of people. His birthplace and the places where he had engaged in political activity became sacred spaces and were visited by pilgrims. In the countryside, the cult of Mao became part of the universe of popular saints and was the focal point of daily life, work, and hours of indoctrination. Families gathered around his image in the morning before going to work to venerate him and draw inspiration to act virtuously, and in the evening on return from work, they again gathered around the sacred icon to express gratitude. In the cities, processions and parades to express approval of Mao were ritual activities that were repeated incessantly every day and night, with a frenzied, obsessive, and jarring rhythm, as the Soviet student recalls:

The drums beat by night, in the morning, and all day long, close-by and in the distance. It is impossible to escape the sound. The rumbling is only breached by raucous voices and shouts: "Long live Mao Tse-tung," "We will defend President Mao!" "Glory to the Great Helmsman!" Parades in the university quarter and in the city streets; endless rallies. . . .

In the first row, four students hold an enormous portrait of President Mao framed in red velvet and rimmed with flowers and green branches. Next come flags of a bright red color and usual form, and long narrow standards on tall poles, whose silk is light and quivering. Thus the procession of men under flags looks heavy and cumbersome, although the people, in the flush of youth, walk with a spring in their step. The flags are followed by a band. A drum is obligatory and is often accompanied by high-pitched Chinese gongs.

Behind the band there comes a well-ordered procession, and occasionally activists walk alongside armed with the ubiquitous sloganizing leaflets. The slogans are shouted rapidly in a hoarse voice.[46]

The writer Alberto Moravia, who visited China in 1967, gave a graphic description of the Maoist liturgy:

Then down below, deep in the whitish haze, something colored appeared, pulsated, and began to move. It was a red flag, one of the many that for about a year in these parts are taken on processions from one end of the city to the other for any number of reasons.

We stop and wait. Shortly afterwards the flag approached and we could see the entire procession. It was made up of young men and women, or in other words, Red Guards, as can be inferred from their scarlet armbands. They were all in blue trousers, white shirts, and they all carried Mao's little red book gripped tightly in their hands. The standard-bearer at the head of the march carried the flag on a bamboo pole that fits into his belt. He was followed by two girls who held up a large portrait of Mao framed in gold and decorated with red festoons. Behind the portrait came the demonstrators in single file. This was a typical demonstration, and once you have seen one you have seen them all. It is perhaps worth pointing out that the style of these processions, like that of propaganda performances with songs, music, and dance, is a religious style, and the religiosity is rustic and traditional. Replace the red flag with the standard of a confraternity and Mao's portrait with the portrait of a patron saint, and you will find that nothing has really changed. The Red Guards are certainly the most modern political movement in the communist world, but their style cannot help being Chinese, which means appropriate to a country like China whose population mainly consists of the peasantry.[47]

All Chinese were subjected to an intense and incessant indoctrination campaign. One hundred fifty million copies of Mao's selected works were printed and distributed, and a billion copies were printed of the *Little Red Book*, a collection of quotations of Mao's thought that became the catechism of the Maoist religion and a guide to all Chinese in every moment of their existence and of relevance to all their activities.[48] The collective pedagogy, based on a daily, pervasive, and incessant indoctrination, became one of the principal tools in the Maoist anthropological revolution to "reform thought" and create the "good communist" and "new man." This involved a radical transformation of identity, which finally freed people from individualism and immersed them mind and body in the social collectivity. The "new man" was to devote his entire life to his party and had to be willing to die for it, too. In 1966 the Italian writer Goffredo Parise felt that China was an immense seminary "where they study and implement Marxism-Leninism not as a science but as a political theology and where six hundred and fifty million seminarists are organized and subdivided into a hierarchy that is more or less that of any other religious community."[49] After the Revolution, the Chinese had taken on "the spirit, the organization, and forms of a religious community":

> What then occurred with Mao Tse-tung's revolution?
>
> Something occurred that had not occurred for millennia and that was the creation not only of a relationship between the Chinese people and their new ruling class but also an identification of the former with the latter. Something else occurred that was unheard of for millennia: this identification of the Chinese people with their ruling class proved in its revolutionary practice to be not only a political experience but also a politico-religious one in which the ancient Confucian rationalistic tradition concurs with the new ideology of Mao Tse-tung.
>
> Put very succinctly, these are the reasons why China resembles a seminary of political theology where the will of the individual, which never counted for anything in the past because it had to conform to that of the family, continues to not count for anything because it has to conform to the ideology of everybody together.[50]

The transformation of Maoism into a political religion, which is inherent in the ideological dogmatism and political monopoly of the Communist Party, resulted from an initiative from above and the spontaneous participation of the masses from below, producing a politico-religious syncretism in which Maoist ideology mixed with Confucianism, Taoist mysticism, and popular religiosity.[51] Moravia considered the "religious nature of the Cultural Revolution" to result from the "Confucianization of Marx's thought by Mao" and the "Confucianization which the Chinese masses instinctively and spontaneously imposed on Maoism, which is a form of Marxism that has already transformed into something more Chinese."[52] Moravia then added, "this is not an intellectual operation, as in Mao's case, but rather a religious operation, in the general sense of the term," which was for the most part the consequence of the rural religious tradition of the Chinese people.[53]

The Cultural Revolution was an experience of collective exuberance, in which violence and the sacred were daily mixed up together with enthusiasm, fanaticism, and terror, both in the city and in the countryside. The Red Guards triggered the hounding of the "class enemies," particularly intellectuals, university teachers, school teachers, technicians, and party members, all accused of treachery, revisionism, and disloyalty to the thought and commandments of the "Great Helmsman." The rituals of confession and repentance became an everyday practice. Those who were accused of not having fully assimilated the new collective consciousness and the correct understanding of Mao's thought were subjected to an immediate trial carried out by the Red Guards. It has been calculated that about a million Chinese lost their lives during the Cultural Revolution, while millions of others were subjected to periods of reeducation and "brain-washing" through forced labor and the constant study of Mao's thought.

The consecration of the cult of Mao was sealed at the Tenth Congress of the Chinese Communist Party, which was held in April 1969. It reaffirmed the primacy of his power and his thought as the supreme teachings for the party, after having purged the majority of his rivals, but at the same time it marked the end of the Cultural Revolution. In the years that followed, Mao reined in the violence of the Red Guards, while China's domestic and foreign policies gradually shifted in a more realistic direction, a process that accelerated after his death in 1976 and the abandonment of his utopia, but without dismantling the totalitarian regime. The myth of Mao survived the repudiation of his policies and, following a brief period when his star was falling during the eighties, it revived on the back of its commercial use and the spontaneous myth of the masses: his embalmed body is still venerated in the mausoleum dedicated to him in Tienanmen Square.[54]

## New States, New Religions

The expansion of the sacralization of politics during the second half of the twentieth century was also brought about by the new national states that emerged from the collapse of the colonial empires. In the Western world, it arose from democracy and nationalism and developed through the principles, values, myths, rituals, and symbols that legitimized the new institutions founded on popular sovereignty and favored the integration of the population and the formation of a sense of belonging and national identity. This was not exactly what happened in the postcolonial states. Here, the sacralization of politics was the main vehicle for legitimizing the new political institutions and forming a national identity in political entities created by the territorial conformations of the old colonial borders with populations often composed of a great variety of ethnic, linguistic, and religious groups who had little more in common than their subjection to colonial rule. In most cases, these new states were formed in societies that were entirely untouched by secularization. The need to unify this heterogeneous mosaic was the principal reason for attempting to establish a civil or political religion, according to the democratic or authoritarian nature of the regime.

The adoption of symbols and rituals, the establishment of national holidays, and the organization of parades and large collective ceremonies were an important feature of the sacralization of politics in new African and Asian states, and were certainly the most visible ones.[55] But equally important was the development of a system of ideas, principles, and values with the purpose of providing a set of shared beliefs on the meaning and purpose of collective life to give a sense of political identity and national consciousness to heterogeneous populations in terms of race, ethnicity, religion, and language, whose cultures still retained the identification of power with the sacred.

In the majority of new states, democracy was short-lived or stillborn. The prevailing regime in Africa and Asia, even in noncommunist countries, was an authoritarian political system, which in some cases replicated the characteristics of a totalitarian state: the attribution of the monopoly of political power to a single party, the dominance of a charismatic leader, a repressive and terrorist police apparatus, the organization of the masses for their control and indoctrination, a planned anthropological revolution to regenerate and mold the nation in accordance with the principles and values of an ideology presented as an absolute and indisputable truth and, as has already been said, the establishment of a system of beliefs, myths, rituals, and symbols that sacralize the new nation, its history, and its institutions, while demanding devotion and loyalty from the ruled.

This last feature was common to all the new states, even those governed by democratic regimes like Israel. Another common feature appears to have been the role of the charismatic leader, at least during the period of achieving independence and founding the new state: Ben Gurion in Israel, Bourguiba in Tunisia, Nasser in Egypt, Nkrumah in Ghana, Senghor in Senegal, Nyerere in Tanzania, Sékou Touré in Guinea, and Sukarno in Indonesia. All these personalities were invested with charismatic authority and became, often intentionally, the center of a system of myths, rituals, and symbols that conferred an aura of sacredness upon the new state, its origins, its institutions, and its policies—although not all of them demanded to be deified as did Kwame Nkrumah.[56] The majority of charismatic leaders not only symbolized the unity of the nation, but also carried out the role of theologians and teachers. They took on the task of developing the principles, values, and commandments of the doctrine that defined the meaning and sense of collective life, interpreted the history and will of the new nation, and indicated goals that needed to be achieved by the population. The historian Jean Lacouture has observed that in African states, the sacralization of the power through the figure of the leader had a fundamental role in reconciling religious tradition with modern politics.[57]

What counts is the deification of the power, the religious dimension that it takes on, and the allusions it evokes, but not the origin, nature, and specificity of this sacralization, as long it has been Africanized. God, Allah, Imana and even Karl Marx can provide the necessary scale for the leader's power, if Sékou Touré or Julius Nyerere naturalize them as Africans. It matters little which text inspires the leader; it matters only the passion of that inspiration.

Thus, the continuous expansion on the black continent of two great monotheist religions not only has not upset the traditional realities of black power, but has not provoked the violent clashes that have occurred elsewhere. As Africanized religion became dissociated from political power in a growing number of societies, it became this syncretic melting pot that reconciled not only Yahweh and Allah, but also God and Caesar. If you examine some of the basic texts reflecting Nkrumah's power, particularly the litanies dedicated to Osagyefo Kwame Nkrumah, you will find an incredible fusion of animism, Judaism, Islamism, Christianity, Marxism, and techniques of power developed by the inventors of totalitarianism.[58]

The relationship between religious tradition and modern politics had a decisive role in attempts to construct secular religions and often determined their outcomes. As we have seen, this was very much the case in Western states where the deification of politics took place after secularization, and was therefore even truer of new states in the Third World, where secularization had not yet commenced and traditional religions continued to be the sole source for legitimizing power. The results of the encounter between traditional religion and new secular religion were varied and gave rise to different experiences of the sacralization of politics that are difficult to generalize. We will examine a few examples.

In some cases, the attempt to establish a civil religion by reconciling religious tradition and modern politics, in accordance with the needs of the new state, became bogged down because of hostility from the dominant religion, as occurred in Malaysia.[59] In other cases, such as Sri Lanka following the establishment of the republic in 1972, the civil religion was grafted onto the Buddhist tradition and even incorporated mythical and ritual elements handed down from ancient political traditions that still survived in Singhalese popular culture. Thus the sacralization of politics appeared to conform with the population's religious confessions and its most ancient and venerable beliefs.[60]

Akmed Sukarno's regime (1959–1965) carried out a similar experiment in the form of "guided democracy." A great deal of energy was expended in inventive slogans, symbols, and rituals to unify Indonesian national consciousness among a mainly Muslim population that was scattered over thousands of islands. Sukarno proposed the doctrine of *Pantja Sila* as the foundation for a civil religion that exalted the Indonesian nation as an example to humanity. Pantja Sila was based on five principles: nationalism, internationalism (or humanitarianism), democracy (or consent), social prosperity, and faith in God.[61] He felt he had found an effective formula for the coexistence of civil religion and traditional religion by making faith in the existence of God the common principle. However, the experiment does not appear to have had lasting results after he was deposed in 1965 for his communist sympathies.[62]

In other new states such the Union of South Africa, the religious tradition was the principal factor in the construction of an Afrikaner civil religion, following independence in 1948. In this case, the sacralization of politics involved interpreting the history and destiny of the Boers as a people chosen by God. The Calvinist religion was used to assert that a sacred pact had been established between God and the people who, having suffered under British domination through the nineteenth and twentieth centuries, had finally reached the promised land of independence with a republican constitution that implemented the divine will to assert and preserve the primacy of the white and Christian race.[63]

Sacralization of politics in the state of Israel was wholly unique. It passed through various phases involving various types of civil religion, which can be distinguished mainly by their attitudes toward religious tradition, the Diaspora, and the Holocaust, as well as different ways of understanding the nature of the new state.[64] For example, the laborite Zionism and statist socialism of Ben Gurion, the founder of the Israeli state in 1947, interpreted the Jewish nation in entirely secular terms and conceived the birth of the new state as the redemption of the Jewish people from the decadence of the Diaspora, and as the advent of the "new Jew" who was active, combative, and heroic, in contrast with the Jew of the ghetto, who was perceived as passive, submissive, and insecure. Neither of these two civil religions placed memory of the Holocaust at the center of its "sacred history." The conflict between these different traditions of civil religion has altered in recent years, and they have been replaced by a new civil religion that reconciles religious tradition with modern politics by making the memory of the Holocaust central to its interpretation of history and the existence of the state of Israel.

A definitive assessment of the sacralization of politics in newly created states has been made difficult by the great variety of its manifestations. However, it is possible to put forward some general considerations using the interpretation developed by the sociologist David Apter. He adopted the concept of political religion to include the nature and the meaning of this phenomenon as it manifested itself in most of the new states in Asia and Africa during the second half of the twentieth century. Apter defines political religion as a "potent symbolic force" for legitimizing the state, integrating the population, and mobilizing the collectivity to achieve given political aims.[65] Political religion confers sacredness on the state, the regime, and the leader, it provides a mythical representation of a glorious past and sanctifies the conquest of independence, after a period of decadence and suffering, as a regenerative event or "rebirth" that demands the nation free itself of its legacy of decadence so that it can take on its appropriate role in the world.[66] The purpose of political religion in new nations is to confer a sacred nature on authority and achieve unity of the state by removing all the divisions that it had inherited from the past to create a healthy and harmonious community in which each individual lives and works for the good of the nation. Parliamentary democracy, from this point of view, is rejected as a Western colonialist institution foreign to the culture and traditions of the new nations, as it is a system of government based on division and conflict between parties, and therefore considered unsuited to the requirements of a new state that has to assert and develop its own unity. The leader, the party, and the political religion are institutions that embody unity of the nation, express its will, and define its meaning and the ultimate aim of its collective existence. The task of political religion is to provide a sense of belonging and identity and to maintain the unity of the nation through a state of permanent mobilization to achieve its political objectives: for this reason it demands the total politicization of collective life, absolute faith in the leader's authority, and the individual's devotion to the nation to the point of sacrificing his or her life. In this sense, Apter argues that the strictly religious nature of political religions is the provision of an interpretation and definition of the meaning and purpose of life by promising immortality to individual lives devoted to the achievement of the nation's transcendent aims, while the nation itself is perceived as a collective entity that is eternal.[67] This, however, reveals factors that, according to Apter, produce the decline of political religion: the inability to provide an effective response to existential problems and the fate of the individual faced with death; flagging enthusiasm for the myths of regeneration and the national mission in the face of material failures; the advent of new generations that did not take part in the revolutionary fervor of the nation's founders and who are more inclined toward pragmatic and individualistic concepts of life, are impatient of authoritarianism, demand freedom to decide their own destiny, and do not believe their rulers' idealistic appeals. All this makes rebellion against the political religion inevitable or at least means that it cannot last. "If revolt against church religion is iconoclastic, the revolt against political religion tends to be cynical."[68]

OLD DEMOCRACIES: THE WANING OF CIVIL RELIGION?

After the Second World War, the sacralization of politics continued to exist in the Western world where democratic systems prevailed, and manifested itself in the mythical, ritual, and symbolic forms that it had taken on during the nineteenth century and the early decades of the twentieth. These forms remained more or less unchanged as they were originally structured to confer sacredness on the nation, but an attempt was made to reconcile this sacredness with the principle of individual liberty. Moreover, the experience of totalitarian religions and their pernicious consequences did not encourage an intense and showy deployment of mythical, ritual, and symbolic mechanisms for binding the citizen to the state. This was certainly the reason why the sacralization of politics as a state-run manifestation was almost entirely missing in such nations as Germany and Italy, which were restored to democracy after their involvement in totalitarian experiments. But even in these countries, as in other Western nations, forms of the sacralization of politics, with varying degrees of durability, continued to be produced by highly ideological social and political movements, particularly radical and revolutionary ones, which put forward absolute truths and fundamental solutions to eliminate the evils of this world.

In other Western democratic states, the sacralization of politics depended mainly on whether or not there was a tradition of civil religion and on the different configurations of the relationship between the religious and political dimensions, especially in relation to the autonomy of political institutions from the traditional religion and the Established Church.

In England, for example, the head of state and head of the Anglican Church continued to be the same throughout the second half of the twentieth century, an indissoluble bond between religion and politics in their traditional meanings, thus making it practically impossible at a national level to create an autonomous religious dimension of politics *qua* politics, as occurred in the United States and France. However, religious pluralism and nonconfessional recognition of the civil role of the monarchy as the symbolic embodiment of the nation has favored, according to some scholars, the formation of a civil religion that is distinct from the religious confessions in that its prime object is the cult of the nation itself, its history, its traditions, its heroes, its war dead, and its institutions, as well as observance of moral, social, and political values that are acknowledged by the majority of citizens, whatever church they belong to, as the essential constituent principles of British unity and collective identity. This civil religion finds its symbolic unitary center in the monarchy's national role, and its most solemn ritual is the coronation, by which the nation carries out an act of collective communion through its sovereign and reconsecrates its unity by reasserting its loyalty to shared values.[69] In continental Europe, there were other monarchical states in which traditional religion continued in the second half of the last century to fulfill the role of legitimizing the political order through the consecration of the monarch, even though society, culture, and politics had undergone a process of secularization. But it appears that even in these states, which include Sweden, Norway, Denmark, and Holland, the development of secularization and nationalism led to the emergence of some elements of a civil religion, with myths, rituals, and symbols that legitimize the institutions and represent the nation as an entity that is perpetual and transcends the life of individual citizens, and to which citizens have a duty of loyalty and devotion.[70] But in these cases, as in the English case, it is reasonable to ask whether the presence of a civil religion currently constitutes an effective source of legitimization of the political order and a viable representation of shared common values.

As far as European democratic republics are concerned, consistent traces of the sacralization of politics during the twentieth century can be found only in France, where there was a varied tradition of civil religiosity that, commencing with the glorification of the French Revolution as the great founding event of modern France, developed after the Great War the symbiosis between religion of the fatherland and cult of the republic founded on the principles of individual freedom and equality of the citizens, in spite of having experienced bitter and divisive religious and ideological conflicts.[71] Following the lacerating experience of the Vichy regime (1940–1944), the republican myth that emerged from the long internecine war definitively asserted its hegemony as a "true civil religion," complete with its own Pantheon, martyrology, hagiography, varied and omnipresent liturgy, and "prolific polytheism," in which its sacred nature associates the living and the dead. It invented its own myths and rituals, established its own altars and temples, and using a public symbolism created a "permanent educative show" consisting of statues, frescoes, toponymy, and school textbooks.[72] The celebration of national holidays and the liturgy of commemoration helped consolidate the republican myth in spite of the troubled events of the Fourth Republic (1946–1958) and the ideological conflicts of the Cold War, which also involved contrasting perceptions of the tradition of the Revolution and the myth of the republic.[73]

We can therefore speak of a "civil religion à la française,"[74] which passes through various metamorphoses and manages eventually to find a form of syncretic coexistence between civil religiosity of the republican fatherland and popular Christian religiosity.[75] This phenomenon particularly typified the presidency of Charles de Gaulle (1958–1968). Catholic and nationalist, but also an exponent of the values of revolutionary and republican France, de Gaulle was the prime mover behind the new civil religion now reconciled with the Catholic tradition. He believed in the "religion of French greatness,"[76] and his idea of France had a sacred majesty: "France has emerged from the depths of the past. She is a living entity. She responds to the call of the centuries. Yet she remains herself through time."[77] Since 18 June 1940, when he took on the task of delivering his nation from defeat and the shame of the collaborationist government of Vichy, de Gaulle was convinced that he had maintained the greatness of France in the world. As president, he represented very effectively his mystical concept of the nation through the mastery of his prose and oratory, compelling symbolic gestures, and the impressiveness of his tall and domineering figure. This left a clear imprint on the symbolic representation of the national political liturgy.[78]

François Mitterrand, who was a tireless opponent of de Gaulle, became president (1981–1995) and inherited the general's sense of the dramatic and the theatrical in the liturgical representation of the president's role as the high priest of the nation and the republic, while clearly adapting it to his own personality of sophisticated intellectual and socialist politician. A ritual event to display the civil religion occurred on 21 May 1981 shortly after Mitterrand's election to the presidency of the republic when he visited the Pantheon, the most important temple of the republican religion. He went there on his own with the bearing of a pious man engaged in a solemn homage to great men venerated by a grateful nation.[79] Eight years later at the celebrations of the second centenary of the Revolution, the republic made a gesture of syncretic reconciliation between the republican civil religion and popular Christianity by transferring the remains of Abbot Henri Baptiste Grégoire to the Pantheon. The Catholic prelate had been the acknowledged leader of the Constitutional Church after the Civil Constitution of the Clergy (1790), although his reburial in the Pantheon did not meet with the approval of the church hierarchy.[80]

In the United States, the tradition of civil religion was upheld between the wars mainly by the priestly role of the president.[81] There was intense activity involving the symbolic representation of the civil religion through ceremonies, holidays, parades, and rituals that commemorated events and heroes of America's "sacred history" and celebrated the fundamental values of the civil community by bringing together national and local traditions.[82] President Franklin D. Roosevelt (1932–1945) made considerable use of symbolism to mobilize emotional and mythical resources around the New Deal and the fight against Nazi and fascist totalitarianism by calling upon the divine mission of American democracy with particular reference to the myth of Lincoln.[83] At the end of the Second World War, imperial antagonism to the Soviet Union gave a further impulse to the intensification of the civil religion. In the face of the enthusiasm and activism the communist religion generated among millions of people through-out the world during the Cold War, some intellectuals and politicians, both secular and religious, believed that there was a need to rekindle the citizens' faith in the principles and values of democracy to fortify them against the seductiveness of totalitarian religions and to make them more proactive in challenging them. This appeal had already been launched between the wars by the liberal philosopher and educationalist John Dewey, who was an ardent exponent of a democratic religion that had to be taught and cultivated in schools as the common faith of American citizens.[84] The appeal was repeated in the early fifties by the American sociologist J. Paul Williams, who warned that the American nation was drifting into decadence because its citizens no longer had any faith in its ideals and political values. Some religious vigor needed to be restored to democracy if this danger was to be avoided: "Democracy must become an object of religious dedication. Americans must come to look on the democratic ideal (not necessarily American practice of it) as the will of God or, if they prefer, the Law of Nature."[85] There was therefore a need for "systematic and universal indoctrination" to instill "the faith that the democratic ideal accords with ultimate reality, whether that reality be conceived in naturalistic or supernaturalistic terms." Government agen-cies and not just churches and synagogues "must teach the democratic ideal *as religion*" by establishing regular public ceremonies to glorify com-mon values, renew the commitment to a life of devotion to them, and inculcating a spirit of sacrifice toward the fatherland as the highest duty.[86]

It was in fact precisely during the fifties that the religious dimension to American politics was considerably bolstered by the portrayal of the Cold War as a crusade against atheist communism, and the exaltation of the American nation's universal mission. God had entrusted the United States with the task of revitalizing humanity by spreading democracy through-out the world. At the same time, the myths, rituals, and symbols of the civil religion continued to be an integral part of the citizens' collective life, or rather part of the life of the American population that felt integrated into society and the political order.[87] This climate of renewed enthusiasm for religious patriotism was the setting for the popular anticommunist campaign that Senator Joseph McCarthy initiated in 1950 during the democratic presidency of Harry Spencer Truman (1945–1953) and which continued until 1954. Favored by the crusading spirit of Cold War anti-communism, the sacralization of politics gained considerable momentum under the republican presidency of Eisenhower (1953–1961), a man of sincere religious feelings who was convinced that "our form of govern-ment has no sense unless it is founded in a deeply felt religious faith, and I don't care what it is."[88] As we have seen, it was under his administration that the United States Congress adopted "In God We Trust" as the official motto of the American nation and added the phrase "A Nation under God" to the pledge of allegiance to the flag.[89]

The civil religiosity of conservative republicanism, with its powerful charge of nationalistic pride, was followed in the early sixties by the renewed religiosity of democratic republicanism, which under the first Catholic president, John F. Kennedy (1961–1963), was more directed toward civil and social values. During his inaugural address, Kennedy made several references to God and renewed the American nation's sacred pact: "Here on earth God's work must truly be our own."[90] The president's Catholic faith meant the civil religion was no longer in hock to the Protestant tradition and conferred upon it a greater universality. It became a civil religion in which an increasing number of Americans could identify. But the enthusiasm instilled by the young president's charismatic personality and his message of democratic renewal changed into tragic desperation on news of his assassination, which millions of Americans following the president's death and funeral on television experienced as a national tragedy because it undermined their identity and faith in the goodness of the "chosen people."[91] As occurred with Lincoln, the assassination and funeral created an aura of saintly martyrdom around the dead president. The Kennedy myth was thus incorporated into the American civil religion, which according to some observers was revitalized by the experience. However, it was no longer conducted in a nationalistic and triumphalist manner, but reflected the American nation's humility and awareness of its reliance on universal values that went back to its origins and were the very essence of its mission to the world.[92]

It was during this period that Robert Bellah, with explicit reference to Kennedy, his presidency, and his assassination, asserted that there was an American civil religion that was not a nationalistic faith but an awareness of the duties of the American nation to transcendental values. As I have already said, this sociologist's arguments gave rise to a lengthy debate that is still continuing.[93] However, subsequent events in American history—the battle for civil rights in the name of those excluded from a civil religion that belonged to whites and the better-off, the Vietnam War which destroyed the myth of an American mission, the youth rebellion which desecrated patriotism's fundamental myths, and lastly the assassinations of Robert Kennedy and Martin Luther King Jr. in 1968—were a terrible blow to that belief in the intrinsic goodness of American democracy. They created enormous difficulties for the nation's identity and undermined the central pillar of its civil religion. Attempts to restore patriotic pride and the myths and rituals of the civil religion were made during the republican presidency of Richard Nixon (1969–1974), whose rhetoric made considerable use of religious terminology to define his political actions.[94] However, the early demise of his presidency, which was dragged down by the

Watergate scandal, aggravated the crisis of confidence among Americans and continued to unsettle their collective consciousness even when it came to the celebrations and collective rituals of the second centenary of the Revolution, an important occasion for renewing the myths of the nation's foundation, the bonds that hold it together, trust in its institutions, and faith in the values of its civil religion.

In the early seventies, the civil religion appeared to be in decline. Robert Bellah declared in 1971, "The American civil religion is an empty and broken shell,"[95] the pact with God had been broken, and "the main drift of American society is to the edge of the abyss."[96] The decline of the American civil religion appeared irreversible even to scholars, such as the historian of religions Catherine Albanese, who had no doubts about its existence stretching back to the birth of the nation.[97] Other academics, mainly exponents of the traditional religions, argued that there never had been a religious dimension to politics in American society that was distinct and independent from the traditional confessions and churches. "I would gladly assist at the burial of the conceptual confusion created by the claim that civil religion is in fact a religion," the Lutheran minister Richard J. Neuhaus told a seminar on civil religion in 1986.[98] Others feared the monopolization of myths and symbols of the civil religion by the new political and religious Right. Indeed, the myths, rituals, and symbols of the civil religion came back into fashion during the republican presidency of Ronald Reagan (1981–1989), who was convinced that the United States had a world mission founded on its faith in God, its ideals, and its force of arms. He knew very well how to play the part of the nation's high priest by continually calling for God's blessing on the chosen people of America and their power, and he wanted to lead the final ideological crusade against communism, the Empire of Evil, before realistically commencing a new policy of détente which would be the prelude to the end of the Soviet system.[99]

Later presidents did not fail to invoke God's help in their speeches or to pay homage to the myths and rituals of the civil religion, although they did not place the same emphasis as their predecessors on the priestly functions of the presidency. Leaving aside the question of presidential rituals and rhetoric, there is still much debate over whether there is a civil religion in contemporary American society and whether it still has a significant role in the collective consciousness of most American citizens.

Our voyage of exploration among civil and political religions commenced with the United States in the late eighteenth century and concludes with the United States on the eve of the third millennium after having covered two centuries of history and having examined democracies and totalitarian regimes scattered over almost all continents. The historical examples and contemporary accounts that I have cited have amply documented the extent and variety of the sacralization of politics during the last two hundred years and have demonstrated its consequences. The history of this phenomenon has encountered moments of particular intensity and periods of extraordinary exuberance which during the twentieth century coincided with the advent of totalitarian religions and the most tragic and cruel periods of human history. However, it is only right to acknowledge that there have been equally numerous and important examples of the sacralization of politics coexisting with a political system that guarantees individual liberty and the power to remove government from office through legal means.

At the start of the third millennium, civil and political religions appear everywhere to be receding, and it is not possible, at least from where I stand, to foresee whether they will continue to exist in other forms or whether the sacralization of politics will blossom again. Nor can we know what fruits that might bring. Given the origins and the history of this phenomenon taken as a whole, one might be inclined to think that the sacralization of politics were the fruit of a particular epoch, the first phase in the expansion of modernity, secularization, and industrialization during which the ancient faiths, myths, and institutions that for centuries had been considered sacred and untouchable underwent a continuous and tormented decline and indeed collapse. At the same time, new faiths, new myths, and new institutions emerged to demand an official seal of approval and sacredness. The radical upheavals, irreversible changes, traumatic conflicts, and immense wars that followed one upon another throughout this modern epoch caused or at least favored the creation of a religion of politics. We could consider the sacralization of politics to be an imposing but extraordinary and contingent phenomenon relating to tempestuous cultural, political, economic, and social changes that dominated the process of modernity through the last two hundred years. This is therefore a phenomenon that has run its course or is at least nearing the end of it, together with the epoch that created it. Perhaps these myths and beliefs will meet the same fate as the religions of ancient cities, which have become the object of archaeological studies and historical curiosity. However, you could also look on the sacralization of politics as a dormant but not extinct volcano that could explode again, scattering beliefs, faiths, and collective fanaticism.

Following the experience of totalitarian religions, there are secular free spirits that believe politics should not be sacralized to ensure the cohesiveness of a collectivity that exists as a state entity. They fear that every system of beliefs, myths, rituals, and symbols organized as the official cult of a state could produce intolerance and bigotry. "Witch hunts" are not unknown to civil religions. But there are also some equally secular free spirits who wonder whether democracy can effectively measure up to the formidable challenges of the world of today without a system of beliefs, values, rituals, and symbols, or, in other words, a civil religion that not only confers legitimacy on political institutions, but also provides individuals with an identity and a sense of belonging that is founded on the primacy of the common good and collective solidarity. This question, which had already tormented the Enlightenment precursors of the sacralization of politics, has returned to haunt democratic consciences in the final decades of the second millennium.[100]

Historians should not indulge in prophecy. However, it is legitimate to suggest tentatively that myths and beliefs will not entirely disappear from politics, and neither will the tendency to confer sacredness on secular entities. Such entities can be new or dressed up in new guises, as with the recent and unexpected resurgence of traditional religions that have become politicized in new ways and demand their primacy over the political dimension. We cannot rule out that new figures will emerge from the difficulties, tensions, and conflicts of the next phase of profound, traumatic, and irreversible change who will be convinced that they have finally understood the true meaning and purpose of human existence. Armed with this comprehensive solution to all evils, they will confer a sacred nature on their ideas and movement, and will consider it right and proper to fight a holy war with intransigence, intolerance, and violence in order to establish a better world. The fanaticism of good intentions, all-encompassing truths, and simplistic solutions will always be a breeding ground for the sacralization of politics.

*Chapter 6*

## RELIGIONS OF POLITICS

*Definitions, Distinctions, and Qualifications*

Clear-cut concepts belong to logic, not to history, where
everything is in a state of flux, of perpetual transition
and combination. Philosophical and historical ideas
differ in essence and origin; the former must be as firm
and exclusive as possible, the latter as fluid and open.
—Jacob Burckhardt, *Reflections on History*

### WHAT IS A RELIGION OF POLITICS?

Now that we have reached the conclusion, it would be useful to summarize the basic findings of our investigation of civil and political religions with a few definitions, distinctions, and qualifications. This will enable us to identify the specific features of this phenomenon, and to take up some of the general considerations concerning the sacralization of politics that we brought up in the Introduction.

A definition does not contain the revelation of a truth and it does not express the essence of a reality in a concept; it is only an instrument that directs research and structures the results. As Raymond Aron observed, definitions are never true or false, but only of varying degrees of usefulness and appropriateness.[1] The etymology of the verb "to define" is to mark out borders and therefore to restrict, distinguish, and pin down. The introduction put forward a broad definition of the religion of politics as a historical manifestation of the sacralization of politics in the present era. We now need to develop this definition further in order to identify the precise features of this phenomenon within the context of other symbolic and ritualistic manifestations of contemporary politics.

A religion of politics reflects the manner in which political activity is perceived, experienced, and represented through beliefs, myths, rituals, and symbols that refer to a sacralized secular entity inspiring faith, devotion, and togetherness among believers. A religion of politics manifests itself when a political movement or regime

   a. Consecrates the primacy of a *secular collective entity* by placing it at
   the center of a set of beliefs and myths that define the meaning and the ulti-

mate purpose of the social existence and prescribe the principles for discrimi-
nating between good and evil;

   b.  Formalizes this concept in an ethical and social *code of commandments*
that binds the individual to the sacralized entity and imposes loyalty, devotion, and even willingness to lay down one's life;

   c.  Considers its followers to be *community of the elect* and interprets its
political action as a *messianic function* to fulfill a mission of benefit to all
humanity;

   d.  Creates a *political liturgy* for the adoration of the sacralized collective
entity through the cult of the person who embodies it, and through the mythical and symbolic representation of its *sacred history*—a regular ritual evocation of events and deeds performed over a period of time by the community
of the elect.


## Civil Religion and Political Religion

The religions of politics do not constitute a single homogeneous phenomenon, like links in a chain all made of the same material. As with all religions, they share many common elements; as with all religions they have
many that are entirely different.

   Religions of politics cannot be associated solely with totalitarian movements and regimes, which have explicitly taken on the form of political
religions, whether they refuse to admit it or whether they shout it from
the roof tops, as in the case of fascism and Nazism. For the latter, this
was consistent with the irrationalist concepts of life and politics. As we
have seen, a massive contribution to the sacralization of politics in contemporary history has been made by political movements and regimes
based on rationalist, atheist, and materialist cultural premises, such as the
various strands of communism that derived from Marxism and Leninism
and always took on the essential attributes of a political religion, particularly after taking power. In other words, they sacralized their ideology,
institutions, and ways of perceiving and experiencing politics and the relationship between rulers and the ruled.

   Religions of politics, then, cannot be associated with a single type of
movement or political regime. They can sacralize democracies, autocra-
cies, equality, inequality, nation, or humanity; they can coexist with other
concepts of life and politics or oppose and suppress them; they can defend
and legitimize a political system or attempt to destroy it; they can be
conservative or revolutionary. There are substantial differences between
the civil religions of democratic regimes and the political religions of totalitarian regimes. These differences concern both their content and their
attitude toward other political movements and traditional religious insti-

tutions. Thus we need the analytical distinction between *political religions*, which refer to the sacralization of politics in totalitarian regimes, and *civil religions*, which refer to the sacralization of politics in democratic regimes.[2] We must now examine this distinction more closely and formulate a more elaborate definition.

A *political religion* is a form of sacralization of politics that has an exclusive and fundamentalist nature. It does not accept the coexistence of other political ideologies and movements, it denies the autonomy of the individual in relation to the collectivity, it demands compliance with its commandments and participation in its political cult, and it sanctifies violence as a legitimate weapon in the fight against its enemies and as an instrument of regeneration. In relation to traditional religious institutions, it either adopts a hostile attitude and aims to eliminate them, or it attempts to establish a rapport of symbiotic coexistence by incorporating the traditional religion into its own system of beliefs and myths while reducing it to a subordinate and auxiliary role.

A *civil religion* is a form of sacralization of a collective political entity that does not identify with the ideology of any particular political movement, acknowledges the separation of church and state, and, although postulating the existence of a supernatural being in the theistic sense, it coexists with traditional religious institutions without identifying with any particular religious confession. It acts as a *shared civic creed* that is above all parties and all religions. It tolerates a high degree of individual autonomy in relation to the sacralized collectivity and generally elicits spontaneous consent for compliance with its commandments of public ethics and collective liturgy.

Obviously, this distinction is not so clear-cut when it comes to specific historical examples. Moreover, the possibility that civil and political religion have common elements and affinities cannot be excluded. Historically, the distinction between civil and political religions can appear clear-cut if we compare the civil religion of the United States and the political religion of Nazi Germany or fascist Italy. But a civil religion in special circumstance can change and become as intolerant as a political religion. We will recall that this ambiguity was inherent in Rousseau's concept of civil religion. He held up the primacy of liberty as the essence of republican patriotism, but we can discern in his concept of civil religion the specter of potential dogmatism innate in the sacralization of the body politic and the nation as against the individual. This ambiguity, with all its inherent risks, was already making its presence felt in the French Revolution. Boissy d'Anglas, who spoke of the "blessed era when religion and the state were one and the same," advocated the establishment of a national political religion to educate citizens and instill in them loyalty and obedience to institutions. He held up the "religion of the ancients" as a model that "was both political and national,"[3] whereas Condorcet was against the creation of "a kind of political religion" because he considered it a "chain to bind the spirit" that violated "the most sacred rights of liberty under the pretext of teaching people to love them."[4]

## RELIGIONS OF POLITICS AND TRADITIONAL RELIGIONS

Religions of politics are a modern phenomenon. Their creation presupposes secularization, modernization, the independence of politics from traditional established religions, and the separation of church and state. This does not signify, however, that religions of politics have no connection with traditional religions. The relationship between the sacralization of politics and traditional forms of worship is very complex and varies considerably according to historical circumstance and the nature of the movements and regimes that sacralize politics.

The sacralization of politics does not necessarily involve a situation of conflict and antagonism toward traditional religions, nor does it presuppose the disavowal or complete rejection of a supernatural supreme being. There are cases in which the sacralization of politics occurs as a direct offshoot of traditional religion, and the former coexists peacefully with the latter: this is true of the American civil religion and other civil religions in Protestant states. The relationship between religions of politics and traditional religions is

a. *One of mimicry*, because a civil or political religion consciously or unconsciously adopts the dominant traditional religion's method of developing and representing a system of beliefs and myths, defining dogma and ethics, and structuring liturgy;

b. *Syncretic*, because it incorporates traditions, myths and rituals of the traditional religions, and transforms and adapts them to its own mythical and symbolic universe;

c. *Short-lived*, because in the majority of historical cases, a civil or political religion enjoys a period of vitality of variable length, and then its capacity to inspire faith and enthusiasm starts to expend itself because of the attrition of time, the passing of the circumstances that gave rise to it, generational change, or crisis and collapse in the political movement from which it was created.

The sacralization of politics, as it has been defined here as a merging of the religious and political dimensions, is a new phenomenon peculiar to modern society and mass politics, and it should be kept quite distinct from the modern manifestations of the *politicization of religion*, such as Islamic fundamentalist movements that take power in order to implement their own religious principles in society and the state. This opens a whole field of study that lies outside the subject matter of this book. We can merely mention in passing a possible line of inquiry. There is the question of the possible influence that political religions—as experiences in the symbiosis between religion, politics, and modernity—might exert consciously or unconsciously on the new return to the politicization of traditional religions and the various fundamentalisms that also tend to mix fanaticism with technology, myth with organization, and sacredness with modernity.

## New Politics, the Invention of Tradition, and the Personality Cult

We also need to clarify some particular features of civil and political religions as systems of beliefs, myths, rituals, and symbols that distinguish them from other ritual and symbolic manifestations to be found in all political movements and regimes. A religion of politics is a different phenomenon from "new politics" as defined by George Mosse in his study into the nationalization of the masses in Germany.[5] "New politics" only concerns the production of symbols and rituals, or the "aesthetics of politics" as Mosse calls it. He refers to the "creation of a political style,"[6] understood as a means to increase one's profile through rituals, symbols, festivals, and monuments to the new concept of nation and popular sovereignty. "New politics" or the "aesthetics of politics" do not always express the sacralization of politics. There are examples of "new politics" involving movements and regimes that do not profess a civil or political religion: the authoritarian regimes that do not attempt to establish their own political creed but use traditional religions as arsenals of myths, rituals, and symbols to adapt the "new politics" to mass society. Franco's regime in Spain was a typical example of this. Its use of the sacred, through various forms of liturgical representation linked to the Catholic tradition, aimed to satisfy "political needs by adapting a traditional symbolic heritage in ideological mode" rather than developing and establishing its own independent system for sacralizing politics.[7] As the political scientist Antonio Elorza has observed, "Francoism [unlike fascism and Nazism] is not a political religion, but the expression of the totalitarian propensity of some Catholic servicemen."[8]

   Similar clarifications need to made for the distinction between the sacralization of politics and the "invention of tradition" as defined by Eric Hobsbawm as "a set of practices, normally governed by overtly and tacitly accepted rules and of a ritual or symbolic nature, which seek to inculcate certain values and norms of behavior by repetition, which automatically implies continuity with the past."[9] Religions of politics, like traditional religions, also contain some element of the "invention of tradition," but recognition of this fact does not mean that the phenomenon is no more than the artificial production of myths and rituals to be exploited for the legitimatization of power in the eyes of the masses, because civil and political religions also concern beliefs, values, and principles that attempt to define the meaning and fundamental purpose of a collectivity's existence. This distinction between instrument and invention on the one hand, and belief and faith on the other, also appears in Hobsbawm's more recent work, in which he defines socialism as "a system of hope and belief, which had some characteristics of a secular religion"[10] and places it in the context of the secular religions of the twentieth century: "The Short Twentieth Century had been an era of religious wars, though the most militant and bloodthirsty of its religions were secular ideologies of nineteenth-century vintage, such as socialism and nationalism, whose god-equivalents were either abstractions or politicians venerated in the manner of divinities."[11]

As the historian Renato Moro has very incisively pointed out, the sacralization of politics is a "theological" problem and not simply a question of ritual, and for this reason cannot be interpreted solely in terms of its use to manipulate the masses. Such analysis would reduce the origin and meaning of civil or political religion to an "exclusive construction of national symbols and rituals from above" for "essentially utilitarian purposes" and "in terms of political immediacy," while entirely ignoring "the elements of faith and belief, and ultimately examining the fundamental nature of this mentality."[12]

Religions of politics are not merely concerned with a method of government exercised by a political class, which invents its own tradition to legitimize its power and interests through myths, rituals, and symbols; neither is it exclusively concerned with the need in a mass era to display abstract political ideas and myths through the dramatic and symbolic representation of an "aesthetics of politics." By religion of politics, we mean a way of interpreting life and history, and perceiving politics—not just the calculations of power and vested interests. Moreover, a religion of politics takes these interpretations and perceptions much further—to the point where they define the meaning and final cause of existence. In order to achieve its aims, a religion of politics can obviously make use of an invented tradition and of the aesthetics of politics to inculcate faith and devotion toward the sacralized political entity among the masses.

A final clarification concerns charismatic leaders and personality cults, which are without question of doubt the most conspicuous and widespread manifestation of the sacralization of politics. It would be difficult to understand the history of civil or political religions without examining both the political and the mythical roles exercised by their charismatic leaders, who excite enthusiasm, passion, faith, and devotion around them—the typical attitudes of a religious movement. It must be stressed that the sacralization of politics is not restricted to the cult of the charismatic leader. Religions of politics are expressions of collective movements and therefore cannot be considered merely creations or derivations of individual charisma. Such an interpretation would result from an overly narrow view that leaves out lasting and well-established collective and institutional manifestations of the sacralization of politics that are completely unrelated to a personality cult but refer to the consecration of a collective entity alone.

### FINAL CONSIDERATIONS FOR A CONCLUSION THAT IS NOT FINAL

In recent years, the increasing research into civil and political religions has confirmed the need for greater critical understanding of the application of these concepts and the avoidance of generalized, vague, and indiscriminate use. At the same time, it has underscored the usefulness of such studies as an essential contribution to the history of contemporary beliefs as they adopt a cognitive approach that refrains from defining its own "truth." The Anglican priest and historian of the church and Christianity Owen Chadwick has written that the historian's task is not "to answer questions on whether a belief is true," but to devote his "endeavor to questions appropriate to [his] discipline, why belief arose, how it was believed, how its axioms affected society, and in what manner it faded away."[13]

Whatever one's concept of religion or theory of "true" religion, the study of totalitarianisms as religious phenomena does not in any way involve stretching the truth or distorting historical realities. The same is true of the sacralization of politics utilized by democratic movements and regimes in ways and forms that lead the political dimension to take on a religious one, which may or may not derive from a traditional religion but does center upon sacralization of a secular entity. If we broaden our view, we can observe how the problem of the sacralization of politics in contemporary history covers an extensive and complex reality that goes beyond civil and political religions that have achieved institutional status: a reality to which we can gain access if we understand that "many apparently profane events, which may even be of a political or entirely economic nature, prove to have profoundly religious associations on close examination," as the historian of religions Raffaele Pettazzoni has written.[14] Indeed, he had no qualms about including the civil and political ideals of the *Risorgimento* and the Resistance in a brief history of religion in Italy.

There are various ways of interpreting religions of politics through definitions of religious phenomena in general, as we saw in the first chapter, but I believe that none of these theories—the *crowd manipulation*, the functionalist, the fideistic, and the numinous—can be sufficient in itself to explain the sacralization of politics as a phenomenon, just as they are not sufficient for the analysis of the traditional religions. A religion of politics, like any other religion, can contain *crowd manipulation* features, can fulfill the functions of social cohesion and the legitimization of power, can satisfy the religious sentiment of the masses, and can be the genuine expression of a numinous experience. It is the task of the academic to investigate these elements and assess the part that each plays in the actual life of real religious manifestations. Any preconceived preference for a single interpretation could compress the complexity of the phenomenon into a narrow perspective and impede a realistic historical understanding of its nature. On the other hand, it is important to note that to study a political movement as a secular religion in any manner is to study only one of its aspects; it does not amount to a complete explanation of its nature and historical meaning.

Whether or not we believe in the existence of secular religions, we cannot deny proven historical facts. Mass fanaticism, enthusiasm for myths, personality cults, dogmatic ideologies, and implacable hatred all in the name of a sacralized entity: these are the tragic realities of contemporary history. They occurred on such a vast scale and were associated with ideologies, political systems, historical traditions, and economic, social, and geographic situations so different as to create a massive and highly complex phenomenon whose special characteristics make it particular to the twentieth century and above all the period between the two world wars. We also need to investigate the origins, nature, and meaning of this phenomenon, and to understand rationally its novelty and specificity, while taking into account its position in history. In spite of the sudden fault lines and unexpected surges, continuity always coexisted with change, and the past flowed into the present, while at the same time breaking with it. In history the new often has the appearance of the ancient, and the ancient is often imbued with unexpected and unpredictable innovation.

At the beginning of the third millennium, the sacralization of politics appears everywhere to be in retreat. Totalitarian religions have been destroyed, rejected, or at very least abandoned. Even in democratic regimes, where the presence of a civil religion was never domineering or burdensome, the sacralization of politics appears to be restricted to a residual and prosaic ceremonial involving government and the governed in homage to fading beliefs and myths that have become a sham and are no longer relevant.

However, it is impossible to say whether the sacralization of politics has disappeared entirely from today's world or whether or not the conditions exist for its eventual reappearance.

Following the collapse of the communist religions, the sacralization of the nation has in many places undergone an unexpected and often violent reawakening. This has brought with it the threat of new political religions based on exclusive, intolerant, and fundamentalist nationalism with powerful racist connotations. In a very different way, the question of civil religions is again topical in democratic regimes, as it expresses an ethical and political need for those who wish to deal with the crisis of democracy, which is exposed to the risks and dangers of internal fragmentation and social disintegration due to gradual increase in demands by individuals and groups for greater autonomy. Such fragmentation naturally challenges the shared ideals and political institutions that represent a collective identity which now looks increasingly artificial and unreal. Faced with such phenomena, it is difficult to say whether the current decline in the sacralization of politics is a passing phase or an irreversible trend. The springs from which beliefs and myths flow to bestow a sacred nature on politics are unlikely to dry up in the near future, but it is still impossible to predict in what ways new civil and political religions could be formed or what the outcomes could be.

This book could make a useful contribution to the analysis of the phenomenon and help us to reflect on the problems its poses for democratic society, but as the Introduction made clear, this study has examined the sacralization of politics as a historical experience in the past, and not as a current or future need, opportunity, or threat.

# NOTES

## CHAPTER ONE
### A NEVER-NEVER RELIGION

1. A. Piette, *Les religiosités séculières*, Paris 1993, p. 44. For a general discussion of secular religion, see also E. B. Koenker, *Secular Salvations: The Rites and Symbols of Political Religions*, Philadelphia 1965; W. Stark, *The Sociology of Religion: A Study of Christendom*. I. *Established Religion*, London 1966; *Religione e politica*, Padova 1978; J.-J. Wunenburger, *Le sacré*, Paris 1981; J.-P. Sironneau, *Sécularisation et religions politiques*, Le Haye-Paris-New York 1982; C. Rivière, *Le liturgie politiche* (1988), Como 1998; R. Díaz-Salazar, S. Giner, F. Velasco (ed.), *Formas modernas de religión*, Madrid 1994; R. Moro, "Religione e politica nell'età della secolarizzazione: riflessioni su un recente volume di Emilio Gentile," *Storia contemporanea*, 2, 1995, pp. 255–325; J.-P. Willaime, *Sociologie des religions*, Paris 1995; A. Elorza, *La religione politica. I fondamentalismi* (1995), Rome 1996.

2. R. Aron, "L'avenir des religions séculières," in id., *L'âge des empires et l'avenir de la France*, Paris 1946, p. 288.

3. G. Stanton Ford (ed.), *Dictatorship in the Modern World*, Minneapolis 1935.

4. A. Keller, *Church and State on the European Continent*, London 1936, p. 68.

5. See F. A. Voigt, *Unto Caesar*, London 1938.

6. E. Voegelin, "Le religioni politiche" (1938), in id., *La politica: dai simboli alle esperienze*, Milan 1993.

7. M.-J.-A.-N. Condorcet, "Premier mémoire sur l'instruction publique," in *OEuvre de Condorcet*, Paris 1847, vol. 7, p. 212.

8. Quoted in J. D. Schultz, J. G. West Jr., I. MacLean (ed.), *Encyclopedia of Religion in American Politics*, Phoenix (Ariz.) 1999, p. 53.

9. L. Settembrini, *Ricordanze della mia vita*, ed. M. Themelly, Milan 1961, p. 96.

10. K. Polanyi, "The Essence of Fascism," in J. Lewis, K. Polanyi, D. K. Kitchin (ed.), *Christianity and the Social Revolution*, London 1937 (1935), p. 385.

11. R. Niebuhr, "Christian Politics and Communist Religion," in ibid., p. 468.

12. See R. Bellah, "Civil Religion in America," *Daedalus*, 1, 1967, pp. 1–21.

13. Ibid., p. 8. For the main arguments, see also D. R. Cutler (ed.), *The Religious Situation, 1968*, Boston 1968; E. A. Smith (ed.), *The Religion of the Republic*, Philadelphia 1971; R. E. Richey, D. G. Jones (ed.), *American Civil Religion*, New York 1974; G. Gehrig, *American Civil Religion: An Assessment*, Storrs (Conn.) 1979; M. W. Hughey, *Civil Religion and Moral Order: Theoretical and Historical Dimensions*, Westport (Conn.) 1983; N. Lehmann de Silva, *A Religião Civil do Estado Moderno*, Brasilia 1985; H. Kleger, A. Müller (ed.), *Reli-*

*gion des Bürgers. Zivilreligion in Amerika und Europa,* Munich 1986; R. Schieder, *Civil Religion. Die religiöse Dimension der politischen Kultur,* Gütersloh 1987. A brief summary of the debate can be found in J. A. Mathisen, "Twenty Years after Bellah: Whatever Happened to American Civil Religion?" *Sociological Analysis,* 2, 1989, pp. 129–46.

14. As the literature on political symbolism is immense, I will only mention a few general works: M. García Pelayo, *Miti e simboli politici* (1964), Turin 1970; M. Edelmann, *Gli usi simbolici della politica* (1979), Naples 1987; D. I. Kertzer, *Riti e simboli del potere* (1988), Rome–Bari 1989; Rivière, *Le liturgie politiche;* L. Sfez, *La symbolique politique,* Paris 1988; G. Fedel, *Simboli e politica,* Naples 1991; G. Navarrino, *Le forme rituali della politica,* Rome–Bari 2001.

15. The bibliography on the sacralization of politics has increased considerably in the last few decades. Recent contributions include E. Gentile, "Fascism as Political Religion," *Journal of Contemporary History,* 2–3, 1990, pp. 229–51; P. Brooker, *The Faces of Fraternalism: Nazi Germany, Fascist Italy, and Imperial Japan,* Oxford 1991; J. Thrower, *Marxism-Leninism of Soviet Society: God's Commissar,* Lewiston 1992; E. Gentile, *The Sacralization of Politics in Fascist Italy,* trans. Keith Botsford, Cambridge (Mass.) 1996; Piette, *Les religiosités séculières;* S. Giner, "La religión civil," in Díaz-Salazar, Giner, Velasco (ed.), *Formas modernas de religión,* pp. 129–71; J. Casanova, *Public Religions in the Modern World,* Chicago 1994; H. Maier, *Politische Religionen. Die totalitären Regime und das Christentum,* Freiburg 1995; S. Behrenbeck, *Der Kult um die toten Helden. Nationalistische Mythen, Riten und Symbole 1923 bis 1945,* Neuburg a.d. Donau 1996; A. J. Klinghoffer, *Red Apocalypse: The Religious Evolution of Soviet Communism,* Lanham (Md.) 1996; H. Maier (ed.), *Totalitarismus und politische Religionen,* Paderborn, Germany, 1996; H. Maier, M. Schäfer (ed.), *Totalitarismus und politische Religionen. Konzepte des Diktaturvergleichs,* Paderborn, Germany, 1997; P. Berghoff, *Der Tod des politischen Kollektives. Politische Religion und das Sterben und Töten für Volk, Nation und Rasse,* Berlin 1997; Y. Karow, *Deutsches Opfer. Kultische Selbstauslöschung auf den Reichsparteitagen der NSDAP,* Berlin 1997; M. Ley, *Apokalypse und Moderne. Aussätze zu politischen Religionen,* Vienna 1997; M. Ley, J. H. Schoeps (ed.), *Der Nationalsozialismus als politische Religion,* Bodenheim 1997; B. Unfried, C. Schindler (ed.), *Riten, Mythen und Symbole. Die Arbeiterbewegung zwische "Zivilreligion" und Volkskultur,* Leipzig 1997; C. E. Bärsch, *Die politische Religion des Nationalsozialismus,* Munich 1998; M. Huttner, *Totalitarismus und Säkulare Religionen. Zur Frühgeschichte totalitarismuskritischer Begriffs- und Theoriebildung in Großbritannien,* Bonn 1999; "Identità nazionale e religione civile in Italia," *Rassegna italiana di Sociologia,* 2, 1999; K. G. Riegel, "Transplanting the Political Religion of Marxism-Leninism to China: The Case of the Sun Yat-sen University in Moscow (1925–1930)," in K. H. Pohl (ed.), *Chinese Thought in a Global Context,* Leiden-Boston-Cologne 1999, pp. 327–58; Y. Déloye and O. Ihl, "Deux figures singulières de l'universel: la république et le sacré," in *La démocratie en France. 1. Idéologies,* ed. M. Sadoun, Paris 2000, pp. 138–246; E. Gentile, "The Sacralization of Politics: Definitions, Interpretations and Reflections on the Question of Secular Religion and Totalitarianism," *Totalitarian Movements and Political Reli-*

*gions*, 1, 2000, pp. 18–55; H. Maier (ed.), *Wege in die Gewalt. Die moderne politischen Religionen*, Frankfurt a.M. 2000.

16. See R. J. Neuhaus, "From Civil Religion to Public Philosophy," in L. S. Rouner (ed.), *Civil Religion and Political Theology*, Notre Dame (Ind.) 1986; M. Spiro, "Religion: Problems of Definition and Explanation," in M. Banton (ed.), *Anthropological Approaches to the Study of Religion*, New York 1966; G. A. Kelly, *Politics and Religious Consciousness in America*, New Brunswick–London 1984.

17. See R. Robertson, *The Sociological Interpretation of Religion*, Oxford 1972.

18. G. Mosca, *Elementi di scienza politica* (1895), Bari 1953, vol. 1, pp. 283–85.

19. A. Aulard, *Le culte de la raison et le culte de l'Etre suprême, 1793–1794*, Paris 1892. However, when he was later examining the relationship between Christianity and the French Revolution, Aulard admitted that Christianity had been in great danger and that "Christianity's dangerous adventure at the time of the cult of Reason and the Supreme Being was the most significant episode in the religious history of the French Revolution" (A. Aulard, *Le christianisme et la révolution française*, Paris 1925, pp. 9–10).

20. G. Ferrero, *Il potere* (1942), Milan 1981, pp. 157–59.

21. A more sophisticated and updated version of this interpretation is put forward by E. J. Hobsbawm and T. Ranger, *The Invention of Tradition*, Cambridge, U.K. 1983.

22. G. Le Bon, *Psychologie du socialisme* (1895), Paris 1920, p. 95.

23. G. Le Bon, *The Crowd: A Study of the Popular Mind* (1895), Atlanta 1982, p. 60.

24. Ibid., pp. 103–4.

25. G. Le Bon, *Psychologie des foules* (1895), Paris 1920, p. 194.

26. G. Le Bon, *Leggi psicologiche della evoluzione dei popoli* (1894), Milan 1927, pp. 161–65.

27. R. Michels, *Political Parties. A Sociological Study of the Oligarchical Tendencies of Modern Democracy* (1911), New York n.d., p. 67.

28. H. De Man, *Il superamento del marxismo* (1927), Bari 1929, pp. 133–43.

29. E. Durkheim, *The Elementary Forms of Religious Life* (1912), trans. Carol Cosman, Oxford 1985, 2001, p. 46.

30. Ibid., p. 320.

31. Ibid., p. 11.

32. Ibid., p. 174.

33. E. Durkheim, "De la définition, des phénomènes religieux," in *Année sociologique*, 11, 1899, p. 20.

34. Durkheim, *The Elementary Forms*, p. 161.

35. A. Mathiez, *La Théophilantropie et le culte décadaire (1796–1801)*, Paris 1904; id., *Les origines des cultes révolutionnaires, 1789–1792* (1904), Geneva 1977; id., *Contributions a l'histoire religieuse de la révolution française*, Paris 1907.

36. Ibid., pp. 31–33.

37. R. Otto, *The Idea of the Holy: An Inquiry into the Non-Rational Factor in the Idea of the Divine and Its Relation to the Rational* (1917), London and New York 1958.

38. Ibid., p. 5.

39. Ibid., p. 33.
40. A. Tilgher, "Numinosità del dopoguerra" (1938), in id., *Mistiche nuove e mistiche antiche*, Rome 1946, p. 47.
41. Ibid.
42. B. Croce, "Per la rinascita dell'idealismo" (1908), in *Cultura e vita morale*, Bari 1953, p. 35.
43. Durkheim, *The Elementary Forms*, p. 322.
44. Ibid., pp. 322–23.
45. M. Eliade, *The Sacred and the Profane* (1957), San Diego–New York–London 1959, pp. 203–5, 209.
46. See P. E. Hammond (ed.), *The Sacred in a Secular Age*, Berkeley 1985; J. A. Beckford (ed.), *New Religious Movements and Rapid Social Change*, London 1986; G. Filoramo, *I nuovi movimenti religiosi. Metamorfosi del sacro*, Rome–Bari 1986; C. Rivière, A. Piette (ed.), *Nouvelles idoles, nouveaux cultes. Dérives de la sacralité*, Paris 1990; Wunenburger, *Le sacré*; G. Kepel, *La revanche de Dieu*, Paris 1991; G. Filoramo, *Le vie del sacro. Modernità e religione*, Turin 1994.
47. R. Bastide, *Il sacro selvaggio* (1975), Milan 1979, p. 195.
48. Ibid., p. 206.
49. Rivière, *Le liturgie politiche*, p. 145.
50. Filoramo, *Le vie del sacro*, p. 25.
51. Ibid., p. 28.
52. Ibid., p. 35.
53. S. Giner, *La religione civile*, in *Religio. Ruolo del sacro, coesione sociale e nuove forme di solidarietà nella società contemporanea*, ed. C. Mongardini and M. Ruini, Rome 1998, pp. 153–54.
54. Sironneau, *Sécularisation et religions politiques*, pp. 196–97.
55. Quoted in Ley, *Apokalypse und moderne*, p. 12.

CHAPTER TWO
CIVIL RELGIONS AND POLITICAL RELIGIONS

1. See M. Henry, *The Intoxication of Power: An Analysis of Civil Religion in Relation to Ideology*, Dordrecht 1979.
2. C. Schmitt, "Teologia politica" (1922), in id., *Le categorie del politico*, Bologna 1972, p. 61. On the similarities between the concept of God and the concept of the state, see D. Nicholls, *Deity and Domination: Images of God and the State in the Nineteenth and Twentieth Centuries*, London–New York 1989.
3. Quoted in A. Aulard, *Le culte de la raison et le culte de l'Etre suprême 1793–1794* (1892), Paris 1909, pp. 8–9. See A. Mathiez, *Les origines des cultes révolutionnaires 1789–1792* (1904), Geneva 1977, pp. 15–16.
4. Quoted in N. Luhmann, "Grundwerke als Zivilreligion. Zur wissenschaftlichen Karriere eines Themas," in *Religione e politica*, Padua 1978, p. 51.
5. G.-F. Coyer, *Dissertations pour être lues: la première sur le vieux mot de patrie; la seconde sur la nature du peuple*, The Hague 1755, pp. 20–21.

6. B. Franklin, *Proposal Relating the Education of Youth in Pennsylvania* (1749), quoted in C. L. Albanese, *The Sons of the Fathers: The Civil Religion of the American Revolution*, Philadelphia 1976, p. viii.

7. J.-J. Rousseau, *Scritti politici*, ed. M. Garin, vol. 2, Bari 1971, p. 62.

8. J.-J. Rousseau, "Book IV, Chapter VIII—Civil Religion," in *The Social Contract*, trans. G.D.H. Cole, London: Everyman, 1973, pp. 270–71.

9. Ibid., p. 273.

10. Ibid., p. 276.

11. Rousseau, "Chapter IV—Education," in *Considerations on the Government of Poland*, completed but not published in 1772.

12. *Ibid.*

13. Rousseau, "Book II, Chapter VII—The Legislator," in *The Social Contract*, p. 115.

14. See S. E. Ahlstrom, *A Religious History of the American People*, New Haven 1976; M. E. Marty, *Pilgrims in Their Own Land. 500 Years of Religion in America*, New York 1984; K. D. Wald, *Religion and Politics in the United States*, Washington 1992.

15. A. de Tocqueville, *Democracy in America* (1835), London 1994, vol. 1, chap. 17, p. 308.

16. Ibid., vol. 1, chap. 17, p. 305.

17. F. Grund, *The Americans in Their Moral, Social, and Political Relations*, London 1837, vol. 1, p. 294.

18. See Marty, *Pilgrims in Their Own Land*, pp. 154 ff.

19. See E. L. Tuveson, *Redeemer Nation: The Idea of America's Millennial Role*, Chicago 1968; Albanese, *The Sons of the Fathers*; E. Marienstras, *Nous, le peuple. Les origines du nationalisme américain*, Paris 1988.

20. C. Cherry (ed.), *God's New Israel. Religious Interpretations of American Destiny*, Englewood Cliffs 1971; Albanese, *The Sons of the Fathers*; Marienstras, *Nous, le peuple*.

21. W. Zelinsky, *Nation into State: The Shifting Symbolic Foundations of American Nationalism*, Chapel Hill–London 1988, pp. 20 ff.

22. B. Schwartz, *George Washington: The Making of an American Symbol*, New York 1987. On the development of myths, rituals, and symbols relating to the American civil religion, see M. Curti, *The Roots of American Loyalty*, New York 1946; R. B. Nye, *This Almost Chosen People*, Toronto 1966; J. O. Robertson, *American Myth, American Reality*, New York 1980; P. Shaw, *American Patriots and the Rituals of Revolution*, Cambridge (Mass.) 1981; J. Bodnar, *Bonds of Affection: Americans Define Their Patriotism*, Princeton (N.J.) 1996; A. Boime, *The Unveiling of the National Icons: A Plea for Patriotic Iconoclasm in a Nationalist Era*, Cambridge 1998; C. E. O'Leary, *To Die For: The Paradox of American Patriotism*, Princeton (N.J.) 1999.

23. Albanese, *The Sons of the Fathers*, p. 107.

24. J. H. St. J. Crèvecoeur, *Letters from an American Farmer*, ed. Susan Manning, Oxford 1997, pp. 42–44.

25. R. Bellah, *The Broken Covenant: American Civil Religion in Time of Trial*, New York 1975, pp. 36–60.

26. H. Melville, *Moby Dick* (1851), New York 1967, pp. 104.

27. H. Melville, *White Jacket* (1850), quoted in Zelinsky, *Nation into State*, p. 286, n. 15.

28. See W. J. Wolf, *The Religion of Abraham Lincoln*, New York 1963.

29. Ibid., p. 159.

30. See Zelinsky, *Nation into State*, pp. 46–48.

31. L. Lewis, *Myths after Lincoln*, New York 1929.

32. F. Merk, *Manifest Destiny and Mission in American History*, New York 1956; E. McNall Burns, *The American Idea of Mission*, New Brunswick 1957; A. K. Weinberg, *Manifest Destiny*, Gloucester (Mass.) 1958.

33. Quoted in P. Bairati (ed.), *I profeti dell'impero americano*, Turin 1975, p. 247.

34. See R. V. Pierard, R. D. Linder, *Civil Religion and the Presidency*, Grand Rapids (Mich.) 1988, p. 153.

35. See R. H. Abrams, *Preachers Present Arms*, Scottsdale (Pa.) 1969; J. F. Piper, *The American Churches in World War I*, Athens (Ohio) 1985.

36. See C. Garrett, *Respectable Folly: Millenarians and the French Revolution in France and England*, Baltimore–London 1975.

37. M. Ozouf, *La festa rivoluzionaria (1789–1799)* (1976), Bologna 1982, pp. 416–35.

38. M. Ozouf, "Religione rivoluzionaria," in F. Furet, M. Ozouf, *Dizionario critico della rivoluzione francese* (1988), Milan 1989, pp. 535–45.

39. M. Ozouf, *L'homme régénéré*, Paris 1989, pp. 116–57.

40. Ozouf, *La festa rivoluzionaria*.

41. Quoted in A. Mathiez, *Les origines des cultes révolutionnaires 1789–1792* (1904), Geneva 1977, p. 21.

42. Ibid., pp. 17–29.

43. A. de Tocqueville, *The Old Regime and the Revolution* (1856), ed. François Furet and Françoise Mélonio, Chicago and London 1998, pp. 99–101.

44. See *Libre pensée et religion laïque en France. De la fin du Second Empire à la fin de la Troisième République*, Strasbourg 1980; D. G. Charlton, *Secular Religions in France, 1815–70*, New York 1963; P. Hutton, *The Cult of the Revolutionary Tradition: The Blanquists in French Politics, 1864–1893*, Berkeley–Los Angeles–London 1981; E. Berenson, *Populist Religion and Left-Wing Politics in France, 1830–1852*, Princeton (N.J.) 1984.

45. Y. Déloye and O. Ihl, "Deux figures singulières de l'universel: la république et le sacré," in *La démocratie en France. 1. Idéologies*, edited by M. Sadoun, Paris 2000, pp. 138–246.

46. R. Sanson, *Les 14 juillet. Fête et conscience nationale 1789–1975*, Paris 1976; *Les usages politiques des fêtes au XIX–XX siècles*, ed. A. Crobin, N. Gérôme, and D. Tartakowsky, Paris 1994; O. Ihl, *La fête républicaine*, Paris 1996.

47. A. Prost, "Les monuments aux morts. Culte républicaine? Culte civique? Culte patriotique?" in P. Nora (ed.), *Les lieux de mémoire*, vol. 1, *La République*, Paris 1984, pp. 195–225.

48. F. Heer, *Europe, Mother of Revolutions* (1964), London 1971, p. 47.

49. Quoted in ibid., pp. 317–19.

50. L. Feuerbach, *Principi della filosofia. Necessità di una trasformazione*, in *La sinistra hegeliana*, Bari 1966, p. 309. See J. H. Billington, *Fire in the Minds of*

*Men: Origins of the Revolutionary Faith*, New York 1980; M. Carrouges, *La mystique du surhomme*, Paris 1948; J. Talmon, *Political Messianism: The Romantic Phase*, London 1960; id., *Myth of the Nation and Vision of Revolution: Ideological Polarization in the Twentieth Century*, London 1981.

51. C.J.H. Hayes, *Nationalism: A Religion*, New York 1960. On nationalism as deification of the nation, see R. Rocker, *Nationalism and Culture*, Los Angeles 1937; G. L. Mosse, *Germans and Jews: The Right, the Left, and the Search for a "Third Force" in Pre-Nazi Germany*, New York 1970; B. G. Shafer, *Faces of Nationalism. New Realities and Old Myths*, New York 1972; G. L. Mosse, *Toward the Final Solution: A History of European Racism*, London 1978; id., *Masses and Man: Nationalist and Fascist Perceptions of Reality*, New York 1980; P. H. Merkl, N. Smart (ed.), *Religion and Politics in the Modern World*, New York–London 1983; *Religion, Ideology and Nationalism in Europe and America*, Jerusalem 1986; G. Hosking, G. Schöpflin (ed.), *Myths and Nationhood*, London 1997.

52. G. L. Mosse, *The Nationalization of the Masses*, New York 1974.

53. A. J. Mayer, *Il potere dell'Ancien Régime fino alla prima guerra mondiale* (1981), Rome–Bari 1982, pp. 124–34; E. J. Hobsbawm and T. Ranger, *The Invention of Tradition* (1983).

54. For a few examples of the sacralization of politics as a function of national identity during the nineteenth and twentieth centuries, see F. Schellack, *Nationalfeiertage in Deutschland von 1871 bis 1945*, Frankfurt a.M. 1990; B. Tobia, *Una patria per gli italiani. Spazi, itinerari, monumenti nell'Italia nuova (1870–1900)*, Rome–Bari 1991; U. Levra, *Fare gli italiani. Memoria e celebrazione del Risorgimento*, Turin 1992; G. L. Mosse, *Confronting the Nation: Jewish and Western Nationalism*, Hanover (N.H.)–London 1993; J. R. Gillis (ed.), *Commemorations: The Politics of National Identity*, Princeton (N.J.) 1994; R. Koselleck, M. Jeismann (ed.), *Der politische Totenkult. Kriegerdenkmäler in der Moderne*, Munich 1994; M. Ridolfi, "Feste civili e religioni politiche nel "laboratorio" della nazione italiana (1860–1895)," *Memoria e Ricerca*, 5, 1995, pp. 83–108; R. Alings, *Monument und Nation. Das Bild vom Nationalstaat in Medium Denkmal; zum Verhältnis von Nation und Staat in deutschen Keiserreich 1871–1918*, Berlin–New York 1996; C. Brice, "Pouvoirs, liturgies et monuments politiques à Rome (1870–1911)," in M. A. Visceglia, C. Brice (ed.), *Cérémoniel et rituel à Rome (XVIᵉ–XIXᵉ)*, Rome 1997; I. Porciani, *La festa della nazione. Rappresentazione dello Stato e spazi sociali nell'Italia unita*, Bologna 1997; J. Vogel, *Nationen im Gleichschritt. Der Kult der "Nation in Waffen" in Deutschland und Frankreich, 1871–1914*, Göttingen 1997; C. Brice, *Monumentalité publique et politique à Rome. Le Vittoriano*, Rome 1998; S. Behrenbeck, A. Nützenadel (ed.), *Inszenierungen des Nationalstaats. Politische Feiern in Italien und Deutschland seit 1860/71*, Cologne 2000.

55. B. Mussolini quoted in E. Gentile, *Il mito dello Stato nuovo*, Rome–Bari 1999, p. 116; A. Gramsci, *Cronache torinesi 1913–1917*, ed. S. Caprioglio, Turin 1980, p. 329. For some aspects of the sacralization of politics in democratic, socialist, and working-class movements during the nineteenth and twentieth centuries, see M. Dommanget, *Histoire du premier Mai*, Paris 1972; *Libre pensée et religion laïque*; V. L. Lüdtke, *The Alternative Culture: Socialist Labor in Imperial*

*Germany*, Oxford 1985; M. Ridolfi, *Il partito della repubblica. I repubblicani in Romagna e le origini del Pri nell'Italia liberale (1872–1895)*, Milan 1989; G. C. Donno (ed.), *Storie e Immagini del 1̊ Maggio*, Manduria-Bari–Rome 1990; "La trasformazione della festa," *Memoria e Ricerca*, 5, 1995; B. Unfried, C. Schindler (ed.), *Riten, Mythen und Symbole. Die Arbeiterbewegung zwischen "Zivilreligion" und Volkskultur*, Leipzig 1997; D. Mengozzi, *La morte e l'immortale. La morte laica da Garibaldi a Costa*, Manduria–Rome–Bari 2000; V. Peillon, *Jean Jaurès et la religion du socialisme*, Paris 2000.

56. On the decisive influence that the Great War and the cult of fallen soldiers had on the sacralization of politics during the twentieth century with particular reference to the myth of the nation, see A. Prost, *Les Anciens combattants et la société française 1914–1939*, vol. 3, *Mentalités et idéologies*, Paris 1977; K. D. Bracher, *Il Novecento secolo delle ideologie* (1982), Rome–Bari 1984; G. Canal, "La retorica della morte. I monumenti ai caduti della Grande Guerra," *Rivista di storia contemporanea*, 4, 1982, pp. 659–69; R. N. Stromberg, *Redemption by War: The Intellectuals and 1914*, Lawrence (Kansas) 1982; M. Lurz, *Kriegerdenkmäler in Deutschland*, vol. 3, *Der 1.Weltkrieg*, vol. 4, *Weimare Republik*, Heidelberg 1985; R. Shipley, *To Mark Our Place: A History of Canadian War Memorials*, Toronto 1987; A. Becker, *Les Monuments aux morts, mémoire de la Grande Guerre*, Paris 1988; A. R. Young, "'We throw the torch': Canadian Memorials of the Great War and the Mythology of Heroic Sacrifice," *Journal of Canadian Studies*, 4, 1989–1990, pp. 5–28; J. W. Baird, *To Die for Germany: Heroes in the Nazi Pantheon*, Bloomington-Indianapolis 1990; C. Maclean and J. Phillips, *The Sorrow and the Pride: New Zealand War Memorials*, Wellington 1990; G. L. Mosse, *Fallen Soldiers: Reshaping the Memory of the World Wars*, New York and Oxford 1990; Koselleck, Jeismann (ed.), *Der politische Totenkult*; A. Gregory, *The Silence of Memory: Armistice Day 1919–1946*, Oxford-Providence 1994; E. Gentile, "Un'apocalisse nella modernità. La Grande Guerra e il Mito della Rigenerazione della politica," *Storia contemporanea*, 5, 1995, pp. 733–87; J. M. Winter, *Sites of Memory, Sites of Mourning: The Great War in European Cultural History*, Cambridge, U.K., 1995; Alings, *Monument und Nation*; J. F. Vance, *Death So Noble. Memory, Meaning, and the First World War*, Vancouver 1997; K. S. Inglis, *Sacred Places: War Memorials in the Australian Landscape*, Melbourne 1998; A. King, *Memorials of the Great War in Britain: The Symbolism and Politics of Remembrance*, Oxford–New York 1998.

57. G. Amendola, *La democrazia italiana contro il fascismo (1922–1924)*, Milan–Naples 1960, pp. 193–94.

58. N. Papafava, "Il fascismo e la costituzione," *La Rivoluzione Liberale*, 28 August 1923.

59. Archives Ministère des Affaires Étrangères, Paris, Europe, 1918–1940, Italy, vol. 62, 2 November 1922.

60. R. De Nolva, "Le mysticisme et l'esprit révolutionnaire du fascisme," *Mercure de France*, 1 November 1924.

61. H. W. Schneider, *Making the Fascist State*, New York 1928, pp. 216–30.

62. H. W. Schneider and S. B. Clough, *Making Fascists*, Chicago 1929, pp. 73–75.

63. Ibid., p. 189.

64. H. Heller, *L'Europa e il fascismo* (1931), ed. C. Amirante, Milan 1987, p. 99.

65. M. Prélot, *L'empire fasciste*, Paris 1936, pp. 226–28.

66. See E. Gentile, *The Sacralization of Politics*; R. Suzzi Valli, "Riti del ventennale," *Storia contemporanea*, 6, 1993, pp. 1019–55; C. Galeotti, *Mussolini ha sempre ragione. I decaloghi del fascismo*, Milan 2000.

67. See H.-J. Gamm, *Der braune Kult. Das dritte Reich und seiner Ersatzreligion. Ein Beitrag zur politischen Bildung*, Hamburg 1962; F. Heer, *Der Glaube des Adolf Hitler. Anatomie einer politischen Religiosität*, Munich 1968; K. Vondung, *Magie und Manipulation. Ideologischer Kult und politische Religion des Nationalsozialismus*, Göttingen 1971; G. Mosse, *The Nationalization of the Masses*; U. Tal, *"Political Faith" of Nazism Prior to the Holocaust*, Tel Aviv 1978; Id., *Structures of German "Political Theology" in the Nazi Era*, Tel Aviv 1979; J. Rhodes, *The Hitler Movement: A Modern Millenarian Revolution*, Stanford (Calif.) 1980; S. Behrenbeck, *Der Kult um die toten Helden: Nationalistische Mythen, Riten und Symbole 1923 bis 1945*, Neuburg a.d. Donau 1996; M. Ley and J. H. Schoeps (ed.), *Der Nationalsozialismus als politische Religion*, Bodenheim 1997; C. E. Bärsch, *Die politische Religion des Nationalsozialismus*, Munich 1998; M. Burleigh, *The Third Reich: A New History*, New York 2000, pp. 1–25, 252–67.

68. D. Cantimori, "Germania giovane: conservatorismo," *Vita nova*, March 1928, pp. 292–93.

69. K. Polanyi, "The Essence of Fascism," in J. Lewis, K. Polanyi, D. K. Kitchin (ed.), *Christianity and the Social Revolution*, London 1937 (1935), p. 360.

70. R. Aron, "Bureaucratie et fanatisme" (July 1941), in id., *L'homme contre les tyrans*, Paris 1946, p. 51.

71. Quoted in J. Fest, *Hitler*, Harmondsworth 1977, pp. 518–19.

72. See C. Lane, *The Rites of Rulers: Ritual in Industrial Society: The Soviet Case*, Cambridge, U.K., 1981; M. Agursky, *The Third Rome: National Bolshevism in the USSR*, Boulder 1987; D. G. Rowley, *Millenarian Bolshevism, 1900 to 1920*, New York–London 1987; W. van den Bercken, *Ideology and Atheism in the Soviet Union*, Mouton de Gruyter–Berlin–New York 1989; R. Stites, *Revolutionary Dreams: Utopian Vision and Experimental Life in the Russian Revolution*, New York–Oxford 1989; J. von Geldern, *Bolshevik Festivals 1917–1920*, Berkeley–Los Angeles–London 1993; J. Thrower, *Marxism-Leninism as the Civil Religion of Soviet Society*, Lewiston (Maine), 1993; A. J. Klinghoffer, *Red Apocalypse: The Religious Evolution of Soviet Communism*, Lanham (Md.) 1996; V. E. Bonnell, *Iconography of Power: Soviet Political Posters under Lenin and Stalin*, Berkeley–Los Angeles–London 1997; O. Figes, B. Kolonitskii (ed.), *Interpreting the Russian Revolution: The Language and Symbols of 1917*, New Haven 1999.

73. F. Gerlich, *Der Kommunismus als Lehre vom Tausendjährigen Reich*, Munich 1920, quoted in M. Huttner, *Totalitarismus und säkulare Religionen*, Bonn 1999, pp. 208–12.

74. R. Fülöp-Miller, *Il volto del bolscevismo* (1926), Milan 1930, p. 47.

75. Ibid., pp. 53–54.

76. N. Berdjaev, *Un nouveau Moyen Ages. Réflexions sur les destinées de la Russie et de l'Europe* (1923), Paris 1926, p. 261.

77. B. Russell, *The Theory and Practice of Bolshevism* (1920), London 1949, p. 9.

78. Ibid., pp. 7–8.

79. Ibid., pp. 8.

80. Ibid., pp. 73–74.

81. J. M. Keynes, *Essays in Persuasion* (1931), London 1951, pp. 297–98.

82. See N. Tumarkin, *Lenin Lives! The Lenin Cult in Soviet Russia*, Cambridge (Mass.) 1983.

83. Quoted by R. A. Medvedev, *Let History Judge: The Origins and Consequences of Stalinism* (1971), New York 1989, p. 617.

84. Ibid., pp. 617–20.

85. Quoted by E. J. Hobsbawm, *Age of Extremes: The Short Twentieth Century 1914–1991* London 1995, p. 66.

86. H. J. Laski, *Faith, Reason and Civilisation: An Essay in Historical Analysis*, London 1944, p. vi.

87. Ibid., p. 167.

88. H. J. Laski, *Reflections on the Revolution of our Time*, London 1943, p. 71.

89. Ibid., p. 72.

90. Ibid., p. 72.

CHAPTER THREE
THE LEVIATHAN AS A CHURCH

1. G. Salvemini, "Il mito dell'uomo-dio," *Giustizia e Libertà*, 20 July 1932.

2. F. Neumann, *Behemoth: The Structure and Practice of National Socialism 1933–1944* (1944), London 1967, p. 96.

3. P. Tillich, "The Totalitarian State and the Church," in *Social Research*, November 1934, pp. 416–18.

4. J. Benda, *The Treason of the Intellectuals* (1927), New York and London 1969, p. 4.

5. Ibid., pp. 22–23.

6. C. Sforza, *Dictateurs et dictatures de l'après-guerre*, Paris 1931, p. 17.

7. Ibid., p. 240.

8. W. Drabovitch, *Fragilité de la liberté et séduction des dictatures*, Paris 1934, p. 152.

9. Ibid., p. 176.

10. O. Forst de Battaglia, "The Nature of Dictatorship," in id. (ed.), *Dictatorship on Its Trial by Eminent Leaders of Modern Thought*, London 1930, p. 364.

11. L. Rougier, *Les mystique politique contemporaines et leurs incidences internationales*, Paris 1935, p. 18.

12. K. Loewenstein, "Autocracy versus Democracy in Contemporary Europe," *American Political Science Review*, October 1935, pp. 574–75.

13. S. Weil, "Let's Not Fight the Trojan War Again," translated from the Italian version, "Non ricominciamo la guerra di Troia," in id., *Sulla guerra. Scritti 1933–1943*, ed. D. Zazzi, Milan 1998, pp. 57–58.

14. G. Leibholz, "Il secolo XX e lo Stato totalitario del presente," *Rivista internazionale di Filosofia del Diritto*, January–February 1938, pp. 1–40.

15. Ibid., p. 31.

16. Ibid., p. 32.

17. G. Leibholz, *Die Auflösung der liberalen Demokratie in Deutschland und das autoritäre Staatsbild*, Munich–Leipzig 1933.

18. Leibholz, *Il secolo XX*, p. 35.

19. Ibid., p. 11.

20. See R. Rocker, *Nationalism and Culture*, London 1937.

21. Ibid., p. 269.

22. Ibid., pp. 61–62.

23. E. Voegelin, *Die politischen Religionen*, Stockholm 1939. Page nos. refer to "Le religioni politiche" (1938), in id., *La politica: Dai simboli alle esperienze*, Milan 1993, p. 25.

24. Ibid., p. 26.

25. Ibid., p. 31.

26. Ibid., p. 74. In an autobiographical work of 1973, Voegelin referred to his essay on political religions and wrote that in using the term he conformed to "the usage in the literature that interpreted ideological movements as variants of religious experience." He also added that, although it upheld the substantial validity of his interpretation, he would no longer use the term *religions* "because it is too vague and because it distorts the real question of those experiences by confusing them with other questions, such as those of dogma and doctrines" (ibid., p. 120).

27. R. Aron, "L'ère des tyrannies d'Élie Halévy," *Revue de métaphysique et de morale*, February 1939, p. 306.

28. R. Aron, "Bureaucratie et fanatisme" (1941), in id., *L'homme contre les tyrans*, Paris 1946, pp. 50–66.

29. Ibid., p. 59.

30. Ibid., p. 60.

31. R. Aron, "L'avenir des religions séculières," in id., *L'âge des empires et l'avenir de la France*, Paris 1946, p. 288.

32. Ibid., pp. 288–89.

33. Ibid., p. 317.

34. Ibid., p. 290.

35. J. Huizinga, *In the Shadow of Tomorrow* (1935), London–Toronto 1936, p. 1.

36. K. Jaspers, *La situazione spirituale del tempo* (1931), Rome 1982, p. 175.

37. Aron, *L'avenir des religions séculières*, p. 303.

38. Ibid., pp. 307–8.

39. R. Aron, *Machiavelli e le tirannie moderne*, Rome 1998, pp. 322–23.

40. W. Gurian, "The Totalitarian State," in *Proceedings of the Philosophical Catholic Association*, 1939, p. 55.

41. Ibid., p. 62.

42. Ibid., pp. 63–4.

43. Ibid., p. 66.

44. W. Gurian, "The Rise of Totalitarianism in Europe," in S. Pargellis (ed.), *The Quest for Political Unity in World History*, Washington, D.C.: 1944, pp. 297–304, on p. 303.

45. W. Gurian, "Totalitarian Religions," *Review of Politics*, 1, 1952, pp. 3–14.

46. Rougier, *Les mystique politique contemporaines*, p. 89.

47. A. Cobban, *Dictatorship: Its History and Theory*, London 1939, pp. 284.

48. Ibid., p. 225.

49. F. A. Voigt, *Unto Caesar*, London 1938, p. 37.

50. Proceedings of the American Philosophical Society, *Symposium on the Totalitarian State*, Philadelphia 1940.

51. F. Morstein Marx, *Totalitarian Politics*, in ibid., p. 2.

52. Ibid., pp. 36–37.

53. C.J.H. Hayes, *Totalitarianism in Western Civilization*, p. 96.

54. S. Neumann, *Permanent Revolution: The Total State in a World at War*, New York and London 1942, pp. 130–31.

55. Ibid., p. 186.

56. Morstein Marx, *Totalitarian Politics*, p. 36.

CHAPTER FOUR
THE INVASION OF THE IDOLS

1. L. Sturzo, "Idolatria collettiva," in *El Matì*, 19 December 1933, published in id., *Miscellanea londinese*, vol. 2, Bologna 1967, p. 286.

2. E. Gounelle, "Editorial," in *La Revue du Christianisme Social*, 6, 1937, pp. 113–14.

3. G. Bevilacqua, "Sgombrare l'idolo," in *Studium*, January 1940, p. 15.

4. A. Messineo, "La crisi della persona umana," in *La Civiltà cattolica*, 3, 1943, p. 33.

5. A. Messineo, *La nazione*, Rome 1942, p. 190.

6. Ibid., pp. 200, 202.

7. Ibid., p. 194.

8. Ibid., p. 201.

9. Ibid., p. 202.

10. J. Maritain, *Umanesimo integrale* (1936), Rome 1946, pp. 219–21.

11. A. Keller, *Church and State on the European Continent*, London 1936, pp. 57, 59.

12. A. Messineo, "Le concezioni monistiche della vita sociale," *La Civiltà cattolica*, 1, 1940, p. 432.

13. C. Dawson, "Religion and the Totalitarian State," *The Criterion*, vol. 14, no. 54, October 1934, pp. 1–16, on p. 3. This argument was then more fully developed in his later work, *Religion and the Modern State*, London 1935.

14. W. A. Visser't Hooft and J. H. Oldham, *The Church and Its Function in Society*, London 1937, pp. 74–77.

15. J. H. Oldham, *Church, Community and State: A World Issue*, London 1935, pp. 9–10.

16. See *The Churches Survey Their Task. The Report of the Conference at Oxford, July 1937, on Church, Community, and State*, London 1937. A full account of the conference proceedings, the text of some reports, and its final resolutions are contained in "Les Conférences Œcuméniques d'Oxford et d'Edimbourg," *La Revue du Christianisme Social*, 6, 1937. The final resolution also appears in C. Boyer, D. Bellocci (ed.), *Unità cristiana e movimento ecumenico. Testi e documenti*, Rome 1963, pp. 130–36.

17. N. Ehrenström, "L'Eglise et l'Etat," in *Les Conférences*, pp. 197–98.

18. *The Churches Survey*, pp. 81–83.

19. Ibid., pp. 130–61.

20. Ibid., pp. 58.

21. See N. Ehrenström, *Christian Faith and the Modern State: An Ecumenical Approach*, London 1937, pp. 213–14.

22. Dawson, "Religion and the Totalitarian State," *The Criterion*, vol. 14, no. 54, October 1934, p. 12.

23. D. De Rougemont, "Mutare la vita o mutare l'uomo," in *Il Comunismo e i cristiani*, Brescia 1945, p. 193. This work is an Italian translation of a collection of writings by F. Mauriac, J.-A. Ducattillon, N. Berdjaev, A. Marc, D. De Rougemont, and H. Daniel-Rops, *Le Communisme et les chrétiens*, ed. H. Daniel-Rops, Paris 1937.

24. L. Barde, "L'état soviétique. Ses principes. Sa technique," in *La société politique et la pensée chrétienne*, Lyon 1933, p. 153.

25. P. Cuche, "L'état fasciste. Ses principes. Sa technique," in ibid., p. 130.

26. A. Roullet, "La personne et les faits dans les régimes totalitaires," in *La personne humaine en péril*, Lyon 1938, p. 149.

27. Ibid., p. 164.

28. Ibid.

29. Ibid., p. 167.

30. Ibid., p. 160.

31. Ibid., p. 169.

32. Ibid., p. 175.

33. J. Delos, "Classes et régimes totalitaires," in *Le Problème des classes dans la communauté nationale et dans l'ordre humain*, Lyon 1940.

34. Ibid., pp. 258–59.

35. *The Churches Survey*, pp. 144.

36. N. Berdjaev, "Communist Secularism," in P. Dearmer (ed.), *Christianity and the Crisis*, London 1933, p. 565.

37. Ibid., p. 566.

38. Ibid., p. 577.

39. Keller, *Church and State*, pp. 68–69.

40. Ibid., pp. 70–91.

41. *Il Comunismo e i cristiani*, p. 5.

42. Ibid., pp. 6–7.

43. See J. Lewis, K. Polanyi, D. K. Kitchin (ed.), *Christianity and the Social Revolution*, London 1937 (1935).

44. Ibid., p. 22.

45. Ibid., p. 25.

46. Ibid., p. 102.

47. Ibid., p. 410.

48. Ibid., p. 415.

49. Ibid., p. 442.

50. Ibid., pp. 460–61.

51. Ibid., pp. 463–65.

52. Ibid., p. 468–69.

53. Maritain, *Umanesimo integrale*, p. 38.

54. Ibid., p. 40.

55. H. Daniel-Rops, "Il sale della terra," in *Il Comunismo e i cristiani*, p. 226.

56. F. Pellegrino, "L' 'attacco a fondo' del comunismo sovietico," *La Civiltà cattolica*, 3, 1941, pp. 173–74.

57. C. A. Moreschini, "Russia, rivoluzione comunista e URSS," *Studium*, November 1942, p. 323.

58. M. Bendiscioli, *Neopaganesimo razzista*, Brescia 1937, p. 18.

59. A. Hilckman, "Il nazionalsocialismo di fronte al cristianesimo e alla Chiesa," in *Vita e Pensiero*, 8 August 1932, pp. 461–68.

60. Ibid.

61. Ibid.

62. Cf. M. Bendiscioli, *La Germania religiosa nel III Reich. Conflitti religiosi e culturali nella Germania nazista*, Brescia 1936; id., *Neopaganesimo razzista*; M. Hermant, *Idoles allemandes*, Paris 1936; N. Micklem, *National Socialism and the Roman Catholic Church*, London 1939.

63. R. d'Harcourt, "Les catholiques et le IIIᵉ Reich," *La revue des deux mondes*, 15 March 1934, pp. 302, 315–16.

64. R. d'Harcourt, "En Allemagne, l'insurrection du spiritual," *La revue des deux mondes*, 1 December 1934, p. 533.

65. A. Béguin, "Le néo-paganisme allemande," *La revue des deux mondes*, 15 May 1935, pp. 280–306.

66. *Christendom on Trial: Documents of the German Church Struggle, 1938–1939*, London s.d., p. 4.

67. R. Kenyon, *Fascism and Christianity*, London 1935, pp. 11–15.

68. Keller, *Church and State*, p. 219.

69. Maritain, *Umanesimo integrale*, p. 221.

70. M. Prélot, *L'empire fasciste*, Paris 1936, p. 134.

71. R. Lloyd, *Revolutionary Religion: Christianity, Fascism, and Communism*, London 1938, pp. 8, 34 and 32.

72. A. Brucculeri, "Il concetto cristiano dello Stato," *La Civiltà cattolica*, 3, 1938, p. 22. The article was later expanded upon in id., *Lo Stato e l'individuo*, Rome 1938. See also id., *Meditazioni politiche*, Rome 1943.

73. Brucculeri, p. 22.

74. Ibid., p. 31.

75. Brucculeri, *Lo Stato e l'individuo*, p. 37.

76. Ibid.

77. L. Brucculeri, "Fra le vittime della Guerra," *La Civiltà cattolica*, 4, 1940, p. 176.

78. Ibid., p. 41.

79. Brucculeri, *Meditazioni politiche*, p. 113.

80. Ibid., p. 199.

81. L. Brucculeri, "Nazionalismo e amor di patria secondo la dottrina cattolica," *La Civiltà cattolica*, 1, 1915, p. 133.

82. Ibid., p. 135.

83. Ibid., p. 143.

84. L. Sturzo, *I discorsi politici*, Rome 1951, p. 388.

85. "Allocuzione di S. S. Pio XI pronunciata nel concistoro segreto del 14 dicembre 1925," *La Civiltà cattolica*, 1, 1926, p. 15.

86. "Allocuzione di S. S. Pio XI pronunciata nel concistoro segreto del 20 dicembre 1926," *La Civiltà cattolica*, 1, 1927, p. 11.

87. Ibid., p. 19.

88. "Principii di dottrina cattolica circa lo Stato e la convivenza civile," *La Civiltà cattolica*, 1, 1927, p. 105.

89. Ibid., pp. 99–100.

90. "Lettera enciclica di S. S. Pio XI sulle condizioni della Chiesa in Germania (14 marzo 1937)," *La Civiltà cattolica*, 2, 1937, pp. 196–97.

91. Ibid., p. 205.

92. Ibid., p. 214.

93. *Tutte le encicliche dei Sommi Pontefici*, ed. E. Momigliano, Milan 1964, p. 1088.

94. Quoted in *Tutte le encicliche dei Sommi Pontefici*, p. 855n.

95. Ibid., p. 851.

96. Ibid., pp. 971–72.

97. Ibid., p. 970.

98. G. Passelecq and B. Suchecky, *L'enciclica nascosta di Pio XI*, Milan 1997.

99. Ibid., p. 173.

100. A. Gemelli, "Cristo o Barabba?," *Vita e Pensiero*, 4 April 1937, pp. 179–85.

101. Brucculeri, "Il concetto cristiano," p. 21.

102. F. L. Ferrari, *"Il Domani d'Italia" e altri scritti del primo dopoguerra (1919–1926)*, ed. M. G. Rossi, Rome 1983, pp. 125–26.

103. I. Giordani, *Rivolta cattolica*, Turin 1925, p. 85.

104. Ibid., p. 147.

105. Ibid., p. 144.

106. Ibid., p. 42.

107. Ibid., p. 48.

108. Ibid., pp. 72–73.

109. L. Sturzo, "Spirito e realtà," *La Rivoluzione liberale*, 15 January 1924.

110. L. Sturzo, *Italia e fascismo* (1926), Bologna 1965, p. 205.

111. Ibid., p. 258.

112. L. Sturzo, "Divinità vecchie e nuove," *Res Publica*, June 1932, and published in id., *Miscellanea londinese*, vol. II, Bologna 1967, p. 95.

113. L. Sturzo, "Federico secondo," *Res Publica*, August 1932, and *Miscellanea londinese*, p. 339.

114. Sturzo, *Idolatria collettiva*, pp. 286–87.

115. L. Sturzo, "The Totalitarian State," *Social Research*, 3, 1936, pp. 222–35.

116. L. Sturzo, *Politica e morale (1938)*. *Coscienza e politica (1953)*, Bologna 1972, p. 29.

117. Ibid., pp. 35–36.

118. Ibid., pp. 32–33.

119. L. Sturzo, "La politica nella teologia morale," *Nouvelle Revue Théologique*, September–October 1938, later published in id., *Politica e morale*, p. 299.

120. Ibid., pp. 306–7.

121. "Fascismo e Vaticano nel 1938," *La vie intellectuelle*, 10 February 1939, now in L. Sturzo, *Scritti storico-politici (1926–1949)*, Rome 1984, p. 179.

122. Sturzo, *Politica e morale*, p. 35.

123. L. Sturzo, "Il primato della morale," in *The Catholic Herald*, 7 October 1933, now in id., *Miscellanea londinese*, pp. 271–72.

124. A. Brucculeri, "Chiesa e civiltà," *La Civiltà cattolica*, 1, 1940, p. 178.

125. Ibid., p. 177.

126. Ibid., p. 181.

127. Gemelli, *Cristo o Barabba?*, pp. 179–80.

128. A. Messineo, "La via dolorosa della Chiesa in Germania," *La Civiltà cattolica*, 2, 1937, pp. 217–30.

129. *The Churches Survey*, pp. 139–46.

130. Ibid., pp. 187–240.

131. Ehrenström, *Christian Faith and the Modern State*, p. 216.

132. Roullet, "La personne et les faits," p. 174.

133. G. Bevilacqua, "Le vie a Dio," *Studium*, November 1938, pp. 209–10.

134. I. Giordani, "Indemoniati," *Il Frontespizio*, April 1938, pp. 211–15.

135. M. Campo, "Torbide religiosità moderne," *Vita e Pensiero*, November 1940, pp. 470–80.

136. N. Micklem, *The Theology of Politics*, London 1939, pp. x–xvi.

137. Keller, *Church and State*, p. 91.

138. J. Lewis, *Communism: The Heir to the Christian Tradition*, in Lewis, Polanyi, and Kitchin (eds.), *Christianity and the Social Revolution*, London 1937 (1935), pp. 473 ff.

CHAPTER FIVE
TOWARD THE THIRD MILLENNIUM

1. Quoted by C. Cherry (ed.), *God's New Israel: Religious Interpretations of American Destiny*, Chapel Hill (N.C.) and London 1998, p. 295.

2. Ibid., pp. 301–2.

3. G. Leibholz, *Politics and Law*, Leyden 1965, p. 118.

4. B. Croce, *Scritti e discorsi politici (1943–1947)*, vol. 1, Rome–Bari 1973, p. 52.

5. B. Croce, "Perché non possiamo non dirci 'cristiani'" (1942), in id., *Discorsi di varia filosofia*, vol. I, Bari 1959, pp. 11–23.

6. B. Croce,"Soliloquio di un vecchio filosofo" (1942), in id., *Discorsi di varia filosofia*, vol. 2, p. 291.

7. S. Weil, *Sulla guerra. Scritti (1933–1943)*, ed. D. Zazzi, Milan 1998, p. 129.

8. R. Aron, *L'homme contre les tyrans*, Paris 1946, p. 200.

9. Ibid., p. 282.

10. Ibid., p. 201.

11. Ibid., p. 190.

12. J. Huizinga, *Lo scempio del mondo*, Milan 1948, p. 88.

13. H. J. Laski, *Faith, Reason and Civilisation: An Essay in Historical Analysis*, London 1944, p. 46.

14. Ibid., p. 37.

15. Ibid., p. vi.

16. See J. Monnerot, *Sociologie du communisme*, Paris 1949.

17. R. Aron, *La mentalità totalitaria*, Rome 1955, p. 22.

18. See R. Aron, *L'opium des intellectuelles*, Paris 1955.

19. Aron, *La mentalità totalitaria*, pp. 23–24.

20. See *Il dio che è fallito* (1950), Milan 1980.

21. See P. Hollander, *Political Pilgrims: Travels of Western Intellectuals to the Soviet Union, China and Cuba*, New York 1981.

22. Quoted in E. B. Koenker, *Secular Salvation: The Rites and Symbols of Political Religions*, Philadelphia 1964, pp. 33–34.

23. See L. S. Beckford, *La formación del hombre nuevo en Cuba*, Havana 1986.

24. Quoted in R. R. Fagen, "Mass Mobilization in Cuba: The Symbolism of Struggle," *Journal of International Affairs*, 2, 1966, p. 258.

25. W. Leontieff, "Che cosa non va nel socialismo cubano," *Comunità*, June 1971, pp. 57–58.

26. See F. C. Barghoorn, *Soviet Russian Nationalism*, New York 1956; J. McDowell, "Soviet Civil Ceremonies," *Journal for the Scientific Study of Religion*, 3, 1974, pp. 265–79; C.A.P. Binns, "The Changing Face of Power: Revolution and Accommodation in the Development of the Soviet Ceremonial System. Part II," in *Man*, 1980, pp. 170–87; C. Lane, *The Rites of Rulers: Ritual in Industrial Society: The Soviet Case*, Cambridge, U.K., 1981; Ead., *From Ideology to Political Religion: Recent Developments in Soviet Beliefs and Rituals in the Patriotic Tradition*, in C. Arvidsson, L. E. Blomqvist, *Symbols of Power*, Stockholm 1987, pp. 87–97; M. Heller, *Cogs in the Soviet Wheel: The Formation of Soviet Man*, London 1988; W. van den Bercken, *Ideology and Atheism in the Soviet Union*, Mouton de Gruyter–Berlin–New York 1989; J. Thrower, *Marxism-Leninism as the Civil Religion of the Soviet Society*, Lewiston (Maine), 1992; N. Tumarkin, *The Living and the Dead: The Rise and Fall of the Cult of World War II in Russia*, New York 1994; A. J. Klinghoffer, *Red Apocalypse. The Religious Evolution of Soviet Communism*, Lanham (Md.) 1996.

27. See H. Matthews, *Castro* (1969), Milan 1971.

28. V. Georgescu, "Politics, History and Nationalism: The Origins of Romania's Socialist Personality Cult," in J. Held (ed.), *The Cult of Power: Dictators in the Twentieth Century*, New York 1983, pp. 129–42.

29. D. Chirot, *Modern Tyrants: The Power and Prevalence of Evil in Our Age*, New York 1994, p. 240.

30. See Eum Seuk Houn, *Les brillantes empreintes*, Pyöngyang 1990, p. 161. See *The Red Dynasty*, Seoul 1982, pp. 28–68.

31. See P. Grangereau, *Au Pays du Grande Mensonge. Voyage en Corée du Nord*, Paris 2000, p. 39.

32. See Eum Seuk Houn, *Les brillantes empreintes*, pp. 145 ff.

33. Quoted in Grangereau, *Au Pays du Grande Mensonge*, p. 38.

34. Ibid., p. 51.

35. Ibid., p. 50.

36. See K. G. Riegel, *Konfessionsrituale in Marxismusleninismus*, Cologne 1985, pp. 178 ff.

37. See J. Lewis (ed.), *Party Leadership and Revolutionary Power in China*, Cambridge (Mass.) 1970.

38. Quoted in M. Meisner, *Marxism, Maoism, and Utopianism*, Madison 1982, p. 162.

39. Ibid., p. 164.

40. V. Lilli, *Dentro la Cina rossa*, Milan 1961, p. 107.

41. Ibid., pp. 131–32, 209.

42. E. Snow, *The Long Revolution*, London 1973, p. 68.

43. Ibid., p. 169. An important account of the Mao personality cult is provided by his personal physician Zhisui Li, *The Private Life of Chairman Mao*, London 1994.

44. Jiping Zuo, "Political Religion: The Case of the Cultural Revolution in China," *Sociological Analysis*, 1, 1991, p. 101.

45. A. Zhelokhovstyev, *La rivoluzione culturale vista da un sovietico* (1968), Milan 1971, pp. 57–58.

46. Ibid., pp. 104–105.

47. A. Moravia, *La rivoluzione culturale in Cina* (1967), Milan 1973, pp. 40–41.

48. See Meisner, *Marxism, Maoism*, p. 165.

49. G. Parise, *Cara Cina*, Milan 1968, p. 37.

50. Ibid., pp. 39–40.

51. See C. Jochim, *Chinese Religions: A Cultural Perspective*, Englewood Cliffs (N.J.) 1986, pp. 56–60; Meisner, *Marxism, Maoism*, pp. 175 ff.; Zuo, *Political Religion*, pp. 103–4.

52. Moravia, *La rivoluzione culturale*, p. 37.

53. Ibid., p. 52.

54. See G. F. Barmé, *Shades of Mao: The Posthumous Cult of the Great Leader*, Armonk–London 1996.

55. See D. I. Kertzer, *Riti e simboli del potere* (1988), Rome–Bari 1989; C. Rivière, *Le liturgie politiche* (1988), Como 1998.

56. See D. E. Apter, "Nkrumah, Charisma and the Coup," in D. A. Rustow (ed.), *Philosophers and Kings: Studies in Leadership*, New York 1970, pp. 112–47.

57. See J. Lacouture, *Quattro uomini quattro rivoluzioni* (1969), Milan 1973, pp. 15–93.

58. Ibid., pp. 265–66.

59. See D. Regan, "Islam, Intellectuals and Civil Religion in Malaysia," *Sociological Analysis*, 2, 1976, pp. 95–110.

60. See H. L. Seneviratne, "Continuity of Civil Religion in Sri Lanka," *Religion*, 1, 1984, pp. 1–14.

61. See J. D. Legge, *Sukarno: A Political Biography*, London 1972, pp. 184 ff.

62. See S. S. Purdy, "The Civil Religion Thesis as It Applies to a Pluralistic Society: Pancasila Democracy in Indonesia (1945–1965)," *Journal of International Affairs*, 2, 1982–83, pp. 307–16.

63. See T. D. Moodie, *The Rise of Afrikanerdom: Power, Apartheid, and the Afrikaner Civil Religion*, Berkeley–Los Angeles 1975; L. Thompson, *Il mito politico dell'apartheid* (1985), Turin 1989; B. Cauthen, *The Myth of Divine Election and Afrikaner Ethnogenesis*, in G. Hosking, G. Schöpflin (ed.), *Myths and Nationhood*, London 1997, pp. 107–31.

64. See C. S. Liebman, E. Don-Yehiya, *Religion in Israel: Traditional Judaism and Political Culture in the Jewish State*, Berkeley 1983.

65. D. E. Apter, "Political Religion in the New Nations," in C. Geertz (ed.), *Old Societies and New States: The Quest for Modernity in Asia and Africa*, London 1963, p. 77.

66. Ibid., pp. 79–83.

67. Ibid., pp. 89–92.

68. Ibid., p. 96.

69. See G. J. Merriman, *Great Britain: A Study of Civic Loyalty*, Chicago 1929, pp. 8–19, 40–49; E. Shils, M. Young, "The Meaning of the Coronation," *Sociological Review*, 1, 1953, pp. 63–81; J. G. Blumler, J. R. Brown, A. J. Ewbank, T. J. Nossiter, "Attitudes to the Monarchy: Their Structure and Development during a Ceremonial Occasion," *Political Studies*, 2, 1971, pp. 149–71; R. Bocock, *Ritual in Industrial Society: A Sociological Analysis of Ritualism in Modern England*, London 1975, pp. 98–117; P. Ziegler, *The Crown and the People*, London 1978; R. Bocock, "Religion in Modern Britain," in R. Bocock, K. Thompson (ed.), *Religion and Ideology*, Manchester, U.K., 1985, pp. 207–33; I. Hayden, *Symbol and Privilege: The Ritual Context of British Royalty*, Tucson (Ariz.) 1987. For the principal opposing and mainly republican views of the interpretation of the monarchy as an institution of the English civil religion, see N. Birnbaum, "Monarchs and Sociologists," *Sociological Review*, 1, 1955, pp. 5–23; T. Nairn, *The Enchanted Glass: Britain and Its Monarchy*, London 1988; E. Wilson, *The Myth of British Monarchy*, London 1989.

70. See *The Church and Civil Religion in the Nordic Countries of Europe*, Geneva 1984; O. Riis, "On Civil Religion," *Religionsvidenskabeligt Tidsskrift*, 1985, pp. 3–29; A. I. Wierdsma, "The Meaning of a State Coronation: The Inauguration (1814–1980) as Ritual of Civil Religion in the Netherlands," *The Netherlands Journal of Sociology*, 1, 1987, pp. 31–44.

71. See *Libre pensée et religion laïque en France. De la fin du Second Empire à la fin de la Troisième République*, Strasbourg 1980; Y. Déloye, O. Ihl, "Deux figures singulières de l'universel: la république et le sacré," in *La démocratie en France. 1. Idéologies*, ed. M. Sadoun, Paris 2000, pp. 138–246.

72. P. Nora, "De la République à la Nation," in P. Nora (ed.), *Les lieux de mémoire*, vol. 1, *La République*, Paris 1984, p. 651.

73. See G. Namer, *La commémoration en France de 1945 à nos jours*, Paris 1987; *Les usages politiques des fêtes aux XIX<sup>e</sup>–XX<sup>e</sup> siècles*, ed. A. Crobin, N. Gérôme, D. Tartakowsky, Paris 1994.

74. J.-P. Willaime, "La religion civile à la française et ses metamorphoses," *Social Compass*, 4, 1993, pp. 571–80. See M. Agulhon, *Les métamorphoses de Marianne. L'imagerie et la symbolique républicaine de 1914 à nos jours*, Paris 2001.

75. The term, which was suggested by the historian Emile Poulat, refers broadly to the prevailing Christian religious culture in France. See Willaime, *La religion civile*, p. 572.

76. L. Hamon, *De Gaulle dans la République*, Paris 1958, p. 49.

77. C. De Gaulle, *Memoirs of Hope: Renewal and Endeavor*, New York 1971, p. 3.

78. See S. and I. Hoffmann, *The Will to Grandeur: De Gaulle as Political Artist*, in Rustow (ed.), *Philosopher and Kings*, pp. 248–315; P. Viansson-Ponté, *Les Gaullistes*, Paris 1963; F. Roy Willis (ed.), *De Gaulle: Anachronism, Realist, or Prophet?* New York 1967; M. Agulhon, *De Gaulle. Histoire, symbole, myth*, Paris 2000.

79. See P. Garcia, *Le Bicentenaire de la Révolution française*, Paris 2000, pp. 61–75.

80. See P. Ory, *Une nation pour mémoire. 1889, 1939, 1989, trois jubilés révolutionnaires*, Paris 1992, pp. 226–27.

81. See M. D. Gustafson, "The Religious Role of the President," *Midwest Journal of Political Science*, 4, 1970, pp. 708–22; R. S. Alley, *So Help Me God: Religion and the Presidency, Wilson to Nixon*, Richmond 1972; M. D. Gustafson, "President Hoover and the National Religion," *Journal of Church and State*, 1, 1974, pp. 85–100; C. V. LaFontaine, "God and Nation in Selected U.S. Presidential Inaugural Addresses, 1789–1945: Part Two," *Journal of Church and State*, 3, 1976, pp. 513–21; M. Novak, *Choosing Our King: Powerful Symbols in Presidential Politics*, New York 1974; R. V. Pierard, R. D. Linder, *Civil Religion and the Presidency*, Grand Rapids (Mich.) 1988, pp. 161 ff.

82. See D. Classberg, *American Historical Pageantry: The Uses of Tradition in the Early Century*, Chapel Hill–London 1990; N. Prevots, *American Pageantry: A Movement for Art and Democracy*, Ann Arbor–London 1990; J. Bodnar, *Remaking America: Public Memory, Commemoration, and Patriotism in the Twentieth Century*, Princeton (N.J.) 1992.

83. See A. H. Jones, *Roosevelt's Image Brokers*, Port Washington (N.Y.) 1974; G. L. Mosse, "L'autorappresentazione nazionale negli anni Trenta negli Stati Uniti e in Europa," in M. Vaudagna (ed.), *L'estetica della politica. Europa e America negli anni Trenta*, Rome–Bari 1989, pp. 3–22; M. Vaudagna, " 'Drammatizzare l'America!': Simboli politici del New Deal," *L'estetica della politica*, pp. 77–102.

84. See J. C. Dawson, "The Religion of Democracy in Early Twentieth Century America," *Journal of Church and State*, 1, 1985, pp. 47–63; M. E. Marty, *Pilgrims in Their Own Land: 500 Years of Religion in America*, New York 1984, pp. 403 ff.

85. J. P. Williams, *What Americans Believe and How They Worship* (1952), New York 1962, p. 484.

86. Ibid., pp. 491, 488.

87. See J. J. Pullen, *Patriotism in America: A Study of Changing Devotions 1770–1970*, New York 1971, pp. 107 ff.

88. Quoted in Pierard and Linder, *Civil Religion and the Presidency*, p. 184.

89. See W. L. Miller, *Piety along the Potomac: Notes on Politics and Morals in the Fifties*, Boston 1964.

90. Quoted in J. G. Hunt (ed.), *The Inaugural Addresses of the Presidents*, New York 1997, p. 431.

91. See B. B. Greenberg, E. B. Parker, *The Kennedy Assassination and the American Public*, Stanford (Calif.) 1965, particularly the essay by S. Verba, "The Kennedy Assassination and the Nature of Political Commitment," pp. 348–60.

92. See J. S. Wolfe, " 'The Kennedy Myth': American Civil Religion in the Sixties," Ph.D. diss., Berkeley 1975.

93. See the bibliographical reference in note 13 to chapter 1.

94. See C. P. Henderson, *The Nixon Theology*, New York 1972.

95. R. Bellah, *The Broken Covenant. American Civil Religion in Time of Trial*, New York 1975, p. 142.

96. Ibid., p. 158. See also D. Anthony and T. Robbins, "Spiritual Innovation and the Crisis of American Civil Religion," *Daedalus*, 1, 1982, pp. 215–34.

97. See C. L. Albanese, *America: Religion and Religions*, Belmont (Calif.) 1981.

98. R. J. Neuhaus, "From Civil Religion to Public Philosophy," in L. S. Rouner (ed.), *Civil Religion and Political Theology*, Notre Dame (Ind.) 1986, p. 98.

99. See Pierard, Linder, *Civil Religion and the Presidency*, pp. 257 ff.

100. F. Ferrarotti, *Una fede senza dogmi*, Rome–Bari 1990; G. E. Rusconi, *Possiamo fare a meno di una religione civile?* Rome–Bari 1999.

## Chapter Six
### Religions of Politics

1. R. Aron, *L'oppio degli intellettuali* (1955), San Casciano 1958, p. 63.

2. For similar distinctions between these two concepts whose arguments do not always agree with those expounded in this work see C. Lane, *The Rites of Rulers. Ritual in Industrial Society: The Soviet Case*, Cambridge 1981, pp. 42–44.

3. Quoted in A. Mathiez, *La Theophilanthropie et le culte décadaire (1796–1801)*, Paris 1904, p. 23.

4. M.-J.-A.-N. Condorcet, *Premier mémoire sur l'instruction publique*, in *OEuvre de Condorcet*, Paris 1847, vol. 7, p. 212.

5. G. L. Mosse, *La nazionalizzazione delle masse* (1974), Bologna 1975.

6. Ibid., p. 8.

7. G. Di Febo, *Teresa D'Avila: un culto barocco nella Spagna di Franco (1937–1962)*, Naples 1988, p. 24; see Ead., "Franco, la cerimonia de santa Bárbara y la 'rapresentación' del nacionalcatolicismo," in X. Quinzá Lleó, J. J. Alemany (ed.),

*Ciudad de los hombres, ciudad de dios*, Madrid 1999, pp. 461–74; Ead., *La cro-ciata e le rappresentazioni del nazionalcattolicesimo*, in *Immagini nemiche. La guerra civile spagnola e le sue rappresentazioni 1936–1939*, Bologna 1999, pp. 27–36.

8. A. Elorza, *La religione politica. I fondamentalismi* (1995), Rome 1996, p. 164.

9. E. J. Hobsbawm, T. Ranger, *The Invention of Tradition*, Cambridge, U.K., 1983, p. 1.

10. E. J. Hobsbawm, *Age of Extremes: The Short Twentieth Century 1914–1991* (1994), London 1995, p. 388.

11. Ibid., p. 563.

12. R. Moro, "Religione e politica nell'età della secolarizzazione: riflessioni su di un recente volume di Emilio Gentile," *Storia contemporanea*, 2, 1995, pp. 309–18.

13. O. Chadwick, *The Secularization of the European Mind in the Nineteenth Century*, Cambridge, U.K., 1975, p. 1.

14. R. Pettazzoni, *Italia religiosa*, Bari 1952, pp. 5–6.